WITHDRAWN
UTSA Libraries

GREAT ATLANTIC ADVENTURES

Also by Edward Rowe Snow

True Tales and Curious Legends

Fantastic Folklore and Fact

Incredible Mysteries and Legends of the Sea

Tales of Sea and Shore

Astounding Tales of the Sea

Unsolved Mysteries of Sea and Shore

Mysterious Tales of the New England Coast

True Tales of Pirates and Their Gold

True Tales of Buried Treasure

GREAT ATLANTIC ADVENTURES

Edward Rowe Snow

⚓

ILLUSTRATED

DODD, MEAD & COMPANY

NEW YORK

Copyright © 1970 by Edward Rowe Snow

All rights reserved

No part of this book may be reproduced in any form without permission in writing from the publisher

ISBN 0-396-06256-3
Library of Congress Catalog Card Number: 74-129958

Printed in the United States of America
by The Cornwall Press, Inc., Cornwall, N.Y.

To our granddaughter
Laura Ann Bicknell

INTRODUCTION

In every book or pamphlet which I have written, and the total now approaches seventy, it has been my plan to give the reader the most accurate account possible of the stories and legends contained in the volume. This present effort is no exception.

Many readers have asked why I began telling stories of the sea and writing books on the subject. I believe it is because all of my ancestors on the male side for eight generations were sea captains except my father. Also, early in life I purchased a canoe that enabled me to visit islands and lighthouses in the vicinity of Winthrop, Massachusetts. The town is a peninsula almost entirely surrounded by the Atlantic Ocean, which gave me countless opportunities to go ashore at many points of interest. At times I would travel by canoe as far as forty miles from my Winthrop home.

In this volume New England and the waters offshore are the locations for many narrations, and Bermuda is given important emphasis. The stories are as far apart in context as my visits out on the marsh behind our present home, and the forgotten Revolutionary battle of Chelsea Creek. Those are matched by the account of the girl who returned home in a

INTRODUCTION

cask of rum, and a fabulous treasure discovered at Bermuda. I trust I have succeeded in passing on to you my interest in all these subjects.

Possibly the two weirdest chapters in the book concern a devil fish and a ship of skeletons.

Many readers indulge vicariously in the experiences of those who sail on the mysterious marine highways, which Conrad chose to call the "savage" ocean. They are often thrilled by and appreciate realism in the stories and accounts presented to them. As often as possible, I have allowed survivors to tell their stories in their original words. In this way I have attempted not only to put the reader into the atmosphere of the event, but also to allow him to hear about it from one who lived through the experience. If I have succeeded in any measure, I shall feel well repaid for my efforts.

Many people have helped in the creation of this volume. In particular I thank our good friend Sister Jean Kennedy in matters pertaining to Bermuda, that collection of magic isles far off in the Atlantic.

Bermudian Will Zuill, whom I have admired for years, also helped me greatly. John F. Lynch of Boston assisted materially in our search for the Franklin medal, which was eventually successful.

Various halls of learning have made my task easier, among them the Ventress Memorial Library, Marshfield; the Allen and the Peirce Memorial Libraries of Scituate; the Boston Athenaeum; the Boston Public Library; the Thomas Crane Public Library of Quincy; the Harvard College Library; the Bostonian Society; the Society for the Preservation of New England Antiquities; the Massachusetts Archives; the Peabody Museum; the American Antiquarian Society in Worcester; the Essex Institute; the Massachusetts Marine Historical League; the National Archives; the Boston Marine Society; the Massachusetts Historical Society; the Maine Historical

Society; the Nathan Tufts Library in Weymouth; and *Yankee* magazine. The late Robb Sagendorph, as always, was an inspiration.

Among those to whom I express my thanks are Dorothy Caroline Snow Bicknell, Mary Brown, Claire Clancy, Arthur J. Cunningham, Richard Dean, Richard W. Dennison, Walter Spahr Ehrenfeld, Patricia Farina, Harland Fay, Leo Flaherty, Dorothy Gammon, Edward B. Garside, Marie Hansen, Ted Hawkesworth, Barbara Hayward, John R. Herbert, Melina Herron, Mrs. William H. Horton, Mrs. Francis Kelleher, Joseph Kolb, Gary Kosciusko, Beverly LaConte, William Francis McIntire, Muriel McKenzie, Maggie Mills, Joel O'Brien, William Pyne, Earle G. Rich, Helen Salkowski, Grace Saphir, Carl Saprito, Tom Smith, Albert Snow, Florence Snow, Winthrop James Snow, Rita Solimini, Janet Sumner, Terry Tucker, Charles R. O. Wood.

My wife, Anna-Myrle, on whom I called for intensive effort in the preparation of the many chapters in this book, responded as usual with her unselfish spirit.

—Edward Rowe Snow

CONTENTS

INTRODUCTION — vii

Part I: Boston and the Northeast

1. PILGRIM ROCK AND PLYMOUTH ROCK — 3
2. MYSTERY MAN OF THE NEPONSET — 14
3. THOMAS MACY, THE EXILE — 22
4. THE NAHANT CANNON — 27
5. THE *MOXIE* TRAGEDY — 31
6. *PERTH AMBOY* — 35
7. MURDER AT MIDDLE BREWSTER — 44
8. THE TRIPLE STORMS OF 1969 — 49
9. THE STORM OF 1898 — 54
10. UNDER BOSTON HARBOR — 64
11. *ROBERT E. LEE* — 67
12. CAPE COD'S CRUMBLING CLIFFS — 74
13. THE PIRATE CRAFT AND THE *KADOSH* — 88
14. ON THE MARSH — 93
15. A MARSHFIELD GHOST — 104
16. THE BATTLE OF CHELSEA CREEK — 110

Part II: Atlantic Tales

1. THE *QUEEN MARY* SINKS A CRUISER — 121
2. MARGARET RETURNS HOME — 130
3. DERELICTS — 132
4. *ANDREA DORIA* AGAIN — 140
5. DOGS OF THE ATLANTIC — 149
6. BARRATRY ON THE *FRANKLIN* — 170

Part III: Bermuda Treasure

1. LUSHER THE UNFORTUNATE — 181
2. *SAN ANTONIO* — 187
3. RUSSELL PEARMAN — 190
4. A LADY OF BERMUDA — 193
5. ROBERT REPOSE — 198
6. JOHN DAVENPORT — 200
7. TEDDY TUCKER — 202
8. HARRY COX — 208

Part IV: Adventures at Bermuda

1. WRECK OF THE *BONAVENTURA* — 213
2. A SHIPWRECK OF 1780 — 216
3. *MADIANA* — 218
4. THE MAIL STEAMER *CURLEW* — 221
5. THE SEA DEVIL — 227
6. BERMUDA'S 1915 WRECK — 231
7. THE *LA PLATA*, WHICH NEVER REACHED BERMUDA — 236
8. SHIP OF SKELETONS — 250

INDEX — 259

ILLUSTRATIONS

Following page 82

Pilgrim Rock
Plymouth Rock
Sir Christopher Gardner
Cannon found off Nahant
Tug *Perth Amboy*
Schooner *Mertis Perry*
Robert E. Lee
Ancient pirate cannon
The marsh
Grave on Boston Common
Gravestone of Margaret Peterson
Bow of the Stockholm after collision
The *Andrea Doria* after collision
The *Andrea Doria* before final plunge
Famous dogs Ruben, King, and Prince
The author with Teddy Tucker
Sea devil
Ship of skeletons

PART ONE

~~~~~~~~~~~~~~~~~~~~~~~~~~

Boston and the Northeast

1

PILGRIM ROCK AND PLYMOUTH ROCK

⚓

NEARLY EVERYONE KNOWS of Plymouth Rock, one of the great landmarks of American history, but relatively few people alive today have even heard of Pilgrim Rock on Clark's Island at the mouth of Plymouth Harbor.

This was the island where the *Mayflower*'s shallop, or work boat, was wrecked during an exploration foray for a suitable settlement. Aboard were eighteen Pilgrims, including my ancestor, Stephen Hopkins. It is likely that the Pilgrims, by accident, must have visited Clark's Island's gigantic rock, now called Pilgrim Rock, before going ashore at Plymouth, so I believe Pilgrim Rock should get a little of the glory that its more illustrious neighbor, Plymouth Rock, has come to receive.

There is no positive proof that any Pilgrim ever set foot on Plymouth Rock. There is much more recorded evidence, as words inscribed on the great boulder at Clark's Island indicate, that the Pilgrims did visit Pilgrim Rock on that island even before landing in Plymouth.

I realize it is of secondary importance whether or not the Pilgrims did physically climb up *on* the Rock at Plymouth.

The vital thing is the symbolism connected with the landing of the Pilgrims in the vicinity of the Rock.

The British poetess Felicia Dorothea Hemans also erred when she spoke of the Pilgrims' landing on a stern and rockbound coast.* When the Pilgrims first came ashore at Pro-

> The breaking waves dashed high
> On a stern and rock-bound coast,
> And the woods, against a stormy sky,
> Their giant branches tossed.

vincetown there were no boulders or rocks in the Cape Cod area anywhere near the size of Plymouth Rock. Of course, one boulder does not make a rockbound coast, and Mrs. Hemans' poem was wholly imaginative in many of its more graphic details.

Nevertheless we owe Mrs. Hemans a vote of gratitude for reminding us of our heritage. What this English poetess said and the way she expressed herself stand as an eternal memorial to the Pilgrims.

Around the turn of the century a prominent Harvard geologist visited Plymouth Rock. He explained why in his opinion it was a physical impossibility for any of the Pilgrims to step or jump up onto the Rock from the awkward shallop. He then made an interesting point. Why would tired Pilgrim explorers, burdened with necessary accoutrements, search out a relatively small rock on which to step?

Across at Clark's Island, however, where the first Pilgrim shipwreck occurred, the massive boulder on which they climbed for a view of the surrounding land and bay has been inscribed with the words: "On the Sabboth Day wee rested 20 December, 1620." The shallop had been wrecked on the island at the height of an intense storm, but later was repaired and reached what is now Plymouth.

Clark's Island was named for the *Mayflower*'s chief mate,

---

* Here is the first stanza in her "Landing of the Pilgrim Fathers":

the first man to step foot on the island. The shallop passengers included Robert Coffin, Stephen Hopkins, William Bradford, Myles Standish, Edward Doty, and thirteen others. Once ashore, the men might have frozen to death if they had not been able to light a fire and dry themselves.

The next morning, a Saturday, they agreed to rest there, dry out their gear and conduct a service of thanksgiving by the Rock, in which they would give the Lord "thanks for His mercies, in their manifould deliverances."

I like to think of that thanksgiving service at Clark's Island as the first real Pilgrim Thanksgiving. Whenever possible, I make it a point to visit Pilgrim Rock, the huge boulder on the island, which still remains unchanged and unmoved, not at all like its sad companion, famous Plymouth Rock itself.

Plymouth Rock has traveled long distances since it came into prominence, with hundreds of pounds of its original weight and shape gone forever.

Early on Monday morning, December 17, 1620, after their Plymouth Bay adventures were over and they had made a careful inspection of the area, the Pilgrims sailed back toward Cape Cod Harbor and the *Mayflower*. Their shallop had been repaired, and on the way back they had no real trouble, even from the Indians. Arriving at the tip of Cape Cod, the adventurers reported to the rest of the company that Plymouth Harbor was a perfect choice for a permanent location. The *Mayflower* sailed to Plymouth, the Pilgrims went ashore, and the rest is history.

The Plymouth settlement, after many trying years, eventually prospered and grew. Historically, it was not until 1769 that the name *Pilgrim* began to achieve importance, even in Plymouth. In that year several young men decided to form a club which they hoped would raise the social tone of Plymouth and bring the name Pilgrim into common usage all over New England. They were anxious to avoid "the many disadvantages and inconveniences that arise from intermixing with the company at the taverns" of Plymouth, the town which had achieved an importance as being the original home of those same Pilgrims.

Among the members of the group was Isaac Lothrop, who became the Old Colony Club's first president. His brother Thomas was elected the first secretary, and there were five other charter members, Elkanah Cushman, John Thomas, Edward Winslow, Pelham Winslow and John Watson. Young Pelham Winslow was the son of Major General John Winslow, who carried out the evacuation of the Acadians from Nova Scotia.*

Eventually, five other prominent south shore residents were invited to join with the charter members of the club. They were Thomas Mayhew, whose ancestor had been proprietor of both Nantucket and Martha's Vineyard; Oakes Angier, descended from Harvard President Uriah Oakes; Cornelius White, whose ancestors included Peregrine White; Alexander Scammell,** who taught the local school; and James Warren, of the *Mayflower* Warrens. Not quite half of the members were Harvard graduates.

One of their first subjects of discussion at the club concerned Plymouth Rock. After considerable research they discovered that no Pilgrim had ever even mentioned Plymouth Rock at any time. Deacon Ephraim Spooner saved the day by giving the members details of the Elder Thomas Faunce legend, and the group decided to accept the legend as fact. Faunce, in 1741 a very old man of ninety-four, had stated that as a boy he had been told that the Pilgrims had

---

* Incidentally, almost one hundred of the Acadians were brought to Plymouth, many of whom later settled along the Jones River. Others moved northward, with Kingston, Duxbury and Marshfield each receiving a considerable number.

** Fort Scammell in the harbor at Portland, Maine, is named for him. Scammell also wrote poetry. He was a major general when mortally wounded at Yorktown.

landed at or near Plymouth Rock. The group decided to go ahead with plans to celebrate the historic landing of the Pilgrims, December 11. Unfortunately, there was a difference of eleven days between the relatively accurate Pope Gregory Calendar, adopted by England in 1752, and the Julian Calendar that the men of Plymouth had been using. The committee changed the date from December 11, adding eleven days. Thus, it was on the morning of December 22, 1769, that a celebration began with the firing of a cannon and the raising of a flag. Members and guests then assembled at the Howland Tavern on Cole's Hill, with a dinner of no less than nine courses awaiting them. The menu ran from baked Indian whortleberry pudding to clams, oysters, codfish, eels, venison, apple pie, cranberry tarts, cheese, sauquetash, and "frost-fish."

Several stanzas of John Dickerson's *Ode on Freedom* were sung, including:

> In Freedom we're born and in Freedom
>   we'll live
> Our right arms are ready,
> Steady, friends, steady!
> Not as slaves, but as Freemen, our
>   lives we will give.

The assembly then dispersed, returning home. Considered a success, the affair was to be repeated as an annual event.

Then came March 5, 1770, when the Boston Massacre occurred on State Street in the heart of Boston. Repercussions from the so-called massacre * soon reached Plymouth, where the people were beginning to question whether they should remain loyal to England or join those who would soon become rebels.

---

* Five men were killed. A massacre, according to the dictionary, is a general slaughter of human beings. Today the Boston Massacre might be called a riot.

James Warren, then a Plymouth selectman, had already gone to Boston to confer with rebel leader Samuel Adams. Early in November 1772 Adams wrote to Warren saying that he wished "our Mother Plymouth would see her way clear to have a meeting and second Boston" by setting up a committee of communication.*

The committee desired by Adams was quickly formed; Warren was made its chairman, and Isaac Lothrop secretary. The Tory-minded residents of Plymouth vainly did what they could to make fun of the committee. With the approach of Forefathers' Day, 1772, the committee suggested to the Old Colony Club that all people concerned get together in a patriotic demonstration. Those in the Old Colony Club, however, replied sharply that Forefathers' Day was none of the committee's business.

By this time many of the Plymouth residents had to make soul-searching decisions, with a goodly number changing from the royalist side to become rebels, and many of those originally favoring the colonists now backing King George and England.

Forefathers' Day arrived. The members listened to a sermon by the Rev. Charles Turner, the Duxbury parson. Torn between the two factions, the pastor decided to talk on a middle-of-the-road subject. Turner preached that he was definitely against sin, which satisfied no one, as most of the audience already were reasonably sure of Turner's attitude in this respect.

About a year later, on December 16, 1773, the Boston Tea Party occurred. A few days afterward James Warren called a special "patriot" meeting during which several resolutions were passed which "applauded" the friends of liberty.

* Warren became Paymaster General of the Continental Army, leaving Mercy Warren, sister of James Otis, to run affairs at Plymouth. Mercy also led a campaign for women's rights and liberation, anticipating Mary Wallstonecraft in the cause of equal rights for all.

The Tories, however, were not idle. Headed by Edward Winslow, they had done everything they could to block the "friends of liberty" meeting. The committee, now anxious to change the tone of the Old Colony Club, asked the members to honor Forefathers' Day by a general statement backing liberty. In no uncertain terms the committee was again told to mind its own business.

A year later Plymouth Rock itself became involved in the confrontation between the opposing factions. Early in the morning of December 22, 1774, Isaac Lothrop and James Warren assembled no less than thirty teams of oxen on the beach near Plymouth Rock to move the boulder to Town Square where it would share honors with the Liberty Pole.

Chains were placed around the venerable rock and the teams of oxen were started forward. Unfortunately, instead of the entire Rock being pulled from its sandy bed, the top broke off and followed the oxen. The lower, larger portion of the Rock settled back to be buried in sand a few days later by a high tide. For once, Plymouth Rock vanished from the beach!

Meanwhile the oxen started up Broad Street with the fragment and arrived at Town Square. There the Rock was placed in the shadow of a large elm tree near the Liberty Pole which had been erected some time before.

Less than four months later, on April 19, 1775, the battle of Lexington and Concord was fought to its fatal conclusion. To give the reader some idea of how the south shore towns stood, I only have to mention that Tory Edward Winslow was the one who guided British Lord Percy to the battleground at Lexington and Concord. Winslow had his horse shot out from under him. Pelham Winslow had gone to Boston to present himself to General Gage as a British Tory now ready to fight for the crown against his old friends and neighbors who had joined with the Continental forces.

Back in 1772 at Marshfield, the local Tories had asked General Gage to make an example of the liberty-loving Marshfield Committee of Correspondence. The Queen's Guard, under the command of Captain Balfour, had been sent to Marshfield to overwhelm "the rabble."

Nevertheless, when the Queen's Guard arrived at the Winslow estate in Marshfield, the Winslows had second thoughts, and advised them against fighting at that time. Apparently it was only the intercession of the Winslows that prevented the "shot heard round the world" from originating in the town of Marshfield in 1772.

Shortly after the battles of Concord and Lexington, His Majesty's ship *Niger* exchanged shots with a fort built on the Gurnet's Nose off Plymouth. One cannon ball passed through the Gurnet Lighthouse, located at the entrance to Plymouth Harbor.

The war for independence finally ended, and the United States began its career as a nation.

On July 4, 1834, the severed portion of Plymouth Rock was moved from the square in Plymouth to the front yard of Pilgrim Hall, and during the next year was enclosed by iron railings.

The base of the rock remained in its bed on the shore. Occasionally it showed its broken surface above the sand after a particularly high tide had washed the sand away from the top. In 1859 steps were taken to erect a granite canopy over the shattered rock.

A monument designed by Hammett Billings was suggested and adopted. The cornerstone of the canopy was laid August 2, 1859. In the chamber between the dome and the capstone were placed the remains of the Pilgrims who had died during the first winter.

In 1880 the people of Plymouth decided to reunite the broken fragments of Plymouth Rock, and so the upper part of the boulder, still in front of Pilgrim Hall, was taken down to the beach.

The two parts of the rock did not fit together because many pieces had been removed from them,* one of them the fifty-pound fragment which will probably always remain in Brooklyn, New York, where it was taken more than a century ago. Eventually, later in 1880, the shattered remains of Plymouth Rock were reunited.

Now accepted as an international symbol, the Rock became the crux of the entire Pilgrim story.

In 1896 the Society of Mayflower Descendants was founded. Strangely enough the very next year the original Bradford manuscript, *Of Plimoth Plantation*, arrived back in America. Bradford's masterpiece related the story of the Pilgrims from 1606 to 1647, but as Bradford had written primarily for family and local interest, no historian realized the importance of the book for many years.

Probably the manuscript had been taken from Boston by a British officer at the time of the evacuation, March 17, 1776. Possibly he had noticed the book in the steeple room of the Old South Church, where it had been part of the Prince Library. The story of how the volume was brought back to Massachusetts is an amazing tale.

It wasn't until 1844 that the Lord Bishop of London, England, Samuel Wilberforce, actually used material from the *Plimoth Plantation* volume. In 1855 John Wingate Thornton and John S. Barry realized that the Lord Bishop must have had access to Bradford's book.

It was traced to the library at Fulham Palace, which is located in outer London. In 1856 in London a copy was made by a professional writer hired for the purpose. In 1897, after negotiations with England were completed, the vital, pre-

---

* An item in a local paper advertised pieces of the Rock on sale for $1.50 each.

cious volume was returned to New England and is now in the State House at Boston.

Although George F. Willison states in his *Saints and Strangers* that the Pilgrims themselves were not familiar with the word "Pilgrim," in rebuttal I offer William Bradford himself who called his companions and himself Pilgrims.

As the years have gone by the Plymouth Rock region has seasonably become crowded with cars and visitors. Since thousands of visitors often come daily from every one of the fifty states, the area around Plymouth Rock is congested. Many controversial plans have been offered by various groups and organizations to solve the traffic problem. One of the latest, to move the Rock to a new location, has been rejected. In March 1970 a new idea was presented which would provide parking for about 150 cars and a Pilgrim historical complex covering 11.67 acres.

The eminent historian Samuel Eliot Morison states in his introduction to the 1952 edition of Bradford's *Of Plymouth Plantation* that the Pilgrims may have landed "anywhere between Captain's Hill and the Rock."

You, the reader, should decide how you wish to interpret the facts that I have brought forth in this chapter. In any case, Plymouth Rock should remain through the centuries as a visual reminder of our ancestors. The ocean, the beach, and the Rock are still there, but the final survivor of the *Mayflower* passengers, Mary Cushman by name, vanished from this world in 1699.

Indeed, the tale of the Pilgrims has everything required for what has become a fascinating story. Through the centuries the Pilgrim spirit has spread from Massachusetts Bay to California, and has united people from widely separated parts of the world now living in the United States.

The compact signed by forty-one Pilgrims in the cabin of the *Mayflower* at Provincetown has been called our first

PILGRIM ROCK AND PLYMOUTH ROCK

Declaration of Independence. The compact emphasized so much that stands for the name Pilgrim today, especially the words, "we do by these presents solemnly and mutually . . . covenant and combine ourselves together into a civill body politick, for our better ordering and preservation. . . ." Plymouth Rock is recognized throughout the world as a symbol of this spirit.

2

MYSTERY MAN OF THE NEPONSET

⚓

> It was Sir Christopher Gardiner,
> Knight of the Holy Sepulchre,
> From Merry England over the sea,
> Who stepped upon this continent
> As if his august presence lent
> A glory to the colony.

IN THIS MANNER Henry Wadsworth Longfellow introduced Sir Christopher Gardiner to his readers. Gardiner, who lived on the banks of the Neponset River on the south shore of Massachusetts for some time, is one of the great enigmas in the history of early New England. Supposedly a knight, he was identified by Charles Francis Adams, Jr., as a man who stands out "in picturesque incongruity against the monotonous background of colonial life." It is almost as though one were to come across a Van Dyke portrait of a cavalier in a New England village church.

Passing across the stage of American seventeenth-century history, he mingles with the life of the seaboard settlements at a period when the seaboard was the frontier. In his wanderings around New England he was almost always accompanied by a mysterious lady in black, and he usually carried a long Spanish rapier under his heavy cloak.

He has been written about on many occasions. As early as 1827 Miss Catharine Maria Sedgwick mentions him in her novel *Hope Leslie*.

"Evidently he came from a Gloucester, England, family, but no one has been able to discover how he received his title. He appeared in America in April of 1630, six months before Boston itself was founded. Claiming that he was weary of the old world, Gardiner was probably a confidential agent of Sir Ferdinando Gorges."

His consort was Mary Grove. It is believed they settled on the banks of the Neponset River near where old ship hulks can still be seen in the vicinity of what was the Lawley yard.*

When John Winthrop arrived, he became preoccupied with Thomas Morton of Merry Mount, and it was not until the latter was sent back to England in the *Handmaid* that Winthrop could devote his attention to Gardiner.

Let us ask Longfellow to continue:

> But a double life was the life he led;
> And, while professing to be in search
> Of a godly course, and willing, he said
> Nay, anxious, to join the Puritan Church,
> He made of all this but small account,
> And passed his idle hours instead
> With roystering Morton of Merry Mount,
> That pettifoger from Furnival's Inn,
> Lord of misrule, riot, and sin
> Who looked on the wine when it was red.

Morton of Merry Mount fame says that during his governing of Merry Mount, "Sir Christopher Gardiner (a Knight)

---

* I have a map drawn by Editor John R. Herbert of the *Boston Herald Traveler* showing the probable location of the Sir Christopher Gardiner estate on the Neponset River.

that had bin a traveller, both by Sea and Land; a good judicious gentleman in the Mathematticks and other Sciences usefull for Plantations, Kimistry, &c., and also being a practicall Engineer came into those parts, intending discovery."

This mysterious individual was one of the most interesting of that group of strange men who came to this country, apart from the Puritans, and perhaps as part of a hostile Church of England conspiracy, designing to rear a new feudal state on the ruins of the Roundhead colony.

In his fascinating romance of "Marry Mount," John Lothrop Motley places Sir Christopher's home just north of Squantum, at the head of a beautiful cove. He also speaks of him as being the renowned Sir Frank de Gorges, a knight of Malta, hero of many naval battles with Turkish and Dalmatian pirates, captain of Venetian free companies, a gallant adventurer in Spain, and a close ally of Sir Ferdinando Gorges in his schemes for renewing the triumphs of Cortés and Pizarro on the coasts of New England.

The Puritans were ruthless with this brilliant and ambitious soldier, who was branded in their colonial records as "a person unmeete to inhabit here." Governor Thomas Hutchinson, in his history of Massachusetts, tells of the unfortunate knight:

"Sir Christopher Gardiner . . . was a Knight of the Sepulchre, but concealed his true character, and came over under pretence of separating himself from the world, and living a life of retirement and devotion. He offered to join several of the churches, but he was suspected to be an immoral man, and not received."

Dr. Maurice Robbins tells me that Gardiner was supposed to have been a Catholic and possibly a member of the Jesuit congregation.

Later it was reported that he was "living with the Indians" at Assawompsett in the region of what is now Middleboro or

Lakeville. With the help of some Indians, Gardiner was captured at or near Assawompsett.

I have always regarded Charles Francis Adams as the outstanding authority on Gardiner. Let us quote from his *Three Episodes of Massachusetts History,* published in 1892. Author Adams believes that Gardiner was sent to the Boston region as an agent of Sir Ferdinando Gorges:

"If he was such an agent,—and there can be little doubt of the fact,—the exact purpose of his coming at this time can only be surmised. It is probable that he was commissioned to act for Sir Ferdinando, and to do whatever circumstances might require, or occasion make possible, to keep the Gorges claims alive.

"He brought over with him a servant or two, and was also accompanied by another companion, 'a comly yonge woman,' as Bradford reports her, whom he represented as being his cousin, but who seems, in fact, to have been his mistress. For some time after his first arrival he does not appear to have been in any way molested. He came to the neighborhood of Boston Bay, and built for himself some sort of a dwelling, though exactly where is not known. Deputy Governor Dudley simply says that it was seven miles from Boston, and on the further side of a river."

Judging by the direction which Gardiner afterward took in his flight, it would seem most probable that he lived on the Neponset, not far from its mouth, and in close vicinity to the former "Massachusetts fields." If he did live there, he was in the midst of Gorges's adherents; for Jeffreys and Morton were but a few miles away, the former at Wessagusset and the latter at Mount Wollaston, while Blackstone, Maverick, and Walford were immediately across the bay about the peninsula of Shawmut.

It would further seem that Gardiner could hardly have failed to meet Morton in London during the summer of 1629, when both were there and in constant communication with Gorges, with whom, also, both were now in correspondence.

"The presence of a man like Sir Christopher in the neighborhood of a young settlement was an event which could not but attract notice. Furthermore, it called for explanation, as every one there had to give some account of himself.

"Gardiner claimed that he had come to the New World simply because he was weary of the Old,—that he sought here no preferment, but was willing to earn his living with the rest; and he even professed himself as desirous of joining some one of the churches. This account of himself seems to have been accepted as satisfactory; perhaps, also, the magistrates were too much occupied to give much thought to him, and, not impossible, they were waiting further developments from their friends and agents in England.

"These came at last in March, 1631, about three months after Morton had been sent away, and from them it appeared that Gardiner was far from being a man of godly life.

"Two women claimed to be married to him, one of whom he had abandoned in Paris, the other in London. The former had then, apparently in hunting him up, found the latter, and a comparison of notes followed. It was known to them that Gardiner had gone to New England, and naturally the agents of the Massachusetts company were applied to for information as to his whereabouts."

In due course of time letters from both wives were transmitted to Governor Winthrop, advising him of the facts in the case. The first, or Paris wife, desired her husband's return to her in hopes of his conversion to better things, while the second, or London Lady Gardiner, sought nothing less than the knight's destruction for his foul abuse, and for robbing her of her estate, of a part whereof she sent an inventory, comprising many rich jewels, much plate, and costly linen. This wife of Sir Christopher further advised the Puritan magistrates that the "comly yonge woman he caled his cousin" was a known harlot, Mary Grove by name, whose immediate return to England in company with Gardiner, her husband, she also greatly desired. Altogether it was a scandalous case.

When the court met in Boston on February 18, 1631, the members decreed that Gardiner "shal be sent as prisoner into England by the shipp Lyon, nowe returning thither." Gardiner evidently had information from Governor Winthrop's Council Chamber almost as soon as decisions were made.

When he saw officers crossing the Neponset River half a mile from his house, Gardiner rapidly armed himself and fled into the woods. His lady, Mary Grove, he left behind. Winthrop later questioned her and she readily admitted she was not married nor had she pretended she was.

The Puritans decided to send her to England to confront Gardiner's two wives, but this was never done.

The magistrates now offered the Indians a reward if they would go and get Gardiner, but they were not to kill him. By this time Gardiner had reached the jurisdiction of the Pilgrims. If we can believe a legend, Gardiner arrived at Saquish, Massachusetts, by boat a short time later.

Part of Plymouth, Saquish was the legendary home of Nancy Hanks, ancestor of Abraham Lincoln. In the year 1631, however, it was the headquarters of another mysterious unidentified associate of Sir Ferdinando Gorges, a man whose name we probably shall never know.*

Here at Saquish Sir Christopher Gardiner tarried briefly,

---

* It is said that when Fort Standish was built at Saquish years later, the underground ruin of the residence of Gorges's follower was discovered and destroyed.

using a secret bookcase trapdoor on two occasions when he suspected officers from the mainland would search the house. Finally he received news which caused him to escape into Duxbury by land. His plan now was to reach the Dutch in New York.

Let us ask another historian to take up his quill pen, Governor William Bradford. This Pilgrim had been kept well informed as to the whereabouts of Gardiner, who was then in the neighborhood of the Taunton River in the general Middleborough area. There the Indians discovered him, and asked Bradford if they could kill him:

"But the Governor tould them no, they should not kill him, but watch their opportunitie and take him. And so they did, for when they light of him by a river side, he got into a canowe to get from them, and when they came nere him, whilst he presented his peece at them to keep them of, the streame carried the canow against a rock, and tumbled both him and his peece and rapier into the water; yet he got out, and having a litle dagger by his side, they durst not close with him, but getting longe pols, they soone beat his dagger out of his hand, so he was glad to yeeld; and they brought him to the Governor. But his hands and armes were swolen and very sore with the blowes they had given him. So he used him kindly, and sent him to a lodging wher his armes were bathed and anoynted, and he was quickly well againe, and blamed the Indians for beating him so much."

By this time, however, all means of taking him back to England had vanished, so the pressure was gradually taken off.

We see him later in Brunswick, Maine, where his consort Mary Groves married Thomas Purchase, a man who is described as "an adventurer of good discretion and perseverance." *

* Mary Groves Purchase died in Boston on January 7, 1656, and Purchase married again.

Meanwhile, Gardiner vanished from the pages of New England history. We know that he was present in the Council Chamber in Boston on February 28, 1634. No further record of Sir Christopher Gardiner has ever come to light.

Again we quote Henry Wadsworth Longfellow:

> Thus endeth the Rhyme of Sir Christopher,
> Knight of the Holy Sepulchre,
> The first who furnished this barren land
> With apples of Sodom and ropes of sand.

3

THOMAS MACY, THE EXILE

⚓

MY GOOD FRIEND at the Massachusetts State House, archivist Leo Flaherty, has under his thumb the background for a thousand historical novels, but so far this bibliophile has resisted all efforts to express himself in archival writing elegance. He tells me that one of the exciting possessions in his vaults is the letter of Yeoman Thomas Macy of Salisbury, Massachusetts, who later went in a small open boat all the way around Cape Ann, Cape Cod, and across to Nantucket.

Macy, an upright citizen of Essex County, admitted one day in 1659 that he had given shelter to vagabonds, or Quakers, as we know them today, in his home. At the time the law prohibited any person from opening his door to a Quaker for any reason at all, and Macy was told to appear before the General Court at Boston to receive his punishment. He decided not to obey the summons. Instead he composed an apologetic, almost fawning letter to the general court. As Samuel Adams Drake states: "He believed that in his case discretion was the better part of valor." At any rate, Macy concluded that it was best to avoid the clutches of the law, and was successful in doing so. Macy's letter follows:

"This is to entreat the honored court not to be offended because of my non-appearance. It is not from any slighting the authority of this honored court, nor from feare to answer the case, but I have bin for some weeks past very ill, and am so at present, and notwithstanding my illness, yet I, desirous to appear, have done my utmost endeavour to hire a horse, but cannot procure one at present.

"I being at present destitute have endeavoured to purchase, but at present cannot attaine it, but I shall relate the truth of the case as my answer should be to ye honored court, and more cannot be proved, nor so much.

"On a rainy morning there came to my house Edward Wharton and three men more; the said Wharton spoke to me, saying that they were traveling eastward, and desired me to direct them in the way to Hampton, and asked me how far it was to Casco Bay. I never saw any of ye men afore except Wharton, neither did I require their names, or who they were, but by their carriage I thought they might be Quakers, and told them so, and therefore desired them to passe on their way, saying to them I might possibly give offence in entertaining them, and as soone as the violence of the rain ceased (for it rained very hard) they went away, and I never saw them since.

"The time that they stayed in the house was about three quarters of an hour, but I can safely affirme it was not an hour. They spake not many words in the time, neither was I at leasure to talke with them, for I came home wet to the skin immediately afore they came to the house, and I found my wife sick in bed.

"If this satisfie not the honored court, I shall subject to

their sentence. I have not willingly offended. I am ready to serve and obey you in the Lord. Thomas Macy."

Three of the men mentioned in Macy's letter, being preachers, could look for no mercy from the Puritan authorities who charged them with going about seducing His Majesty's good subjects to their "cursed" opinions. One of them, Edward Wharton, was an old offender. Two of them, William Robinson and Marmaduke Stevenson, are the same persons who, a little later on, were hanged at Boston.*

Meanwhile Macy and others in the area had already purchased the island of Nantucket. There they intended to sail if the general court decided against accepting Macy's explanation, for Nantucket was not within the jurisdiction of the Bay Colony.

When the general court refused to accept his apology, Macy acted with great speed. He rushed his wife, family, and friends into an open boat with whatever belongings were available, and took Richard Starbuck to help him. They rowed and sailed along the coast to Cape Cod, around the Cape and across the treacherous seas to the far-away island of Nantucket, landing at Madaket, and settling there. It was the autumn of 1659, and they had carried out what was truly a remarkable accomplishment! Macy's descendants soon populated the island, and one of them wrote a history of Nantucket.

John Greenleaf Whittier, in telling the story two centuries later, may have colored the facts a little. Whittier's ballad tells us that Macy's house was suddenly surrounded by a troop of horsemen while Quaker Wharton was hidden inside. Macy argues with the sheriff until the officer starts to seize him. Making an excuse, Macy and his family leave the house and run for the river:

* See my *True Tales and Curious Legends*.

THOMAS MACY, THE EXILE

Ho! speed the Macys, neck or naught,—
   The river-course was near:—
The splashing on its pebbled shore
   Was music to their ear.

    . . .

A leap—they gain the boat—and there
   The goodman wields his oar;
"Ill luck betide them all,"—he cried,—
   "The laggards upon the shore."

Down through the crashing underwood,
   The burly sheriff came;—
"Stand, goodman Macy,—yield thyself;
   Yield in the King's own name."

"Now out upon thy hangman's face!"
   Bold Macy answered then,—
"Whip *women* on the village green,
   But meddle not with men."

    . . .

With skilful hand and wary eye
   The harbor-bar was crossed;—
A plaything of the restless wave,
   The boat on ocean tossed.

    . . .

They passed the gray rocks of Cape Ann,
   And Gloucester's harbor-bar;
The watch-fire of the garrison
   Shone like a setting star.

    . . .

Far round the bleak and stormy Cape
   The ven'rous Macy passed,
And on Nantucket's naked isle,
   Drew up his boat at last

    . . .

An yet that isle remaineth
   A refuge of the free,

As when true-hearted Macy
  Beheld it from the sea.

  .   .   .

God bless the sea-beat island!—
  And grant for evermore,
That charity and freedom dwell
  As now upon her shore!

4

THE NAHANT CANNON
⚓

IN THE YEAR 1932, inspired by Robert Salmon's painting of Swallow Cave, Nahant, I journeyed by canoe with Mrs. Snow across from our Winthrop, Massachusetts, home to visit that delightful area which includes such romantic locations as Dorothy's Cove, Joseph's Beach, Sappho's Rock, John's Peril, and Pulpit Rock. Just before we landed we thought we sighted an unusually shaped lobster buoy, but on drawing closer, the buoy turned into a several-hundred-pound shark, which rolled over on its back and slipped right under the canoe.

We never found out what the shark did after that. We know it did not bump the canoe, for I brought my paddle down on the water with a smack so that it sounded like the report of a gun, after which we paddled desperately for Swallow Cave, reaching it in what for us was record-breaking time.*

Landing on the rocky shore, we explored the cave and attempted to figure out just how forty Narraganset Indians could have crowded into that relatively small space inside the cave.** Then, as the tide was high, we swam to the other end

---
* A few days later fishermen in the same area brought in a shark about eighteen feet long weighing approximately 1,450 pounds.
** See my *Strange Tales from Nova Scotia to Cape Hatteras*, pp. 154-160.

of the cave and wandered out onto the beach at the left. Returning, we took the canoe and paddled over to nearby Pea Island, as I wished to see at first hand Nahant's Shag Rocks, often confused with the Shag Rocks near Boston Light where the *Maritana* was lost in 1861.

It was at Nahant's Shag Rocks that the wreck of the *Elizabeth and Ann* went to pieces in the year 1829, and I was eager to dive down between Shag Rocks and Pea Island to search for some gold that might still be there. I had no thoughts of a cannon at that time. Probably our encounter with the shark less than an hour before prevented me from diving as far down or for as long a time as I had planned, but in any case I found nothing.

More than a third of a century elapsed. Then, in the summer of 1969, scuba divers Thomas Lemoine and Fred Pagent decided to explore the same location where I had gone diving in 1932. After exhausting the area immediately near the island, they went out into deeper water, where to their delight and amazement sometime later they located a huge, cylinderlike object which, after considerable effort, they identified as a cannon five feet long and about six hundred pounds in weight.

Heavily encased in rust, barnacles, sea cement, kelp and seaweed, the cannon was eventually attached to a raftlike arrangement at low tide, and when the tide came in, up came the cannon. Later, after being floated over to Canoe Beach, the relic was taken to the home of diver Lemoine, who lives in Lynn.

The story of the cannon begins more than 140 years ago.

Late in the afternoon of March 6, 1829, Captain William Tewksbury, the famous lifesaver, arrived in Boston from Deer Island with the news that Captain Savage and his entire crew had been lost off Nahant on the *Elizabeth and Ann*. Battered fragments of the craft even then were coming ashore up and down the coast, while oranges and cigars from the ship were strewn all along the ocean beaches from what is now Winthrop Highlands to the end of Deer Island.

When the cabin came up on Point Shirley Beach, the captain's watch was found still hanging on a hook attached to the bulkhead. The quarterdeck later smashed ashore at Cedar Island at the entrance to Shirley Gut.*

The day after the storm the inmates of the poorhouse in Chelsea, along with several laborers, were gathering kelp and seaweed on the rocks at what is now Fort Heath, Winthrop. One young lad, more active than the others, saw a partially submerged plank floating in waist-deep water. There seemed to be a white cloth attached to the wood, so the curious youth waded out into the water to get the plank.

To his astonishment, the boy found the cloth was actually a large canvas bag, torn at one end. It was so heavy that he had trouble lifting it, but the young man managed to bring it ashore. Pulling it up on the rocks, he opened the sack and was overwhelmed by what he found. It was filled with golden doubloons!

The others crowded around him, and began to bother the lad, but the overseer was firm, and told them to keep their distance. Putting his assistant in charge of the group, the foreman took the boy at once to the local Chelsea bank with his treasure.

Incidentally, the hole torn in the canvas bag had allowed many of the gold coins to escape into the ocean. A search was made at the time, but nothing more was found.

The money totaled a handsome fortune. Needless to say, the youth's days as a laborer were over. I have spent countless hours attempting to discover how much money he recov-

---

* The only accurate painting including Cedar Island is Robert Salmon's work showing Shirley Gut, Deer Island, and Point Shirley. The island vanished long before the Gut was filled in.

ered and what he did with the unusual find in his subsequent life history, but except for a related incident years later, I have discovered nothing.

One summer, around 1880, the son of the Reverend Mr. Duffield was playing in the sand on the northern side of Grover's Cliff, Winthrop, when he dug up a coin with his shovel. Taking it to his father, the boy found that he was the happy owner of a gold piece.

Word quickly traveled around, as news of that sort does, and soon the entire shoreline was crowded with people searching for gold. Many of them were lucky. The papers of the period reported the finding of around three hundred dollars from the wreck of the craft.

Whether more money is still buried from the wreck of the *Elizabeth and Ann,* lost back in 1829, is an unanswered question, but the ship's five-foot cannon brought up off Nahant is a delightful reminder of scuba-diving adventure at its happiest.

5

THE *MOXIE* TRAGEDY

⚓

CERTAIN DISASTERS can impress a relatively young person so that he will never forget. Such an event was the loss of the *Moxie*.

On the evening of March 29, 1917, the motorboat *Moxie* left Stone's Wharf in Lynn at about 9 P.M. for a voyage of adventure around Boston Bay. The boat was owned by Hudson Robertson of Lynn. His son, also named Hudson, had taken his father's boat without permission for a few hours' ride. In all there were thirteen aboard, all members of a youthful group known as the Biltmore Club.

Hudson had first invited the McQueeney brothers, Thomas and James, and then John Murphy, Matthew Welch, Lester McClearn, and George Gaffney. When word got around among the club members that Robertson was taking out the *Moxie,* six other boys were allowed to join the group, Francis Gerard, Matthew Pashby, Allen Kelly, Tony Scala, Clarence D. Maloon, and M. Henry Brown, Jr. Indeed it became quite a crowd for a motor craft of relatively modest proportions.

Shortly before eleven o'clock, across Boston Bay in the town of Winthrop, where the Snow family lived, residents were walking along Shore Drive, or what was locally known as The Crest. My older brother, the late Nicholas Snow, had gone to the movies with his friend Lawrence Cox and a few others in his group. There had been an old sea offshore with breaking waves from the storm of a few days before. Hearing the booming of the surf, the boys decided to walk along The Crest and see how the waves were hitting.

By the time the group, walking down Ocean Avenue, reached the shore, one of them thought he heard a cry for help coming from way out on the ocean. The others laughed at him, but everyone crossed the wide Shore Drive and went over to the rail on the stone wall above the sand.

Then came a definite shout through the night from out on the water. "Help! Help!" All the boys heard this new frantic appeal.

As the tide was going out, the boys decided to build a huge bonfire to attract and lead those in trouble offshore toward the beach. Unfortunately, nothing more ever really developed. The minutes passed and the cries grew fainter. Telephone calls made to the Winthrop police resulted in their appeal to Gus Johnson, superintendent of the Winthrop Yacht Club. Commandeering a truck, Johnson and others loaded a dory aboard. Another call to the Nahant Coast Guard ended in vain when the Coast Guard explained that their only boat was out of service. The head of the Nahant Coast Guard then stated that he would call someone who would get a boat to go and help whatever craft was in trouble.

The Coast Guard then telephoned Hudson Robertson, who owned the *Moxie,* and he volunteered to go out. Arriving at Stone's Wharf, he found his boat missing. This was the first he realized that his boy probably had taken the boat out.

Meanwhile, across in Winthrop, those on the shore had listened as the cries for help grew fainter and fainter. Finally they died away altogether.

When Gus Johnson arrived on the scene, my brother and

THE *MOXIE* TRAGEDY

Lawrence Cox helped him carry his dory down to the beach. He launched into a heavy swell. A great breaker came rolling in, caught the dory and capsized it. In the icy March water Johnson was barely able to swim ashore, and the others helped him get out of the breakers. Then followed another long period of waiting, but after vainly staying up until the early hours of the morning, one by one the watchers on shore abandoned their vigil and departed to their homes.

My brother did not know who had been in trouble, of course, but he and his friends were amazed the next morning when they discovered that no less than thirteen boys had been aboard the *Moxie* and probably all had drowned. As the days went by, however, rumor after rumor came in that several of the boys had been picked up or had been sighted on the harbor islands. Of course, every rumor proved false.

A few days after the tragedy the first body was found on one of the Brewster Islands. Then, on the afternoon of April 6, just as this nation was declaring war on Germany, Tom Johnson and I decided to walk along the beach to see if anything could be found of the missing boat *Moxie*. I shall never forget the terror we experienced when we discovered the first body. In all at least six boys washed in on the beach that day between Winthrop Bar and Point Shirley itself. They proved so heavy that ladders had to be brought down and the bodies rolled onto the ladders to be taken up to the shelter of the seawall.

In a relatively short time the parents were notified, and we watched as pitiful scenes took place and identification after identification was made.

A special relaxing of parental discipline occurred that night after Tom Johnson and I discovered the bodies on Winthrop's Short Beach shore. Both Tom's mother and my mother allowed us to go to the movies. It was a school night, and I'll always remember the actor and the picture. Sessue

Hayakawa, who later played the Japanese prison camp commander in the *Bridge on the River Kwai,* was the star in Stevenson's *Bottle Imp.* For those of you who have read the tale, you'll agree it was not the ideal movie to see after what we had gone through.

Two days later the *Moxie* herself was exposed, and I went down at an extremely low tide and examined her. Filled with water, her gunwales were barely above the surface of the sea. As I stood there I thought of the great tragedy that had separated so many happy families.

6

PERTH AMBOY
⚓

GERMANY BROUGHT World War I to the mainland of the United States on Sunday, July 21, 1918. At the time, 10:30 in the morning, the tug *Perth Amboy* was towing four barges three miles off Orleans on Cape Cod, heading from Gloucester to New York. A U-boat opened fire on the tug and her four barges, and continued the attack until noon. The tug was burned by shellfire, and the barges *Landsward, 766, 403* and *740* sent to the bottom. Only one barge was loaded, her cargo consisting of stone. The seamen and their families all were aboard the various craft.

No less than forty-one people were aboard the five craft, including three women and five children. Three men, Captain Charles Ainsleigh of the *Landsward,* John Bolovitch and John Botovich, Austrian members of the *Perth Amboy* crew, were wounded. Captain Ainsleigh was wounded in both arms by shrapnel and was treated in Orleans at the summer home of Dr. J. Danforth Taylor of East Boston.

Before the attack ended large crowds of natives and summer visitors, attracted by gunfire, watched the thrilling encounter taking place just off the shores of Cape Cod.

According to Captain Ainsleigh the U-boat launched three torpedoes at the tug. Not one of them hit. After shelling the tug and barges, the U-boat finally submerged. She was last observed heading south.

The tug was later brought into port, with the effects of her battering clearly visible. Cape Cod residents could not understand why the U-boat would waste shells on a fleet of barges proceeding down the coast. It is believed by some that the real goal of the U-boat was a large northbound collier. Two colliers, the *Arlington* and the *J. D. King*, passed Orleans shortly before the *Perth Amboy* was fired upon, but both safely escaped through the danger zone.

A substantial fogbank lying four miles offshore had hid the U-boat from her approaching victims until the last moment. Proceeding leisurely through the calm summer sea, the *Perth Amboy* was unaware of the presence of danger. Suddenly a deckhand sighted a streak of foam underwater which shot by close to the stern. Before he realized that it was a torpedo, two other missiles slipped by, each wide of its mark. He shouted a warning, and at that moment there was a flash out of the fog and a cannon shell crashed through the wheelhouse.

The U-boat now methodically shot shell after shell at the convoy. One by one the barges were hit at the waterline and disappeared beneath the surface until only the stern of the *Landsward* was visible. The tug herself became a blazing inferno.

Captain J. H. Tapley, who was in his cabin, ran out on deck just as the submarine loomed out of the fogbank with her deck gun flashing out the deadly shells.

An example of the spirit of American youth was shown by eleven-year-old Jack Ainsleigh. When the submarine started shelling, the boy ran into the cabin and returned carrying an American flag. Leaning over the rail, he waved the colors in defiance at the German submarine. He then shouted to his father that he was going to get his gun, a twenty-two caliber rifle, and return some of the shots the U-boat was firing.

Captain Ainsleigh restrained his son, but shortly after this the captain himself was hit by shrapnel as he superintended the launching of a small boat.

Soon all the crew and their families were in rowboats. When the little flotilla of boats entered Nauset Harbor, young Jack Ainsleigh was sitting in the bow of the skiff holding the American flag proudly erect. He was given a rousing cheer by the cottagers who rushed down to the beach to help the survivors ashore.

When the U-boat surfaced that Sunday she had been twelve miles northeast of the Orleans Coast Guard Station. The first notice of the firing was brought to Captain Robert F. Pierce, keeper of the Orleans Station, by the man in the tower. "There's heavy firing offshore up to the north," he said, and the men soon learned a submarine was attacking.

Pierce ordered the surfboat made ready, and then telephoned Superintendent George W. Bowley at Provincetown for final instructions. It was an unheard-of situation in American history. Should the surfboat be launched to save lives at the scene of the sinkings, or should the surfboat be kept ashore until the submarine had gone?

Superintendent Bowley, in good American fashion, ordered the surfboat to proceed to the scene of the U-boat attack, where Captain Pierce was to place himself and crew in readiness to save life.

Launching the surfboat, Captain Pierce arrived in time to see the German submarine standing by on the surface of the water. By this time the loaded barge had already gone down and the other three were on their beam ends in the water. The tug was still on fire. Lifeboats from the four barges and the tug were already pulling away from the sinking and burning vessels.

Captain Pierce discovered that several of the crew of the tugboat *Perth Amboy* had been wounded by gunfire from the submarine, so he did what he could to help them. Meanwhile the U-boat slowly submerged.

Then the other lifeboats followed the surfboat, and eventually all landed without further incident. A special train took the wounded men to Boston.

When interviewed, Captain Pierce admitted the situation had not been a pleasant one. "It looked rather hard to be sent twelve miles away in a small surfboat to a German submarine firing heavy guns on a tow of barges, but orders from the superintendent must be executed and I had no excuse," were his words.

One hundred and forty-seven shots were counted, at least one of which landed on United States soil at Orleans. Aviators from the local Chatham Naval Air Base were up in Provincetown at a baseball game. Five hydroplanes eventually circled the area, and there is a persistent rumor that one plane actually took off in time to drop a monkey wrench on the deck of the U-boat, which submerged shortly afterwards.

The late Walter Walsh Eldridge, or Good Walter as he was called, was at the scene of the U-boat attack a short time after Captain Pierce's surfboat arrived. The U-boat had disappeared, so Walter and his associates went aboard the smouldering tug.

"We got off a few chairs from the *Perth Amboy*," he said. "A short time afterwards a big steamer came by loaded with passengers. We were half expecting to see it blown up, but I guess the U-boat was pretty far away by that time.

"I knew there was a mess out there when I heard the firing, so we started out to see what we could salvage," he said.

Years later, in 1936, Captain Jim Tapley of the *Perth Amboy* decided to write of his experiences that memorable day.

His words follow:

* * *

"This is an account of my encounter with a German submarine during the First World War. I was then captain of the tug *Perth Amboy* owned by the Lehigh Valley Railroad and engaged in the coastwise transportation service, principally between New Jersey ports and ports in New England.

"We left Portland, Maine, about noon on the twentieth day of July, 1918, with a tow of three barges bound for New York. About two A.M. the next morning we cleared from Gloucester, where we had picked up a fourth barge, also for New York. That was Sunday and as fine a summer day as we could wish for. We had passed out by Highland Light on Cape Cod about eight A.M. and since my rest had been broken the night before, I decided to have a little rest before dinner.

"I had been asleep only a short while when I was awakened by a loud explosion, and on going into the pilot house found the man at the wheel as much surprised as myself as to its cause. It was not long before there was a second explosion and I then discovered that a shell had exploded only a short distance from us. It was not until a third shell had exploded that I discovered a submarine about a mile offshore of us and partly submerged. This, I was sure, was the source of the trouble. I had not long to wait before a fourth shell hit the tug and exploded with a terrible report.

"At the time I was partially stunned but soon regained consciousness to find both doors blown off the pilot house and a large hole in the roof over my head. My room adjoining the pilot house was completely destroyed with everything in it. I do not remember seeing the man who had been steering until we were leaving in the boat. The last shell had set the tug on fire around the pilot house, which was then burning rapidly.

"As soon as possible, we launched the boat; this took about four minutes. After seeing that the crew of seventeen men were in it, we started for the shore toward the Coast Guard

Station at Orleans, Massachusetts, which was about two miles away. The submarine then continued to shell the barges, sinking all four of them and doing considerable damage to the tug, which remained afloat and afire.

"After getting in the lifeboat I found that the wheelsman had been badly injured. His right arm had been hit by a piece of shell that had broken it just above the elbow, leaving a hole about the size of a half silver dollar through it. Another piece had hit him in the back making a flesh wound about five inches long and a half inch deep. A third piece had gone through the muscle in his leg just below the knee. As I was standing directly between the man and the submarine when he was hit, it has always been a mystery to me that I escaped with only one slight wound. Several others in the crew had flesh wounds of little consequence, except possibly the cook, who went to the hospital some months later to have several small pieces of shell taken from his leg.

"Upon nearing shore we were met by the Coast Guard boat which gave first aid to the injured man, and as soon as we landed he was rushed to the hospital at Boston where after a long time he was discharged. His arm had been saved by grafting a piece of bone from his leg into it and although it is no doubt much better than an artificial limb, it is far from being what it was before the accident.

"On our arrival at the Coast Guard Station shortly after noon we were given a cordial welcome and were fed and clothed to the best of their ability. Many of the men including myself escaped with very little clothing. I forgot at the time about the others but my full equipment on landing consisted of a suit of underclothes badly soiled with blood from attending the wounded man, part of an outside shirt, the other part of which was used to tie up the man's wounded arm, a pair of socks and a pair of trousers that I had reclaimed by washing and pressing; this had apparently weakened them so that the first time I stooped over there opened up a wide gape in a place that is very embarrassing to any man.

"I secured an outfit as best I could at the Coast Guard Station with the exception of shoes. Later that afternoon we returned to the tug where the Chief Engineer saved most of his clothes, since his room was in the after part of the tug where the fire had not reached at that time. He kindly let me have a pair of his shoes which were several sizes too large, he was wearing size twelve and I size eight. It was no easy task walking in the sand, because the extra size soon became filled with sand which made progress slow until I stopped and emptied them.

"We remained at the Coast Guard Station that night in sight of the tug which continued to burn until late in the evening, when a Coast Guard boat that was sent out from Provincetown apparently put out the fire.

"The next forenoon the tug *Lehigh* arrived alongside the *Perth Amboy* to take her to Vineyard Haven. I then decided to go back on board, but was detained for a while by a United States Intelligence Officer until much against his wishes, I finally left with five members of my crew in our lifeboat and started to row out to the tug. We arrived within a short distance of her, when the *Lehigh,* having gotten her clear from the wire cable that was made fast to the sunken barges, started with her in tow for Vineyard Haven. We tried to attract their attention on board the *Lehigh,* but we were unsuccessful so returned to the shore where we found a sea sled that had been sent up from Chatham and was waiting for us.

"Aboard the sea sled we were soon on our way at a speed of fifty-five miles an hour to join our tug. It looked as though we would soon be on board. It was a very hazy day and when nearing the Shoals of Chatham, we could not see a distance of more than a mile. However, we arrived in sight of the tugs and expected soon to be on board, when one of the engines on our sea sled stopped. The sea sled was equipped with two engines, and with only one of them running she would go around in a circle, so it was impossible to proceed before this engine could be started. The engineer assured us that he would have it fixed in a few minutes, but after what seemed nearly an hour, we were still drifting helplessly with the tide and the engineer was beginning to develop a worried look. Finally a hydroplane was seen circling above us and seeing our signal that was sent by the wigwag system, it was soon along side of us. It was our intention to have this plane transfer us to the *Perth Amboy*, but while discussing the matter, the engineer succeeded in getting the engine started so we proceeded under our own power once more with the plane flying only a short distance above us to see that we had no more trouble.

"It was not long before we were alongside the *Perth Amboy* and on board. We continued on to Vineyard Haven where a large fleet of vessels had been detained until it was considered safe to proceed to Boston. A large crowd awaited us on shore and we were given a grand reception.

"The fire that had been nearly extinguished on the *Perth Amboy* got into the coal bunkers and continued to burn for three days but by pumping water into her through the fire hose and then pumping it out of the hull again it was finally extinguished on Wednesday morning.

"We remained at Vineyard Haven until the fire was out. Then we were taken in tow and proceeded on to New York. Although the upper part of the tug was badly damaged, both by fire and gun shot, the hull, with the boiler and engines, was taken to a shipyard and repairs were begun. While repairs were made, I was given a vacation and then placed on the other tugs until the *Perth Amboy* was ready once more for service in November.

"I have now been going to sea over thirty-nine years and in

looking back over the past as we all are so apt to do, I can say that it seems a short time since the day I started out from home when a boy to go to sea. —Captain James H. Tapley, May 16, 1936."

7

MURDER AT MIDDLE BREWSTER

⚓

ON THURSDAY, January 29, 1970, a news item was released from Des Moines, Iowa, telling of Mr. and Mrs. Edward Briney who rigged a shotgun in their farmhouse to protect the building from thieves. Eventually that shotgun cost them a court decision of more than $55,000.

The Briney family owned an eighty-acre farm near Eddyville in Mohaska County, and had set up the trap gun in a bedroom in 1967 when bothered by intruders.

In July, 1967, a prowler, Marvin Katko, twenty-seven, was wounded in the ankle by the trap gun when he entered the bedroom. Caught, he pleaded guilty to larceny in the night time. Katko was fined fifty dollars and released. He then sued the Briney family for $50,000 plus $5000 court costs and won.

At the sheriff's sale on Tuesday, January 27, 1970, the Briney home was sold for $10,001 to make partial payment to Katko.

When I learned of this strange story, I thought back two generations to the year 1923, when I first heard the weird tale of the boy who died at Boston Light because of similar tactics involving trap guns. It became one of the most unusual trials in Massachusetts history, one which a generation ago was often used in teaching law courses. Although taking place on Middle Brewster Island in Boston Harbor, the murder was actually committed in the jurisdiction of Hull which includes part of Boston Harbor, and so the case itself eventually came up in the Plymouth Superior Court.

It all began on the morning of June 13, 1923. Over at Boston Light, keeper J. Hart was down on the lighthouse pier. Early that morning he had heard a shot from a German Mauser rifle fired at Middle Brewster Island a short distance away. That shot led to the death a few hours later of an Italian lad from Boston's North End. The boy, brought to the lightkeeper's residence, died there on the kitchen floor.

Long before dawn that fatal day Salvatore Ciarmataro and his two sons, Vittorio and Joseph, had left the North End of Boston aboard a motorboat heading for the outer harbor. They were to spend the low-tide part of the day among the Brewster Islands to gather periwinkles, an Italian delicacy. Joseph was put ashore at Calf Island, and Vittorio at Middle Brewster.

Vittorio worked for two hours in the hot sun, and then became thirsty. Unable to locate a well, he went to the home of caretaker Hjalmar Roos in the middle of the island where he knocked at both front and back doors to no avail. Then, as his thirst increased, and although he knew it was wrong, he went from window to window, trying to find one unlocked.

Noticing a window on the back porch open just a little and the shade drawn with a towel hanging beside it, Vittorio reached for the sash to push up the window. A blinding explosion occurred, and Vittorio felt a stunning shock in his stomach. He had been shot by a concealed trap gun.

The unfortunate lad managed to crawl down to the beach, where he collapsed. Across on Great Brewster, his father had gathered his quota of periwinkles when he heard the shot. Ciarmataro walked out on the bar, calling for his son. Hearing a muffled reply, he walked farther along the bar, and then into the ankle-deep water, calling constantly. Again he heard the muffled voice.

"Pa, come. I've been shot."

Noticing another fishing craft starting out from Calf Island, the father shouted in that direction. It was a lobster boat, operated by young Augustus Reekast who had lived on the islands of the outer harbor most of his life. Reekast had heard the shot and also decided to investigate. On the way he stopped to pick up Joseph Ciarmataro. The anxious father still called to Reekast. Ten minutes later the lobsterman landed at Great Brewster where the frightened Salvatore shouted at him.

"My son Vittorio just called to me from Middle Brewster. He says that someone shot him. Can you help?"

"I'll take you right over there," came the reply. They soon reached Middle Brewster and rowed ashore.

Vittorio told them what had happened. They tried as best they could to staunch the flow of blood before carrying the wounded boy to the motorboat. Reekast headed for the boat slip at Boston Light, where Salvatore went ashore. When he returned he told the others that keeper Hart had telephoned for help, and suggested they bring the wounded lad to his kitchen. It was then nine o'clock in the morning.

Twenty minutes later the quarantine boat from Gallop's Island brought a doctor and a nurse who did what they could for the young Italian. Unfortunately, Vittorio died fifty minutes afterward, for the bullet had gone through the boy's body, shattering his spine.

Hull police arrived, and after learning the details, went over to Middle Brewster, where they found the window smashed by the bullet. Chief Frank M. Reynolds managed to open the window. Examining the towel which had hung beside the shade, he discovered that it concealed a stout cord that ran from the sash to the floor where a pulley held it in place.

The cord then led across the room to the kitchen sink and from the sink to the trigger of a powerful German Mauser rifle which had been set in a frame of wood so that it could not move. Chief Reynolds had come upon one of the most diabolical gun traps ever to kill a man!

There seemed to be nothing of any great value in the cottage and apparently no one but Vittorio had been on the island at the time of the shooting. The chief phoned the Boston police from Boston Light and asked them to pick up the caretaker of Middle Brewster, Hjalmar Roos,* who lived in the home on Middle Brewster.

Roos was captured the next day, but he was bailed out by the owner of the island, Melvin Ohio Adams, who of course had no previous knowledge of the booby trap. The trial resulted in a $750 fine for Roos, as it was ruled the boy had been breaking and entering when shot.

Salvatore Ciarmataro, and after his death, the survivors, tried to collect damages for Vittorio's death, and the case was continued for a number of years, until finally in 1931 it was settled by a payment of $6,000. Strangely, Roos was still working as caretaker at Middle Brewster Island all this time.

Years later, in December 1954, I was autographing books at a large Boston department store when someone touched me on the arm. It was Augustus Reekast, who told me he had some information in which I'd be interested. I arranged to have him come back at suppertime when the crowd of autograph seekers thinned out.

Reekast then reminded me of the day when I had gone out in my canoe to visit him and had asked for his story of the shooting. He admitted that he had not told the whole story.

---

* His name is spelled Roose in the newspapers and Roos in the Plymouth court records.

"Roos is now dead, and I am ready to give the details."

He explained that he and Roos had had trouble over lobster traps. Reekast suspected that the other man was hauling traps that were not his. The day before the shooting, Roos tried to run him down, but Reekast maneuvered to get away. Reekast shouted "I'll get you for this," but he had a large load of lobsters, and could not spend the time to chase after Roos that day.

"That gun trap that he set and which was fired when the young Italian boy opened the window was meant to kill me. Only the fact that I had a full load of lobsters to take in to a customer kept his plan from working. When I got back from town Roos's boat was gone, and I guessed right that he had left for South Boston.

"The next morning I got up and hauled a few traps. All of a sudden I heard the shot at Middle Brewster. I knew then that the bullet intended for me had been fired at someone else."

At the Plymouth superior court the indictment returned by the grand jurors at the October sitting in 1923 alleged that "Hjalmar J. Roos, of Hull in the County of Plymouth, in the said county, assaulted and beat Victor Ciarmataro and by such assault and beating did kill Victor Ciarmataro."

On the twenty-sixth of October Hjalmar J. Roos pleaded guilty. The court fined him $750, and ordered him committed until the fine was paid.

As I have already mentioned, Melvin O. Adams, who ran the Narrow Gauge Boston, Revere Beach and Lynn Railroad and owned Middle Brewster Island, paid the fine for caretaker Roos and later the $6,000. When compared to the $55,000 judgment against the Briney family, Adams was indeed relatively lucky.

8

THE TRIPLE STORMS OF 1969

⚓

> The snow had begun in the gloaming,
> And busily all the night
> Had been heaping field and highway
> With a silence deep and white.
>
> Every pine and fir and hemlock
> Wore ermine too dear for an earl,
> And the poorest twig on the elm-tree
> Was ridged inch deep with pearl.
> —James Russell Lowell

ON SUNDAY, February 9, 1969, the first of three outstanding snowstorms hit New England. Most of the Massachusetts residents living south of Boston had almost forgotten that the icy grasp of winter was still a possibility, although there hadn't been a major storm that winter. Even the cities and towns had been lulled into a sense of indifference. The weather report for that Sunday predicted only a modest snowfall. And so it was, when the first big storm came no one was ready for it. The result was chaos.

A northeast gale, rapidly increasing in intensity as it moved across the Bay State, caused more than fifty deaths in New

England. Vast areas were without electricity for forty-eight hours, and telephones in scores of areas were worthless.

It snowed and it snowed and it snowed.*

Thousands upon thousands of cars clogged main area roads. Finally, on February 12, after fifty hours of blizzardlike conditions, Massachusetts gradually began to recover, but it was agonizingly slow. The cars still abandoned on the highways took much longer to remove than was expected. Briefly, the storm had come too fast, the gales were too strong, and the plows too late. As a result the snow-removal costs staggered the imagination of the tired taxpayers.

On the main highways the snow first reduced the key arterial roads to two lanes, then to one, with motorists often forced to drive on and on hoping for an open ramp so that they could get off the expressways. One by one the lanes became hopelessly jammed and the car occupants were faced with the disheartening task of abandoning their vehicles and hiking to comparative safety.

In homes, the fortunate families who had fireplaces were able to keep fairly warm and cook impromptu meals. But others had to seek refuge in schools, churches, motels, and with their neighbors. When electric power was finally restored most of the people were cold, tired, unwashed, unshaven, and hungry.

On Monday, February 10, the Blue Hills Observatory in Milton, Massachusetts, reported that the snowfall had reached 17.3 inches, which increased to 21.6 inches the next day. The wind there had hit eighty-nine miles an hour at the height of the gale.

A portion of the roof of the Sears store in the Mall at Natick, Massachusetts, collapsed from the weight of the snow,

---

* The storm produced the greatest amount of snow since February 4, 1961 when 14.4 inches fell. The 1969 Sunday-Monday total was 11.1 inches.

with the damage estimated at one million dollars. Several other buildings also lost all or part of their roofs.

Crews came from as far away as Hartford, Connecticut, to help the Boston Edison Company restore power. Eighty percent of Needham homes and 90 percent in Dedham were without power for long periods.

At the height of the fiercest gale the *Constitution*, known as Old Ironsides, broke free from her moorings, but was soon returned to her berth at the Charlestown Navy Yard in Boston.

When the storm came to an end, it proved to be the most expensive in Boston history. The State Public Works Commissioner, Edward J. Ribbs, said the bill for snow removal would be $1,800,000.

Late Sunday, February 23, the second February storm began to make its presence known, and all New England was soon bruised and battered. The first flakes began to fall around Boston just before midnight Sunday, with the Weather Bureau predicting a fall of two to four inches.

As the hours of Monday wore on the storm increased in intensity. Gale winds hit the coast that night as the Weather Bureau raised the forecast to nine inches. Still the snow fell. The temperature dropped into the twenties and the dry snow swept by peak winds drifted deeper and deeper, and it was not until Friday afternoon that New England saw the sun. By the gale's end the Blue Hills Weather Observatory reported that thirty inches had fallen.

Public facilities were ready this time, and the snowstorm was not as devastating as the first one. Nevertheless, many people lost their electric power, while still others were marooned in their cars.

When the lights failed at the Snow residence, we resorted to cooking our meals in one of our fireplaces and indeed it was a real return to primitive conditions. At first we enjoyed the novelty, but eventually we began to wonder when the electricity would return. Frankly we were relieved when the lights came back on.

A two- to four-inch snowfall had been predicted. When the storm ended, snow depths were as high as three feet, with drifts over eighteen feet. This storm will be known as the Big Snow of 1969, and the 26.3 inches that fell in Boston must be recorded as the greatest storm in the history of that city's Weather Bureau, although on many other occasions in New England history, starting long before the Weather Bureau operated, there have been heavier snow falls.*

Falling longer and harder along the Massachusetts coast than anywhere else, the snow hit Cape Ann in the Gloucester-Rockport area with almost terrifying results. Badly crippled was the region around Route 133 in Essex, while Beverly and Ipswich were struck overwhelming blows from which the towns could not recover for a week, even with the help of army equipment.

The terrible snowstorms of 1969 brought out the fact that quite often those who operate snowblowers are not qualified in this respect. It is probable that several score people in New England were injured while running snowblowers. Many people were taken to hospitals because of their failure to be moderately careful. It was explained by hospital spokesmen that the accidents usually came when people reached under a machine to clear snow out of the motor while the machine was still running.

Another indication of a changing world was that hundreds and hundreds of cars belonging to skiers were caught on the highways leading back from the skiing areas. This was never a hazard in the old days.

The third storm, that of March 3, which could be classified

---

* The years 1716, 1717, 1741, 1774, 1786, 1857, 1867, and 1878 provide typical examples.

as a weekend gale, saw many commuters stay home rather than take a chance on traveling. Within twenty-four hours most roads were passable, and it was then hoped that King Winter had finished sending storms of such intensity as 1969's first two wintry gales.

9

THE STORM OF 1898

⚓
———

THE "PORTLAND" STORM of 1898 will always be so called for the sidewheeler *Portland,* which went down with all hands during the storm. Many craft met their doom during this storm, including the pilot boat *Columbia,* also lost with all hands. Another pilot boat out in the same gale, the *Varuna,* survived the storm.

Varuna

During a long career in piloting service, the most hazardous experience of the *Varuna* * occurred during the night of the Portland storm, November 26-27, 1898.

When the storm broke she was about twenty miles off Minot's Light, Cohasset. Because of the intensity of the gale, Captain William H. Fairfield had himself lashed to the wheel and remained on duty twenty-four hours, allowing himself to be relieved only after two of his ribs had been broken from beating against the binnacle. The foresail was carried away and ice and snow added to the difficulties encountered.

---

* Built in Chelsea at the Howard & Montgomery yard in 1890, she was 88 feet long and named for the Vedic king of the waters in Hindu mythology. Pilot boats in the early days were schooners without engines. They now have auxiliary power.

However, the *Varuna* survived the storm which sent so many staunch craft to their doom at the bottom of the sea. When the injured Captain Fairfield was carried to his bunk, he shouted out to keep the *Varuna* headed up and to make a straight wake. One of the *Varuna's* boats was crushed and the other damaged. Her lee rail was carried away. The *Varuna's* deck was completely covered with sand blown from sandbars when she was off Cape Cod during the height of the Portland storm.

Discovered in crippled condition by an incoming Philadelphia vessel, she was then towed into port, although a pilot guided the Philadelphia craft as they entered Boston. On arrival there was quite a celebration, with every whistle in the harbor greeting her. She had been feared lost, for her broken rail, bearing the name *Varuna,* had been reported from Cape Cod, where it had been picked up on the shore along with wreckage from the *King Philip, Pentagoet, Addie E. Snow,* and *Portland.*

Columbia

On several occasions I have told the tale of the loss of the *Columbia* at the height of the Portland gale of 1898. New material has been located and is added to the story of the wreck, which has been related at Scituate firesides for over half a century.

The *Columbia's* last known act was to discharge her pilot, Captain William Abbott, aboard the steamer *Ohio,* which later pushed ashore on Spectacle Island. The storm grew worse as the evening wore on, and it is believed that the *Columbia* worked her way out to the vicinity of the Boston Lightship. Then the gale took over. No one escaped the wreck, so conjecture alone must dictate the story of the *Columbia.*

The morning after the wreck Surfman Richard Tobin of

the North Scituate Lifesaving Station had the south patrol along Sand Hills from eight to twelve. His report follows:

"I went down to the beach to the key post about three miles from the station. . . . The seas were coming over with such force that I was washed into the pond back of the ridge. It was blowing so hard that I was obliged to kneel down to get my breath."

At 9:30 Surfman Tobin was on the veranda of the very cottage into which the *Columbia* later crashed. When he returned to the station it was three in the afternoon. The storm was now so intense that no patrol was permitted to leave; in fact the next patrol did not go out until midnight.

Surfman John Curran set out on the south patrol this time, and at 1:45 A.M. he sighted a schooner lying on the beach right in the line of his patrol. She had crashed into a cottage.

The wreckage from the shattered building was lying in heaped confusion on the decks of the careened vessel. Since Surfman Tobin had stood on the veranda of that cottage at 9:30 the *Columbia* had washed up on the beach after that time. No one witnessed the disaster and no one ever knew exactly what took place.

By 3:20 that morning Curran had returned to the station and notified the captain of the lifesaving station, who visited the scene with three surfmen. On the way they found the body of the *Columbia*'s first boat keeper. The bodies of four other men were later discovered in the vicinity. No others ever came ashore.

The wreck of the *Columbia* was complete. The starboard side of the pilot boat had split near the garboard, the planking was torn where she hung and ground on the rocks, and the sternpost was broken to pieces. The foremast was gone, two anchor chains hung from the hawsepipes, and the anchors were missing.

When the *Columbia* took the station offshore the week before the storm, there were four pilots aboard, Captain Thomas Cooper, Captain William Abbott, Captain John Fawcett, and Captain Ellis Olsen.

The following men were drowned: Peter Peterson of Roslindale, the first boat keeper; Edward E. Peterson of Maine, the second boat keeper; Andrew Ellingson of North Bennett Street, Boston, the third boat keeper; an unknown Norwegian, who was the fourth boat keeper; Frank Nelson, 15 Charter Street, Boston, the cook.

Nelson left a widow and two grown children. Ellingson boarded with a brother-in-law and was married, and the others were single.

When the wreck was found, the body of one of the crew, about forty years old, was discovered in the hold.

The *Columbia* was built in 1894 in the yard of Ambrose Martin at Jeffries Point, East Boston, for Captain Thomas Cooper, E. C. Martin, and John and Joseph Fawcett. She was ninety feet five inches over all and was about eighty-five tons registered.

Probably the five men on the pilot boat were dead before the *Columbia* struck the beach, and the fact that both anchors were gone showed that the vessel had attempted unsuccessfully to weather the storm. This opinion was shared by a majority of seafaring men who visited the scene.

The pilot boat *Columbia* was left where she hit on the beach, high above the reach of the normal tides of the years. Too badly damaged for reconditioning, she was made into a museum. Run at one time by Otis Barker, the museum stayed on the Scituate beach for years. Barker introduced many reminders of the "home on the sands," of Dickens's *David Copperfield*, according to historian Ralph M. Eastman, who mentions Old Peggotty and Little Emily. Thousands visited this vessel during the first quarter of the present century, but about the year 1933 the elements began to make inroads on the wreck, and so it was that Scituate officials ordered the pilot boat burned.

Thus ended the career of the Boston pilot boat *Columbia*, the schooner on which five brave men tried unsuccessfully to ride out the Portland gale.

Mertis H. Perry

Out in the same wild, furious gale which destroyed the steamer *Portland* was a fishing schooner, the *Mertis H. Perry*. Through the cooperation of my good friend Torrey Little, I have been able to offer my readers a picture never made public before, a picture of that same schooner after she was wrecked off Brant Rock.

I do not know the photographer, but offer him a tardy congratulation for his excellent work that cold day of November 28, 1898, when he photographed the *Mertis H. Perry*, cast ashore two miles north-northwest of the Brant Rock Lifesaving Station. Five of the fourteen men in her crew lost their lives.

At 8:30 in the forenoon that Saturday morning, the lifesavers of Brant Rock were faced with a terrific job of rescue and assistance. The storm had battered the cottages in furious fashion: one woman and her four children had to be brought to the lifesaving station and, when the doors of the station began to collapse, assisted to the Union Church seventy-five yards to the west.

While the lifesavers were making these and similar strenuous efforts to save the townspeople, a fishing schooner, the *Mertis H. Perry* of Boston, dashed ashore between nine and ten o'clock in the forenoon. No one saw her come ashore, but two of her survivors gave the story.

The schooner left Boston on Monday afternoon, November 21, with a crew of fourteen, bound for the fishing grounds that lie about twelve miles southeastward of Highland Light, Cape Cod. The first part of the trip was uneventful, with the exception that the vessel sought refuge in Provincetown Harbor on the twenty-fourth and twenty-fifth where she rode out a northwester.

The evening of the twenty-sixth, with a catch of about fourteen thousand mixed fish, she started for Boston. The wind at this time was fresh from the northeast and breezing on. Highland and Race Point lights were sighted, but at about 9:30 that night the weather shut in thick with snow and rain. The course laid out was about northwest by north. The sea and wind kept increasing every moment, and at about eleven o'clock the captain wore ship with the intention of edging offshore.

The snow was now driving across the vessel in sheets and the seas were sweeping her decks. There were but thirteen fathoms of water underfoot, and as one anchor failed to bring the schooner head to, the starboard anchor was let go with the chain cable. This fetched her up, but the increasing fury of the gale caused her to drag both anchors and all on board knew that the water was rapidly shoaling.

The captain, almost despairing, ordered the masts cut away. The foremast went first, but hung alongside fast to the jibstay; the mainmast went clear. About half past two in the morning of the seventh, the hemp cable parted and the sailors took the stranded end that led up through the hawsepipe and made it fast to the chain cable, veering the latter to its full scope. Still the craft continued to drag. The lead was put over and the sounding indicated only six or seven fathoms. Finally, at about seven o'clock, the schooner was brought up by her anchor, but hardly had this occurred when the chain cable parted.

There now remained but one thing to do—head her to the westward, strike the beach somewhere, and take their chances.

She was turned before the storm, which swept her along with the force and speed of an avalanche, while the crew, to whom the end did not seem far off, clung desperately to the hoops around the stumps of the masts. Five minutes later the vessel was in the midst of heavy breakers, and almost immediately struck bottom, the seas making a clean breach over her.

She kept pounding in all the while, the flood tide helping her on, until the imperiled men could see the dim outlines of the land through the thick veil of snow. At eight o'clock, when she could not have been more than two hundred yards off, William Bagnall, of Cape Breton Island, suddenly gave up and died, doubtless from the effects of his terrible exposure. The captain, Joshua Pike, said to have been of North Sydney, N.S., had evidently become demented from his awful experience, for he abruptly picked up part of a dory that had been smashed in, and without saying a word, jumped overboard, and was not seen afterward.

A big sea now turned the vessel broadside on and swung the jibboom so far off that those still on board could not reach the bank that way. They hove a line to their shipmates on shore, but before the latter could make it fast, another sea hove the craft back, and six of the remaining men crept along the jibboom and landed safely.

Joseph Veader of Gloucester fell off and was drowned. George Bagnall died from exhaustion, while his comrades were making their escape, and Charles Forbes, who succeeded in getting ashore, was so prostrated that the survivors were obliged to leave him behind, while they themselves went in search of aid to relieve their own distress. They reached the farmhouse of a Mr. Ames, where they were given dry clothing and cared for. Two of the farmhands were at once dispatched for Forbes, but on arriving at the scene of the wreck they found him lying dead on the bluff.

Thus, nine men survived and five perished.

Minot's Light

The keeper of Minot's Light, Milton Reamy,* wrote a letter to the editor of the *Daily Ledger* in Quincy, Massachusetts, shortly after the great Portland gale of 1898, in which he describes the storm and compares it with other previous catastrophies.

"Editor, *Daily Ledger:*

"The terrible blizzard of November 26-27 far exceeded both the great storm of February 1, 1898, and that of the winter of 1888 in violence and destructive power. The official records of the Weather Bureau conclusively prove this. There are no official records of the great spring gale of April 16, 1851, which carried away Minot's Ledge lighthouse, drowning the keepers and proving the inadequacy of lighthouses built on iron supports on sea level sites.

"The latter storm was accompanied by rain, not snow, and the tide rose two feet less than in the late blizzard. As the wind in spring gales is not usually so violent as in the fall and winter storms, and as the actual damage done by it was less than in the last storm, it is highly probable that it too, was storm of less magnitude.

"The lighthouse which preceded the present structure was a round building erected on about a dozen iron rods, making a structure similar in general appearance to Bug Light in Boston Harbor, but of course much larger and higher. These upright rods were held in place by enormous iron nuts, as large around as a man's body, and each weighing several hundred pounds.

"The immeasurable power of the waves demolished it in short time after the gale of 1851 reached its height.

---

* I often met his son, Octavius H. Reamy, who served at both Minot's Light and Graves Light.

"The present tower is built of successive tiers of huge stones and masonry.

"The stones in each tier are laid in the form of a wheel with a round stone or hub, in the centre, and stone blocks, like spokes, radiating from this hub to the circumference or rim, which is also of large blocks, the spaces between the spokes being filled with cross blocks, dovetailed and mortised into the spokes and each other, the whole mass pinned together with enormous copper bolts.

"This tower, which is actually stronger than a solid block of stone would be, can defy the power of the waves in any storm, yet should a heavily laden wreck be thrown upon the tower by the waves its doom would be certain.

"The following is a brief summary of wind velocity during the height of the late blizzard, which the writer copied from the official records of the weather bureau in Boston. 'The wind steadily increased and from 3 A.M. on Sunday to 1 P.M. it blew at a rate of from 40 to 50 miles; the maximum rate being 60 miles at 11 A.M. and nearly that at noon. The extreme rate for any one mile was 72 miles per hour at 11:02 A.M. During the afternoon and night the wind slowly diminished in force. The wind blew from the northeast until 2 A.M. Sunday, the north till 4:20 P.M., then northeast.'"

The following letter from keeper Milton Reamy tells more of the 1898 storm. It was also written to the *Ledger,* and dated December 12, 1898.

"Dear Sir:

"When I arrived on shore from the tower today, where I have been for the last fortnight, I found your letter. As I have been too busy to answer it before you will please excuse me. As regards storms, when at the tower we are shut in and cannot see the storms at their worst. Myself and Mr. Lapans, the 2nd assistant, went out to the tower on Saturday the 26th inst. The weather was fine and the sea as smooth as a mill pond. It remained so until late at night when the wind sprang up from the eastward and increased in force until Sunday morning when it was something terrific. I have never experienced anything like it before, although we have had some terrible storms while I have been keeper of this light. Of course the tower trembled more or less and there was some very heavy pounding by the seas, but there was no damage done that we could see. Perhaps if we could have known how much havoc and damage was being done on sea and shore, we might have been a little anxious for ourselves; it was just as well we did not know.

"We are reasonably sure now that the tower will stand almost any amount of thumping by the seas. While the storm was on, the weather was thick and the windows covered with snow so that we could not see out, but after it cleared up, we saw within a short distance, the masts of three vessels the tops of which were just above the water, and other wrecks of vessels and houses on shore, then we began to realize that the storm was more terrible than we had thought it, and when we came ashore and saw the havoc and damage, and read of the disaster in shipping we thanked God that He had permitted us in His mercy and loving kindness, to meet once more with our friends and dear ones on shore. Sincerely yours, Milton Reamy, Keeper."

10

UNDER BOSTON HARBOR

⚓

ON MANY OCCASIONS I have descended to the bottom of Boston Harbor, either by free diving when I took a dive off the top of the Northern Avenue Bridge, or with scuba equipment when I explored several of the areas where sunken treasure might be brought up.

In an earlier book, *True Tales and Curious Legends,* I tell of Edward Bendall, who built America's first diving bell. More than two centuries were to elapse before one of the most fascinating races in underwater history took place at the bottom of Boston Harbor, in the same general area where Bendall brought up treasure with his diving bell. The race was between three hard-hat divers, and was part of the City of Boston's Fourth of July celebration in the year 1869.

George T. Woodsum of Braintree, an expert in such matters, tells me that the first man to win a hike under the waters of Boston Harbor was George L. Phillips of Marshfield, who on July 4, 1869, walked from T Wharf in Boston to Cunard Wharf in East Boston, clothed in a diver's suit. He came out the victor in the first and only contest of its kind ever known.

In that year, the city fathers were looking for some sort of novel way to celebrate the birthday of the nation. Submarine diving was then in its infancy, and someone conceived the idea of a race by submarine divers. A committee was appointed and the details were arranged. The steamer *Grace Irving* was chartered for the day.

The start was arranged by the spectacular exploding of no less than thirty kegs of powder by Ammi Smith, head of the committee. Phillips later gave the following account:

"It was something new then for anyone to walk below the water. I had been out of the war only a few years, where I served in the Twelfth Massachusetts, and had only been below a few times.

"Three prizes were offered, seventy-five dollars, fifty dollars, and twenty-five dollars. I happened to be the lucky man to win the first prize. It seemed that every sort of craft that would carry anyone was brought into service to carry spectators. United States war vessels were used and the Portland, Augusta, and Bangor boats pulled out of their docks with hundreds of passengers.

"They loaded them on just as long as the police would allow them to do so. Fifty cents a head was the price. Having been married only a short time, I brought my wife, who 'watched' from a schooner with relatives of the other two men.

"Each man had a boat with a crew of four men to steer, two at the pump, and one forward with the lifeline. Something was the matter with my pumps, and I had to change to larger ones which would not go in the boat. I borrowed another boat from a vessel at the wharf that was much heavier than the first one. Everyone thought that because the boat was heavier I would have a harder time to win.

"You see each of us at the given signal of the exploding powder was to climb down the ladder and draw our boats across the harbor.

"It was near noon on a high tide, at the full of the moon.

I found a great deal of soft mud but some hard footing. I had told the men who were taking care of my boat to stop pumping just as soon as we arrived on the other side. They did not understand, so it took me at least a minute longer to get up to the raft. There were three flags and as soon as one of us waved his flag a gun was fired and that marked the time.

"I climbed the ladder and thought that the other two men had won out. Some one cried to me to wave the flag. I had just sense enough to do so. I won the race in seventeen and a half minutes, which was quicker than some of the boats could do it in the fog. Lloyd's time was twenty-two minutes, and Palmer did not get across. He was exhausted and had to be pulled up to his boat. He, however, got twenty-five dollars, the third prize.

"It was kind of queer about those other two men. Lloyd was drowned down in North Carolina. Palmer went out West and became a stage driver. He was shot to death by a road agent years ago."

11

ROBERT E. LEE

⚓

On a cold but pleasant morning in January, 1970, Mrs. Snow and I stood high on the cliffs at Manomet Point, Massachusetts, with a group of Plymouth residents looking out at Mary Ann Rocks. There, forty-two years before, three heroes had perished in the sea just offshore, while returning from a stranded steamer, the *Robert E. Lee*.

It was on the night of March 9, 1928, at the height of a raging snowstorm that the Boston-to-New-York boat *Robert E. Lee* was approaching Manomet Point. It is said that snow drifting into the wheelhouse began to affect the compass, taking her considerably off course, so that the *Lee* hit the Mary Ann Rocks a short time later while running for the Cape Cod Canal. There were 273 men, women, and children aboard.

Captain Harland W. Robinson of the *Lee* later said that the steamer was going at full speed when she struck. Clearing the first series of rocks, she then hit four giant boulders in rapid succession. Slowly she began to ship water on the starboard side.

When the craft piled up on the rocks, crew discipline remained excellent, but a few of the passengers had to be quieted. Some of the steamer lights soon failed, with the entire ship gradually blackening out. As the 400-foot steamer rolled back and forth in the darkness, the uneasy passengers began to wander nervously about the vessel.

After a conference between the captain and engineer, it was agreed that the safest thing to do was to open the sea cocks, and the *Robert E. Lee* slowly settled down on the rocks, finding a sort of cradle. The rolling and pitching ceased, and it was possible for those on the upper decks to go back to bed. Unfortunately, as the tide came in, the water entered the staterooms on the lower deck and rose higher and higher inside the ship. As the tide would be full at two in the morning, the officers were worried as to what might happen at that time. The high tide came, the ship held firm, and that crisis was over.

The next day dawned clear. The Manomet Point Coast Guard Station sent its surfboat under Boatswain's Mate William H. Cashman out to the *Lee,* negotiating with difficulty the giant swells on the way to the Mary Ann Rocks.

Arriving at the scene of the accident, Cashman clambered aboard the *Lee,* where he consulted with Captain Robinson about taking the passengers off the wrecked liner. It was finally agreed that rowing them all ashore would be not only a long and tedious task, but one fraught with the danger of the small boat capsizing in the breakers. By this time several vessels had come to the vicinity to offer assistance. The rescue craft then standing by were instructed to get ready to receive the passengers from regular lifeboats which could be sent over to them.

The large, powerful surfboats at Sagamore and Wood End were sent for, and Boatswain's Mate Cashman finally started back for the shore with his men. He was pleased that satisfactory arrangements had been made.

One cutter filled with passengers had been unloaded at the

patrol boat when the Manomet surfboat started back to the beach. It was then a little after eleven o'clock in the morning, and the surfboat had reached a position just off State Point. She was then making good headway.

Suddenly an enormous wave began to form. Approaching the surfboat, the billow built up higher and higher, gradually raising the stern. Then, with a jar, her bow hit bottom and she pitchpoled,* spilling out every member of the crew. Watchers on the shore saw several of the men come to the surface and struggle in the angry sea.

Three of the crew of eight eventually died as a result of the capsizing, Boatswain's Mate William H. Cashman, Frank Griswold, and Edward Stark. The others were rescued and rushed to the hospital. Joseph Ducharme, Edward Douglas, Alden A. Proctor, Irving Wood, and Earl Sampson all recovered.

Perhaps the most surprised man on board the *Robert E. Lee* was J. J. Keeley of Winthrop, Massachusetts. Sleeping through the confusion of the shipwreck and subsequent excitement, Keeley did not awaken until seven o'clock Saturday morning. He dressed and went down to the ship's barbershop for his morning shave, where he learned that he was aboard a wrecked steamer.

Eventually, every passenger was taken safely from the *Robert E. Lee*. Some were placed on the patrol boats *Bonham, Active,* and the *C. G. 176*. Others returned on the *Red Wing* to Boston, where they arrived at 5:15 Saturday afternoon.

The stranded *Robert E. Lee* attracted so many thousands of people the following weekend that Manomet Point Road had to be closed and then the road to the Idlewild Hotel was blocked off to automobiles. At least 10,000 people visited

---
* Turned over, end over end.

Manomet to see the New York boat on the rocks that March 11 in 1928.*

The tug *Commerce*, with a lighter, arrived on the scene and started unloading cargo to lighten the *Lee*. A short time later the tug *Resolute* arrived to help out, but it was many days before those who believed the *Robert E. Lee* could be saved were vindicated. Most of the watchers thought that the craft would never be released, but they were mistaken, and off she went the latter part of the month.**

On January 20, 1970, I interviewed Paul Bettinger, who was on the cliff the day after the wreck in 1928. When I visited him at his office at his Plymouth newspaper, the *Old Colony Memorial,* he told me of the disaster.

"I was the first one down to the scene, arriving there with my brother, Fritz J. Bettinger. Reaching the shore early, we climbed to the top of the observation tower at the Coast Guard Station there.

"It was a fair day and the sun was shining, quite in contrast to the storm which wrecked the *Lee*. I'll never know why the Coast Guard boat went out. We watched them launching, and that particular launch was photographed by Lester R. MacLellan, a photographer from the *Globe* or the *Herald* in Boston. I've seen the picture.

"Reaching the *Lee,* the Coast Guardsmen went on board, and then evidently agreed with the officers on the *Lee* that the *Lee* was in no danger, for the passengers could be taken off by larger Coast Guard craft later.

* Twenty-eight years later when the *Etrusco* came ashore at Scituate, Massachusetts, more than a million people came to the area to see the freighter before she was "got off."
** Old-time lifesavers recalled other steamers in trouble. The British steamer *Pacqua* was alerted early enough by Coast Guard Coston lights, and backed off without striking. The *Pavonia,* about which I wrote in *New England Sea Tragedies,* hit High Pine Ledge off Duxbury Beach in October, 1886, but suffered no loss of life.

"Starting back from the *Lee,* the lifeboat got in pretty far, roughly a hundred yards from shore, where the water shallowed off so that it wasn't too deep. The waves there were high. Suddenly a great billow came roaring in. I watched as the craft was caught in the stern and lifted high in the air. The wave was so high that the lifeboat bow hit bottom.

"She pitchpoled, going stern over bow, and that was it. Every man was thrown out into the icy seas, and those who could clambered up on the keel. Although near to the shore, the lifeboat was quite a distance from the station. It is probable that before the rescue craft could reach the men the three who were lost had died of shock and exposure.

"When the first boat reached the shore under the cliff, we took Cashman up to the Idlewild Hotel, where Dr. Edgar Hill worked over him for a long, long time. Then he stood up, raised his hands in submission and said, 'No use.'

"I also recall watching some of the passengers who landed at the Plymouth pier later that same day."

The body of Boatswain's Mate William H. Cashman was taken to Boston.* Later he was buried in his Coast Guard uniform in Holy Cross Cemetery.

Ironically, Cashman had re-enlisted for the fifth time. While in service at Brant Rock the preceding year he had requested that he be transferred to the Manomet Station.

One man whose activity has not been remembered as it should be through the years is Russell Anderson of Manomet. The greatest credit is due him for what he did that March day forty-two years ago. As the surfboat pitchpoled, he shouted to his friends nearby.

"We must do something. Come on, let's get a boat."

Running down the beach, he was accompanied by his

---

* Cause of death was decided to have been from "shock and exposure of upsetting of lifeboat and immersion in the ocean for more than an hour."

friend Earl Harper and a State Trooper named Horgan. They found the dory of Frank Brooks overturned but ready. Obtaining oars and oarlocks, all of which took time, the three men slid the dory down the beach and into the sea. After several narrow escapes from breaking waves, they reached the scene of the pitchpoling and began to pull the Coastguardsmen out of the sea. By this time the boat was leaking badly. Noticing the approach of another craft, they started toward shore.*

Launching a second dory into the tumbling seas was Daniel Sullivan, Plymouth, who was assisted by Harry F. Eddy. The two dories brought every Coastguardsman ashore.

The keeper of the Manomet Lifesaving Station later wrote the following statement:

"As captain of the Manomet Lifesaving Station I wish to express the gratitude and appreciation of the men of this station who received such valiant and self-sacrificing assistance from the public and private citizens during the recent disaster to the New York boat, the *Robert E. Lee*. We realize it is impossible to express our thanks to each person individually, as many who did such gallant work are even now unknown to us.

"May we again express our gratitude and appreciation to all who so greatly assisted, and may we assure them that their deeds performed at that time will never be forgotten by the men of this station. —Arthur Young, Captain, Manomet Lifesaving Station."

A bronze tablet in memory of the three men who lost their lives was dedicated on Memorial Day, 1928. Attending the

* On February 2, 1970, I talked with sixty-two-year-old Anderson. He told me that his first rescue on an earlier occasion had been that of a man named Magee, who had gone down for the third time. After bringing Magee ashore, Anderson gave him artificial respiration for more than an hour, finally saving him.

service were members of Plymouth American Legion Post Number Forty, Plymouth Fire and Police departments, State Police, and Coast Guard. Also present were District Commander Wilcox, U.S.C.G., and Senator J. H. Cashman, brother of the victim.

The inscription on the tablet follows:

IN MEMORY OF BOATSWAIN'S MATE WILLIAM H. CASHMAN, SURFMAN FRANK GRISWOLD, SURFMAN EDWARD P. STARK, WHO OF STATION NO. 31 UNITED STATES COAST GUARD, LOST THEIR LIVES IN THE PERFORMANCE OF THEIR DUTY, MARCH 10, 1928, WHEN THE STEAMSHIP ROBERT E. LEE STRANDED ON MARY ANN ROCKS, SOUTHEAST OF THIS STATION.

GREATER LOVE HATH NO MAN THAN THIS THAT HE LAY DOWN HIS LIFE FOR HIS FRIENDS

ERECTED BY THE CITIZENS OF PLYMOUTH, MASSACHUSETTS.

DEDICATED MAY 30, 1928

The *Robert E. Lee* was to survive fourteen more years. On July 30, 1942, the 5184-ton craft went to the bottom in the Gulf of Mexico, sunk by a U-boat. This time the passengers were not so lucky, as there was a substantial loss of life.

12

CAPE COD'S CRUMBLING CLIFFS

⚓

HENRY DAVID THOREAU identified Cape Cod as "this bare and bended arm" of Massachusetts, while Joseph Conrad referred to the ocean that surrounds Cape Cod as a "savage autocrat spoiled by much adulation."

Many of my readers, after visiting Cape Cod, have written to me asking for help in understanding just what is meant by the eternal fight which Cape Cod and the ocean are constantly conducting.

Actually my best answer is this chapter. Soaring over Cape Cod at Christmas time as the "Flying Santa" dropping Yuletide presents to the Cape Cod lighthouse keepers and Coastguardsmen for more than a third of a century, I've come to appreciate from the air what a tremendous fight almost every Cape town has with the sea, the wind, and the sand. The latter sweeps across the roads, being scooped up, thrown about, and piled high in unbelievable drifts by the wind. In contrast, in an overnight storm, the sea can do more than its share of damage to the general state of things in almost any one of the fifteen towns which comprise the Cape. During a single tide the ocean often builds up sand high on the beach or scours it out in unbelievable fashion.

But we could spend countless hours talking and writing about the Cape's sand hills, the wind, and the ocean. Instead, let us discuss our subject from another viewpoint: by examining government station daybooks and journals for factual evidences of Cape Cod changes.

The Three Sisters of Nauset, as the trio of lighthouses there was called for many years, long ago gave up the unequal fight to stay at the edge of the cliffs at Eastham, and now one single, unattended beacon, set back from the cliff, gleams out to warn the sea voyager. Then the proud Marconi Wireless Station finally succumbed to the inroads of nature and slid over the bank at South Wellfleet. Even Eugene O'Neil's residence on the cliffs at the old Peaked Hill Bars Coast Guard Station was overwhelmed in the terrible, devastating storm of March 4, 1931, and quickly went to pieces. There have been scores upon scores of other minor and major disasters along the Cape cliffs down through the centuries.

But for the actual day-by-day deathwatch of two other important government stations I take you first to Chatham and then to Billingsgate.

Almost a quarter century ago, while hiking around Cape Cod, I visited the Atwood House in Chatham as the guest of historian Virginia Harding. While browsing through the records there, we found an old picture of Chatham Lights, then situated on the cliff looking out to sea. The two lighthouses in the picture looked secure and permanent.

"Perhaps the record books of some of the old keepers are here," I wondered aloud, but Virginia Harding said that there were none in the building. However, she did remember a journal or diary kept by the famous Captain Josiah Hardy, the same lighthouse keeper who years ago told her father, Herman Harding, of 365 vessels he sighted in one day. Therefore the home of Captain Hardy's granddaughter became my next objective. After putting the papers and pictures back in order, we locked up the Atwood House and started for the home of Grace Hardy. Ten minutes later we arrived at Miss Hardy's home.

"Oh, yes, I remember your book on lighthouses," said Miss Hardy, after introductions were completed. "Well, why didn't you say something about my grandfather in your lighthouse book?" was her question.

I explained that in every book I had written, there were always a few parts which would have been better had some missing diary or absent journal turned up in time. After the book was published, it would be read by the unknown party who had the missing information. That party was willing and even pleased to furnish it, but, of course, it was then too late, as the book was finished. I had not known of the diary or journal or where to find the information in time.

"I'd be glad to include your grandfather's career in my Chatham section of the book," I concluded, and in this she readily acquiesced.

"Grandfather was keeper of the light from 1872 until 1900, and I have his diary, although it is falling apart and going to pieces from my lending it to so many people. However, I'll show it to you." Her eyes flashed as she got up to bring back the precious journal of Captain Josiah Hardy. Yes, indeed, the little book was in need of rebinding, but I spent a happy hour reading the pages of the keeper's lighthouse diary.

Keepers of other years were Samuel Ney, Joseph Loveland, Samuel Stimson, and Simeon Nickerson. Nickerson's widow took over the duties of keeper at his death, and she was followed during the Civil War by Captain Charles Smith. In 1871 Josiah Hardy became assistant keeper at Chatham twin lights, and on December 6, 1872, he assumed his duties as head keeper, a post which he was to retain until the end of the century. Just before Hardy came to Chatham Light, a great physical change occurred in Chatham.

In the days after the Civil War there were many houses built to the eastward of Chatham Light, and there was at one time a store no less than half a mile to the eastward. But on November 15, 1870, a terrific northeast storm hit the Cape causing extremely high tides and a dangerous surf. As the day lengthened, the storm grew worse, and fishermen everywhere feared for their craft. Suddenly the serious news reached Chatham Village that the beach had broken through, with waves washing under the piles of Hardy's Wharf. It was the beginning of the end as far as the two old lighthouse towers were concerned. At the time of the breakthrough, the edge of the cliff was 228 feet from the brick lighthouse towers.

Four years went by. Keeper Hardy wrote that the twenty-third of November, 1874, was a "day of storms, ushered in by a northeast wind and high course of tides," adding that the bank had suffered severely during the storm. Ten days later Hardy measured the bank to find it 190 feet from the south tower, commenting on the fact that since 1870 thirty-eight feet had been lost, or "an average of not quite ten feet a year." A more serious note is seen in the next entry, that of November 15, 1875.

"It has washed away on an average of fifty feet a year opposite the house of Captain Josiah Hardy and abreast of the lights just thirty-one feet a year." Each month keeper Hardy faithfully made his measurements of the doomed bank. Each month Hardy reported it to the lighthouse authorities, but nothing was done to shore up the banking. "On February 17, 1877, Mr. Lunt, a member of the Harbor Commission visited this station today to ascertain the extent of the washing away of the shoreline." Just eleven days after Mr. Lunt's visit the distance from the bank to the south tower was only ninety-five feet, and on March 31 eleven feet more had fallen! This so discouraged the government that it was decided to abandon all future efforts to save the lighthouse station.

On April 25, 1877, Frederick Tower, assistant engineer of the Lighthouse Board, arrived in Chatham to arrange and lay out the grounds for the new lighthouses across the street on the west side of the road, inland from the sea. Begun in May, the towers were built rapidly, for by then the cliff had reached a point seventy-seven feet from the old south tower. Forty-two feet high, the new towers were one hundred feet apart, with the keeper's dwelling located between. The work was finished September 6, 1877, when the lenses were moved from the old towers to the new towers. They were lighted the same night.

The lights finished, work was rushed on the keeper's dwelling, and his family thankfully moved into the new house in November, when the hungry sea had reached a point less than fifty feet from their old home.

The next year the lighthouse tender *Myrtle* sent ashore two barrels of kerosene and new fixtures to supplant the old fixtures which burned lard oil. On the night of July 4, 1878, kerosene oil was used for the first time in Chatham lighthouse history, and all the fishermen and townspeople rejoiced at the great improvement in the glow.

But the relentless Atlantic Ocean's treacherous currents quickened their pace, and on June 30, 1879, keeper Josiah Hardy wrote in his diary that the old south tower was only seven feet four inches from the bank, having washed away more than twenty-three feet in less than a year.

On September 30 that same year the south tower stood twenty-seven inches from the edge of the cliff, and exactly two months later one-third of the same lighthouse was out over the edge. The townspeople visited the scene daily, speculating on the exact time when the great tower would drop over the bank, and it is said that many bets on that subject were placed by the fishermen sailing up and down the coast.

The spectacular event took place at exactly one o'clock in the afternoon of December 15, 1879. There had been a terrible storm that year, and while it helped the destruction of the south tower, it seemed to aid in the formation of a new barrier beach. The old cistern went over the bank the following July, but after that the cliff fell away at a slower rate. It was not until March 26, 1881, that most of the north tower fell over, leaving a small cone-shaped pile of bricks and mortar. The complete lighthouse foundation never did go over the cliff, for in the presence of Virginia A. Harding, on that May day of 1946, I located several of the red bricks at the top of the cliff.

The reason the cliff halted its rapid pace of washing away can be found in Captain Hardy's remarks of 1881. He tells us that the barrier beach was then making down from the north to reach a point nearly opposite the lights, and if continued it would protect the shore. And so it did, for today the sand stretches out substantially in all directions from the sites of the old lighthouses.

Retiring in 1900, Captain Josiah Hardy was succeeded by Captain Charles Hammond, who died in service at the twin lights. Keeper Allison was in charge when the northern light was moved to Nauset in 1923.

We now turn our attention to Billingsgate Island, that part of the Massachusetts Bay side of the Cape which has suffered greatly from erosion.

Because of agitation by Captain Michael Collins, Billingsgate Light was erected on Billingsgate Island off Cape Cod in 1822. The first light had eight oil lamps with crude reflectors. There was a brick dwelling for the keeper, with an attached brick tower for the light. Around the time of the

Civil War, Billingsgate Point washed away to such an extent that the lighthouse was in danger of falling into the sea.

In spite of current opinions to the contrary, there was a sizable fishing village at Billingsgate for many years. A picture taken around 1870 shows eight houses or buildings in addition to the lightkeeper's home.

We include below items from the lighthouse journal at Billingsgate Island begun by keeper Herman Dill:

JOURNAL OF LIGHT-HOUSE STATION
AT BILLINGSGATE ISLAND
HERMAN DILL, KEEPER

1872

Month of September 5 Arrived the supply vessel with oil

Spt. 14 The lighthouse leeks on the East End

Sept. 21 One hundred and Eight Viserters went up the tower the Last Quarter. 928 Vessels pas the Light House the Last Quarter

November 16 . . . The New Light on Wood End is Vary plain

December 21 . . . Asnowing Again to Knight 4 Knights in Succession

1873

January 12 my oil is so Hard that i hav to Dip it out

January 29 the Island is Cavord over with Snow and ice the tower is a glare of ice and frost.

June 3 the Steem Horn at the High Land of Cape Cod can be heard very Plain

July 21 the tent on town hill Provincetown Can be seen from the Island.

An exceptionally high tide Nov. 18 & flooded tower floor to depth of 2 inches

1874

November 11 A grate Cry of Black fish All hands turned out and Drove on Shore about 3 hundred at Truro

Nov 28 Drove on shore at Island 66 Black fish Also 175 at Eastham About 3 hundred people at the Sean . . . The Sch Ira Kilhren Ran on a Roc and Sunk in Wellfleet Bay. The Wind Blowing very fresh and A Bad Storm.

1875

Jan 29 There is the most ice in and Round this Island that I ever saw Nothing but ice as far as i Can Sea.

Jan. 31 I never saw so mutch ice as there is in Site to Day there is nothing but ice as far as i Can Sea

February 7th it has been very Cold here for the Last Month and the most ice that i ever see in this Rigen. We are almost buried up in it. No salt water to be seen from the Island i have not Seen a Living man for over a month no prospect for the Better I do get the Blues some times to think i Can't (get) here from the main so pend up with ice that i Can Not Move in either Direction for the ice is 15 feet high in some places

Feb. 11 The ice has made a move to go

Feb. 12 I thought the ice was going out but the next day it was all back again with Eight vessels in it hard and fast . . . Those vessels are between Provincetown and this island. it Rains it Blows it Snows it hails Every Day or night for a month and I do not know when it will be any better Weather I hav not put my foot on the Mainland for 37 days and there is no prospect as yet.

February 13 there was snow last night . . . The ice will stay here I can see three men and dog on the ice and one boat i suppose it is an ice boat for Pleasure

February 21 today is Sunday there is no Prospect of getting of this Island this month there is some of the largest Islands of ice that i ever see in this Bay i do not think there is Water enuff to float those islands of ice it has been 47 Days since i have been off this Island.

February 22 the Day that George Washington was born 1732 it has been 143 years . . . There is 11 Boats or ice boats on the ice to Day between this Island and Wellfleet all ICE

> March 1 there is today 13 Schooners in the ice and one Brig and there are two Steamers A triing to get them out the ice is piled 15 or 20 feet high in some places.
>
> March 3 Three men Landed here today from one vessel for cole i supplied them all they wanted and they went to the vessel again on the ice about 3 miles of (f) they had been in the ice 21 days they belong in Gloucester.
>
> March 4 the very Wourst Snow storm for the year it is a Regular Driving Snow Storm and a gail of wind I never saw sutch weather in all my life
>
> March 17 I left this Island for the first time for 70 days.
>
> March 22 five vessels Come down the Bay today the first vessels that has gone out this spring
>
> November 9 A large School of Black fish was landed on this Island today A part Sold for $850 Wind NE
>
> November 16 Tide very high the Island has gon 15 feet.
>
> November 17 i do not know but the Island will All wash away for i never Saw the tide So high since I have been on four years There ought to have been something done last summer
>
> December 13 Was the highest tide that i ever saw here it came in from the North End of the Island . . . it maid A Clean sweep through inside . . . there was from 3 to 5 feet of water
>
> 1876
> March 26 the very worst storm for the winter was Last Night

The above is the last entry ever made by keeper Herman Dill, for the very next day he was found dead at sea in his lighthouse dory. The new keeper, Thomas K. Payne, took charge of the station April 1, 1876. Payne had formerly served at Billingsgate from 1860 to 1869. His entries follow:

> April 17, 1878 Mr. J. F. Walker of Orleans arrived at this Island this morning about 4 OClock brought news to Mr. Sparrow of the death of his Brother by the capsizing of his

Pilgrim Rock at Clark's Island. (Pt. I, Ch. 1)

Plymouth Rock.
(Pt. I, Ch. 1)

Sir Christopher Gardner entering the secret hiding place modeled after Salford Prior in England. This is believed by some to later have been the Nancy Hanks residence at Saquish. (Pt. I, Ch. 2)

Opposite: The tug *Perth Amboy* awaits tide change at Hog Island, Buzzards Bay. The *Perth Amboy* was shelled off Orleans, Cape Cod, by a U-boat during World War I. (Pt. I, Ch. 6) PHOTO BY R. LOREN GRAHAM, SWAMPSCOTT, MASS.

Below: Thomas V. LeMoine of Lynn with the cannon found off Shag Rock, Nahant. (Pt. I, Ch. 4)

Schooner *Mertis Perry* wrecked on the beach at Brant Rock, Massachusetts, 1898. (Pt. I, Ch. 9)
COURTESY OF W. TORREY LITTLE

Robert E. Lee passing the statue of Liberty. (Pt. I, Ch. 11)   PHOTO BY R. LOREN GRAHAM, SWAMPSCOTT, MASS.

Bell of the *Kadosh* brought up by, left to right, William Connolly, Douglas Dapprich, Michael Janiszewski. (Pt. I, Ch. 13)

Two generations at the cannon of the de Crisse. Dorothy Snow Bicknell holds her daughter Laura Ann at the ancient pirate cannon. (Pt. I, Ch. 13)

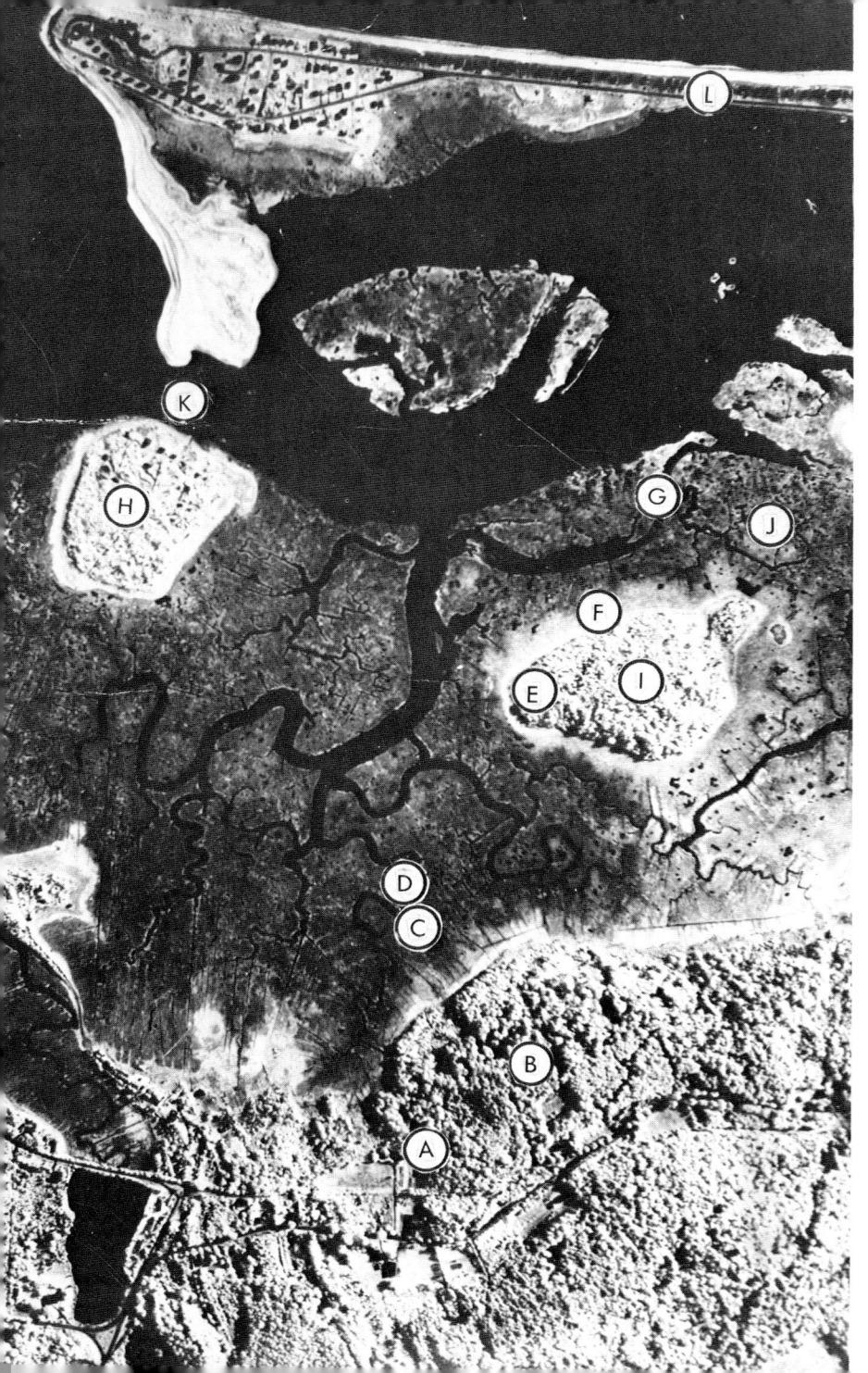

Final resting place of 107 members of the British armed forces on Boston Common. Left, Greg Benjamin of the Bostonian Society; right, Bookman George Gloss of Boston. (Pt. I, Ch. 16)

Opposite: The marsh. Infrared photo taken from one mile in the air. (Pt. I, Ch. 14.) (A) Oxen Trail, or Indian Trail. (B) Flower Hill overlooking marsh. (C) Footbridge forty feet long over mud flats. (D) Marsh Monster, or platform built of shipwrecks and flotsam. (E) Dolly's Rock, northeastern tip of Hen Island. (F) Daddy's Rock. (G) Scene of encounter with Phantom Clam Digger. (H) Trouant's Island. (I) Hen Island. (J) Kedge discovery scene. (K) Present junction of North and South Rivers. (L) Humarock Beach.

Gravestone of Margaret Peterson whose remains were sent home to Machiasport, Maine, in a cask of rum. (Pt. II, Ch. 2)

PHOTO BY PENNELL L. WORCESTER

Ruptured Bow of *Stockholm*, which collided with and sank the *Andrea Doria* south of Nantucket Island in 1956. (Pt. II, Ch. 4) U.S. COAST GUARD OFFICIAL PHOTO

The *Andrea Doria* *(above)* after collision with the *Stockholm,* and *(below)* just before her final plunge. (Pt. II, Ch. 4) U.S. COAST GUARD OFFICIAL PHOTOS

King, who saved many lives from the wreck of the *Harpooner*. (Pt. II, Ch. 5)

Below: Rubens, the only dog known to be able to tie knots. (Pt. II, Ch. 5)

Prince guarding the entrance to the corridor of the Lady in Black at Fort Warren. (Pt. II, Ch. 5)

Mr. Snow (left) showing Teddy Tucker, Bermuda diving expert, treasure from Cape Cod during Snow's reception at Bermuda. (Pt. III, Ch. 7)

Above: Sea Devil flying through the air. (Pt. IV, Ch. 5)

Below: Ship of Skeletons that was discovered floating off Bermuda well over a century ago. (Pt. IV, Ch. 8)

dory on the back side of Cape Cod his son was with him but was rescued by the crew of the Life Saving Station on Nausett beach.

May 17 Caught ten thousand macerel in the deep water wier at Eastham

May 27 I had my dog Rover killed this morning. He was about ten years old. he could not leave the Light House to go to the Shore for fear of a dog owned by Mr. Mayo ugly old dog he has but one friend that is his master

August 16 I like burning Kerosene very much.

Sept 28 I am alone on the Island

Dec 7 A boat arrived here from Wellfleet brought news to J. F. Walker (a fisherman on this island) the death of his mother

1879

Jan 11 Mr. Marrington (the assistant) arrived at 7 OClock . . . had great difficulty in keeping clear of ice.

Jan. 15 To night I have to record the sad news of the death of Robert Marrington . . . This afternoon we saw him about half past two coming up the point towards the Island, at half past three I went down where I suppose he was he was not to be found my search for him was in vain it was about half flood. broken ice & slur all around the island with a high sea wall of ice he must have fell through the ice

Jan. 16 This morning I went in search of Robert Marrington I found his gun where it would be about two feet of warter at half tide both barrel's of his gun were empty how he came to his end will always remain a mystery . . . There was a strong current across the point at the time & ice a moveing

April 28 The body of Robert Marrington was picked up today four miles from this island.

1880

January 1 This is the Twelveth New Year day I have spent on the Island. It is a hard place in the winter season to collect items to write in a journal

Apr. 18 A whale was seen floating about three miles North-West from this Island at three o'clock. . . . a finback whale 65 feet long had been killed by Provincetown parties Capt. Savage and crew . . . towed it into this harbour

Apr. 19 Owners of the whale have arrived, paid $30.00 for picking him up. Has been sold to Wellfleet parties for $190.00.

May 4, Another whale was caught near island and sold for $75.00 (30 ft. long)

1881

January 1 I wish all the readers of this journal a happy New Year

Apr. 7 Eighteen whales have been shot in the Bay the last ten days.

Oct. 31 I found a finback whale which had ran ashore on a bar NW from this Island. J. L. Hopkins and myself killed & secure him, sold him . . . for $100.00 His length was fifty-five feet.

1882

Feb. 22 The middle of the Island was flooded five feet of water within fifteen feet of Lighthouse . . . the Island lost thirty feet.

Early in July keeper Payne became seriously ill. His wife took over the duties connected with running the lighthouse until the end of August when he recovered sufficiently to attend to them himself.

Dec. 1 I have spent fifteen Thanksgiving days at this Station, but yesterday was the most lonesome. I shall not have any man to live with me this winter am going to rough it alone.

1883

Feb. 1 J. L. Hopkins arrived here from Eastham with twenty day mail

Feb. 25 News from the main would be very acceptable.

Apr. 30 A large lot of seals lying on old island I have seen hundreds

July 27 Capt. Heitt of Wesport caught six hundred Tautog in four days near this island

Dec. 4 George T. Dill arrived here from Eastham to stop with me this winter.

Dec. 10 A goose killed today on this island by G. T. Dill sold him for one dollar

On June 30, 1884, Captain Payne retired from the Service at his own request and with a high and honorable record as keeper.

J. W. Ingalls became the new keeper on July 1.

1884
Oct. 31 Mr. Dill is very long doing a small job.

1886
Aug. 9 Getting ready for Inspector, but I ate too many cucumbers, sick last night
November 30 Killed two Mosquitoes this day

1887
Jan. 31 I am ready to go ashore for good

1891
July 23 Deputy Sherrif Leuitel of Barnstable County Ar'd with a Prisoner, Mrs. Hosea Dill on a Murder trial. Came for the Medicine left on the West end of the Id.

1892
March 31 This is our last night on the Island as Keeper. We are packed up and mostly moved. . . . We have had many pleasant hours but many more very lonely ones . . . Remember us friends If any

Good Bye

In 1915 the sea began to undermine Billingsgate Light again. Ropes were used to prevent the tower from falling while men climbed up to remove the lens and lighting apparatus from the old beacon. When the tower was finally abandoned, the light shone on each night without a single interruption. One evening it appeared from the cupola of a private house and later from a temporary structure erected near the old beacon.

The light continued to gleam from the temporary structure, which was reinforced and made permanent. In 1922, however, exactly one hundred years after its first establishment, Billingsgate Light was discontinued.

Today one may sail over much of the area once known as Billingsgate.

What is the future of Cape Cod? Will it be taken over by the sea as writer Jeremiah Belknap hinted in 1791, or will Cape Cod lose more areas of land in the fashion explained by Shebnah Rich in 1883, when his map includes "ILE Nawset" and "PT. Gilbert" extending miles out into the sea. Both of these have long been fathoms deep under water.

On the other hand, Amos Otis said long ago that "where an open sea then was, now the beaches meets the eye."

Shebnah Rich, writing in 1883, explained that there had been almost unbelievable changes in the Cape Cod cliffs and shorelines. That is why, commented Rich, it is so hard to understand wl t ancient writers like Bradford, Morton, and Prince meant when they mentioned Cape Cod shore lines of former centuries.

The harbors, bays, and shores were as unlike the coast of his day as the "descriptions of Sinbad the Sailor, or Ghanges Khan," concluded Rich.

The Cape Cod National Seashore group has taken over much of the area on the Cape which is in the so-called crumbling cliffs region. Let us hope that this worthy organization can help solve what apparently is Cape Cod's eternal problem.

Nevertheless, I do not think that we shall ever have to

worry too much about losing Cape Cod, as many fear. If a few acres disappear from the Cape in one area, usually that loss is compensated in another. In my opinion this balance of gain and loss will continue indefinitely.

13

THE PIRATE CRAFT AND THE *KADOSH*

⚓

The discovery in 1969 of a bell near Harding's Ledge in fifty feet of water has revived interest in a fatal shipwreck which occurred in the area more than ninety-seven years ago.

On September 6, 1969, three divers, William Connolly, Douglas Dapprich, and Michael Janiszewski, recovered the bell from the famed bark *Kadosh,* which was lost on Harding's Ledge in 1872. It was found lying on its side, with a large lobster living inside the bell. The inscription was practically obliterated.

When the bell and a cannon, which I now own, were placed on the 665-ton bark *Kadosh,* they already had a fascinating history. They were originally on a pirate craft, the *Nostra Señora de Crisse,* which anchored off Scituate in 1818.

Aboard the pirate craft were Edward Rosewain, Thomas Warrington, William Holmes, Thomas Chappel, and Thomas Harrison. The first three had captured the craft from Captain John Reed and Mate Joseph, throwing them both into the sea to their deaths. The other two men were actually innocent bystanders of the piratical act.

At sunset, August 29, 1818, the pirate ship *Nostra Señora de Crisse* appeared off the shores of Third Cliff, Scituate. The

THE PIRATE CRAFT AND THE *KADOSH*

three pirates went ashore with a small wooden box of treasure they had obtained from the *de Crisse*. They dug a deep hole in the sand, lowered the box, and covered it over carefully. Then, after taking bearings on several landmarks for future reference, they rowed back to their craft.*

Shortly after midnight, they set sail for the mouth of Sictuate Harbor where they were guided by the tiny gleam of Scituate Light at the entrance to the inlet. Apprehensively, the men dropped anchor not too far from the lighthouse itself and waited for morning. Holmes, a native of Plymouth, hoped to deceive the Scituate residents by claiming that the schooner was his own.

With the coming of dawn fishermen and other inhabitants of Scituate were greatly surprised to see a foreign schooner with a brailed or lug foresail anchored in their harbor. This attracted the notice of the Scituate customs officer who then prepared to make an official visit to the vessel.

Meanwhile Holmes was growing increasingly nervous regarding his coming reception from the people of Scituate. When he saw the customs boat start out for the schooner, he decided to make an escape. As he was going for the boat, he noticed the yawl with the two honest men, Harrison and Chappel, at the oars as they rapidly neared the opposite shore. Holmes realized with sinking heart that the two men were escaping for the purpose of betraying him and that the game would soon be up. He and his two cronies hurriedly jumped aboard the remaining small boat and rowed desperately to the mainland where they decided to separate at once.

In eluding the customs officer they were only postponing their eventual capture. Holmes was later apprehended while

---

* All indications are that the gold and silver in the box amounted to about three thousand dollars. Most of the treasure was never found. If discovered today, it would be worth over ten thousand dollars!

attempting to board the Hingham packet for Boston. Warrington, pretending that his name was Warren Fawcett, was also caught and brought back. Rosewain was the last to be made prisoner. After the three pirates were captured, they were taken to the Boston jail, and on June 15, 1820, the three were hanged.

At an auction sale held at Scituate Pier, William Perkins purchased much of the gear from the pirate craft, including the bell and the cannon. His bark, the *Kadosh,* was made ready for a long voyage.

When in 1871 the *Kadosh* sailed from the port of Boston bound for the Orient, her master, Captain Hedge of Cape Cod, was not feeling at his best. Upon his arrival in Yokohama he was invalided home, and his place was taken by the chief officer, J. A. Mathews.

At Manila the bark was loaded with sugar, hemp, and sappanwood. The long trip back across the world toward Boston was at first uneventful, but on Monday, December 23, 1872, when the *Kadosh* reached Cape Cod, a snowstorm began. Foggy weather soon added to the unfavorable picture and a pilot was desperately needed. None could be found.

The *Kadosh* beat back and forth across the entrance to Boston Harbor, and finally reached a position off Nantasket Beach. Suddenly Captain Mathews heard the distant foghorn from Boston Light, four miles away, and decided to anchor not far from the dangerous Harding's Ledge. Unknown to the captain, the location he chose was about a mile and one half out to sea from Strawberry Hill, Nantasket Beach. It was then noon, Thursday, December 26, and other unfortunate craft were also in trouble.*

As the day wore on the storm increased in fury until the *Kadosh* anchor cables parted, one by one. Almost at once the

---

* See my *True Tales and Curious Legends.* The *Francis* and the *Peruvian* were two Cape Cod losses in the same storm.

bark began to drift shoreward. Suddenly she smashed against a jagged underwater formation, which proved to be part of Harding's Ledge, and her career ended. The *Kadosh* began to break up almost at once.

The crew scrambled into the vessel's two boats. Captain Mathews took charge of the whaleboat, which was considered much safer than the small jolly boat.

Launched first, the jolly boat had ten men aboard, including the chief mate, S. K. Gorsock, and a seventeen-year-old seaman, Cliff Richards. The craft was well manned. Gradually filling with water, the jolly boat managed to survive the dangerous breakers all around, but capsized on hitting the Nantasket shore. Nevertheless, everyone was saved.

Back aboard the *Kadosh,* Captain Mathews had gone below to retrieve his nautical instruments. Finally, he ordered the whaleboat launched into the sea and took the tiller. There were seven others aboard with him as he steered for the distant shore. Almost without warning a giant comber reared up out of the sea directly astern and thundered along toward the frightened men. Reaching the whaleboat the wave began to break and the eight mariners didn't have a chance.

The whaleboat was swamped, and the men were unable to hold onto it long in the icy seas. As their strength failed, they sank to their death.

Their companions, who had landed safely, launched the jolly boat and rowed out in a vain attempt to save any possible survivors. They brought the captain's body ashore, but it was washed into the ocean again that night.

The survivors found a hut near Atlantic Hill where they left a stowaway from the Philippines. Not accustomed to the New England climate, he was nearly dead from exposure.*

---

* What happened to the stowaway later is a mystery. It is said by old Hull residents that the boy was allowed to stay in Hull illegally for the remainder of his life.

The others then hiked through the drifts toward Hingham, where they found a boardinghouse. The next day they started out again. Receiving assistance along the way, they finally reached Boston. When their frostbitten limbs had healed, they shipped out again aboard another Perkins ship, the *Akbar*.

Seven of the eight mariners lost on the *Kadosh* eventually washed ashore. Five were buried at the First Parish Church in Hingham, close to the railroad station there. Captain Mathews' remains were sent to Yarmouth, and Steward John W. Kirby's to Cambridge.

The cannon from the *Kadosh* was rescued, and the cargo of hemp was purchased by several Cohasset residents. The wood was also salvaged, as were small teak and sandalwood cabinets. The sugar was ruined.

14

ON THE MARSH

⚓

OUR MARSHFIELD HOME overlooks the North River and a great marsh area which stretches for miles and miles below us. I can look out through my picture window door and see the marsh, the North River, Scituate's Third and Fourth cliffs, and Trouant's Island which can be reached at low tide by corduroy road. Then, looking far out to sea, I often observe ocean craft such a great distance away that only their superstructure shows over the curvature of the earth.

The only sure thing about the marsh is its uncertainty, especially in wintertime. Each year when the swimming and canoeing season ends, I begin my losing battle against gaining weight, for unless I can get down on the marsh for a good long hike at least once a week, I am doomed in the weight department.* My wife, Anna-Myrle, is very much against unusual activity on the marsh in winter, and she rightfully believes that even in summer the marsh has many areas of danger. Of course in cold weather these dangers are greatly magnified, and I agree that hiking on the winter marsh is almost as dangerous as stepping into an automobile.

---

* It was an even 210 pounds on my birthday, August 22, 1970, with my height six feet one inch.

One day in January, 1970, however, Anna-Myrle did not object too strenuously when I announced my intention of going out in full foul-weather gear to dig a few of the clams we both enjoy so much. An hour later I reached the edge of the salt-water marsh, but discovered that the severe winter had not been kind. I started out over the narrow (eight-inch-wide) forty-foot-long bridge, climbed up on what we call the Marsh Monster * and was disappointed to discover that the tide evidently had been caught by the great ice floes and was much too high.

Nevertheless, after finding that several of my favorite clamming locations were still under water, I decided to double back on my tracks and visit a distant location half a mile away which usually yielded a few clams even close to high-tide time.

Crossing an area of slippery, glistening ice, I skidded and fell heavily on my right hip. After recovering, I started out toward an area known locally as the Phantom Clam Digger's Gully, but again I was disappointed to discover it clogged with floating ice when it should have been relatively bare.

Thinking that I was familiar with the depth of the water I decided to step down into the salty brine, and located a place where the solid floating ice was about ten inches thick. The open water between bank and ice was four feet across and—as I figured—about three feet deep. Getting a good grip on my clam fork, I threw it out on the frozen surface.

Then I stepped down over the edge of the bank. Instead of encountering a sandy bottom, my rubber boot touched slippery underwater ice. Unfortunately, by the time I discovered that the bottom was ice, I had begun to slide and couldn't stop my progress, with my slide terminating right under the edge of the surface of the ice.

I should have been concerned, but started to laugh at my

---

* A wooden structure I constructed out of driftwood, flotsam, jetsam, and lagan.

stupidity. In the old days I would not have stepped down, but instead would have leaped out on the ice. In attempting to be extra cautious I was now in real trouble. The temperature was fifteen above zero, my rubber boots were filled with icy water, and I was at least a mile and a half from home,* making the situation fairly serious.

Crawling out from under the ice, I rolled over on the floating surface to recover the clam fork. Tossing it ashore, I jumped across to solid ground. The squiggling water in my boots bothered me, so I knelt down, tilted up first one leg and then the other in back of me, and in this way drained most of the water from my rubber boots.

Then I hiked back toward Hen Island where I buried the clam fork in a snow drift near Daddy's Rock, and began to walk and jog toward home.

After many adventures of skidding, sliding, and breaking through potholes, I reached the mainland, where I soon had a feeling that both feet were beginning to freeze. The right foot, which had never been the same since my injury suffered while with the Twelfth Bomber Command in North Africa, was stiffening noticeably.** Nevertheless, another twenty minutes found me home and ready for a thawing-out bath. I didn't even catch cold. On the other hand, I came home without clams for the first time in many a moon.

On another wintry occasion I started out from our Summer Street home in Marshfield for a good long hike. Walking down the old oxen path to the marshes, I wondered if I had put on sufficient foul-weather gear, having dressed in rubber hip boots, hooded storm jacket, and oilskin pants, with two

---

* See *Great Sea Rescues*, p. 234, for an escape from an even worse fix in 1918.

** In 1778, under similar conditions while on a shipwreck all night in Plymouth Harbor, Captain James Magee poured rum down his boots to prevent his legs from freezing. His sailors drank their allotment of rum, saved none for their boots, and died within a few hours. Captain Magee survived.

stocking caps on my head at different angles. In spite of all this, the biting wind almost overwhelmed me at first. A thin fall of snow, which covered the oxcart trail in back of our residence, crunched with every step I made, as the temperature that day was far below freezing.

Tracks of rabbits, chipmunks, and squirrels I quickly identified, but it was the relatively large deer hoof marks going across the path that interested me. I also noticed that the animal I have come to know as Reddy the Fox had crossed over from his Hen Island lair. Reaching the marsh itself, I discovered it would be necessary to break through half-frozen inch-thick ice on my way out. Then I came to an area where the ice had not frozen to any dangerous degree, and began to stride along with more assurance. With every step, the sounds of the marsh grass breaking off like pipestems was indeed unusual music.

Finally I came to the rivulet thirty feet wide with the narrow forty-foot bridge, but discovered that the timber spanning the gap was coated with snow and ice. Gingerly inching my way across the bridge—for I had no desire to slip and fall down to the frozen flats ten feet below—I reached the other side of the waterway. Then I started to hike in the general direction of Hanover Flats.* Soon I was trudging along in an ankle-deep combination of ice, salt water, and mud. Reaching the outer limits of Hen Island, which are about a mile from the house the way the marsh rivers and rivulets allow me to go, I skirted the southern shore. For some crazy reason I then decided to make my monthly attempt on a project I had—to rediscover an old wooden kedge. This kedge had been used to assist a very famous ship down the river on her way out to sea two centuries before.

Launched in Pembroke on the North River, the Boston

---

* So named because in earliest days residents of Hanover were entitled to dig clams there. It is Scituate property.

Tea Party ship *Beaver* had been kedged over the shallow flats of the river with the kedge buried in the marsh as an anchor. After getting the Boston Tea Party craft out of the North River and into the ocean, the pilots are believed to have abandoned the kedge, according to Marshfield historian Joseph Hagar.

The kedge was now coveted by one historically-minded South Shore resident, and I had promised to look for it. Although I had seen the kedge more than seven years before, I was unable to find it again, probably because of the waist-high grass in the area. Now that it was winter, the grass was almost gone and I would have a better chance of discovering the outline of the kedge in the coarse marsh grass.

Lining up my sights, I began to look. Five minutes later, to my happiness, there was the kedge. After driving a small staddle spike into the soft marsh earth, I walked over to the nearby island where I located a two-by-four, returned, and drove it deep into the marsh near the kedge as a more noticeable marker.

The next day I paddled out, located the two-by-four and then the kedge, slid the kedge aboard the canoe, and brought it ashore. Later I transferred it to my car and delivered it to my historically-minded friend, receiving in exchange an object I had coveted for a decade.

Although it was formerly the North River, the area where clam digging takes place today in Marshfield is now known as South River Flats because of the 1898 breakthrough which created a new exit or mouth of the river two miles to the north. The river area between was then renamed South instead of North, thus shortening the North River and substantially lengthening the South.

Clam digging in the winter, for those of you who have not tried it, should be done with not one but two pairs of gloves. Thin woolen gloves should be underneath and the cumbersome rubber gloves over them. However, in spite of all precautions, fingers will eventually become more than chilly, and hands may begin to freeze. Especially is this true if there is a bitter, wintry gale sweeping across the flats.

At extreme low tide I can hike right across the marsh and flats, taking the shallow rivulets and salt water streams without fear of getting too wet or muddy, but the margin of safety is small. Often I've started out just a little late and have been able to reach the flats only by long detours which totaled more than a mile. Even then, because of the vagaries of tide, wind, and clogged ice, I have lost out, returning with a minimum of clams. On occasion I've used the canoe as an icebreaker as the *Manhattan* was used in 1969, but honesty forces me to confess that the *Manhattan* was quite a bit heavier and longer than the canoe, and the ice it broke was just a little thicker.

On many occasions out on the marsh I have seen prints of Reddy the Fox. On occasion, if I get out on the marsh before the sun has been up more than half an hour, I can see Reddy running, almost galloping along the shore from his lair, heading for the tender mussels which the low tide offers him. Again, I have caught Reddy less than fifty yards from me on two occasions, and on one particular early morning encounter, Reddy and I stood and stared at each other for at least two minutes, neither gaining any advantage, after which Reddy casually disappeared into the underbrush of Hen Island.

Mink and otter are only rarely seen, and I recall one summer when daughter Dorothy came up from her swim and encountered an otter relatively close at hand.

The muskrats have almost vanished from the marshes, but occasionally the tracks are noticed.

As winter progresses, many of us who endure the extremely cold weather of January and February like to make strenuous attempts to prove that we are tougher than the elements. Actually, I don't think that I am trying to prove anything when I hike out, but I do like to gather a few wintry clams.

One cold day Dorothy and I were hiking along the high-tide area on the frozen surfaces down in back of our Marshfield residence, when Dorothy discovered an oblong-shaped wooden object painted gray, closely resembling a lobster buoy. Both ends were burned off, and we found out later it was a Navy flare. We left it there after reading the inscription.

The flare evidently had been thrown out from a plane, and I wondered what particular disaster prompted a pilot to drop it at sea. Probably we shall never know.

On another occasion, January 26, 1962, I paddled out in my canoe to dig some clams at a favorite location of mine, a nameless island in the middle of the marine approach to the Humarock Bridge, fairly close to Cunningham's Grotto. There was only one objection to a winter visit to the island, for at both high and low tide, it is surrounded by a channel at least six feet deep.

By the time I reached the main part of the river, I realized something I had not noticed before, that the wind gusts were violent ones. Later I checked the weather bureau to find that some of the gusts had reached fifty knots. Nevertheless, using my tandem paddle and with the wind vigorously pushing the canoe, it seemed the logical thing to try for the island where the large two-and-a-quarter to two-and-a-half-inch white paper-shelled clams were awaiting my arrival.

Probably it only took fifteen minutes for the entire trip from our high-tide swimming-pool area. When the canoe slid up on the mud flats and I had put out my anchor, as a matter of habit I turned the canoe over. I have had several other experiences with the wind in the twenty-eight canoes I have owned.

One time back in 1928 on Winthrop Beach, five miles from Boston, I had pulled the canoe up and left it on the shore. While I went home for lunch, a miniature cyclone upended the canoe, and those who saw it happen said it was spinning like a top as it whirled down the beach a total distance of a quarter mile. The damage took four months to repair and all the work was done by my friend, Chester Cole, who still lives in Winthrop.

I recall another incident which occurred during the hurricane of 1954. At the time, I was exploring Jones River from Duxbury and Kingston. Reaching the boatyard at the bend in the river, I was given permission to haul the canoe up above the high-tide mark for the night.

Again, I was not among those who saw what happened to the canoe, but the proprietors of the boatyard told me the day after the August 31 tempest that during that hurricane, Carol by name, the canoe had taken off like an injured swan to describe a parabola right over the boatyard building and land high in the branches of the nearby tree along the edge of the road. I recall that was canoe number twenty-six, which I still have, although I've purchased two more since. Number twenty-six, however, still bears the scars of that canoeish attempt to fly.

Getting back to Friday, January 26, 1962, out on the island, I retrieved my clam fork, changed my paddling gloves to woolen and rubber clam-digging gloves, and started to walk over to where some nice large clam holes were conveniently placed in multiple clusters.

The Snow household then had a capacity of seventy-six clams, and I believed that a good ten minutes digging would produce that many. On that particular island the clams are down about eight to twelve inches, so it does take a little longer than in some other areas.

About ten minutes later I had brought up sixteen of the

reluctant bivalves. I stood up and looked across to check on the canoe, and after having rested briefly, returned to my digging with renewed vigor.*

The next time I looked up, the canoe had vanished! I'd taken my clam-digging gloves off, but I simply dropped the clam fork and started running.

I realized I was in a tough spot. It was a terribly cold day, a strong westerly wind was blowing, and there I was in rubber hip boots on an island entirely surrounded by a deep channel. I could also add that night was coming on.**

Mrs. Snow has definite instructions not to take alarm or call the Coast Guard in winter until three hours have elapsed after I leave the house, and only one hour and a half had gone by.

Did you ever try running in rubber hip boots for a distance of an eighth of a mile in mud that allows you to sink down from two to eight inches?

I ran and finally sighted the two peaks of the canoe. I found out later that one of the strong gusts of wind had snapped the anchor line, rolling the canoe up the beach to a point just a few feet from deep water.

Out of condition, I was terribly tired even before the first hundred yards had been covered, but kept on until I came to a deep area where the incoming tide had created a stream across the mud flats three feet deep. I was well-enough acquainted with this salt-water stream at that time of tide to know that I had to make a quick choice.

If I ran around the rivulet, perhaps another gust would grab the canoe and blow it into deep water beyond my reach. However, if I ran across the rivulet I would go over the top of

* Incidentally, the particular type of clam I enjoy digging is soft-shelled. Extremely fragile, it often collapses at the slightest pressure.
** For those of you not familiar with tides, they never come in or go out at convenient times, and often one must dig just before darkness. It is against the law to dig after dark.

my rubber boots, possibly freezing my feet in the bargain before I got home. If I lost the canoe, I knew it would mean a rubber-booted swim of fifty yards at least and I wasn't looking forward to such an eventuality.

I decided to try for the canoe the quickest way. Wading through the stream, I was soon over the top of my boots, but reached the other side of the muddy bank. There I ran the remaining fifty yards to make a desperate grab before the canoe might blow away again.

The paddles, and I always plan to carry an extra one, were still in the canoe, but my rubber gloves were back at the clam-digging flats. All that was left in the canoe was a soggy mitten I use when taking a kettle of clams from a fire, and another glove usually associated with railroad locomotive engineers. Both were for the left hand. Reversing one, I pulled them on. I still remember how cold and wet they were. The right glove began to freeze, and so I dropped it into the bottom of the canoe. Pulling the craft into ankle-deep water, I stepped in and started paddling against the strong wind. It must have been hitting a thirty knot clip at the moment. Fighting frantically for every inch gained, I was not able to reach Hen Island. There is an outlying marsh island near the Hen Island mainland, and I dragged the canoe up and across the outlying island, slid it down into the creek which separates the marsh island from Hen Island itself, and paddled across to the main part of the marshland immediately surrounding the island.

By this time my right hand was almost frozen. Pulling the glove off, I slid my hand inside my left armpit, for the hand had turned a lobster red. Then and there I decided that sitting in the canoe paddling against the wind would take me too long to reach home, so I pulled the canoe up on the Hen Island marsh and began to haul it towards the solid area above the high-tide mark.

Even this became too much. I found myself resting every

few minutes, sitting on the canoe peak. I decided on a system whereby I would pull the canoe for two dozen steps and then rest, but on the way in I hit some real boggy ground and almost lost my right rubber boot on two occasions.

Finally, gratefully, I reached the row of boulders which indicate the high-tide mark around the island. After stealing a brief rest, I pulled the canoe up into the shrubbery and out of sight where I tied it to one of the saplings.

My next step was to hike around the island on the Branch Creek side, past Dolly's Rock, and across the extensive marshland between Dolly's Rock and the Ox Trail skirting the mainland below Flower Hill.

Ten minutes later I had crossed two substantial hazards, one at the ford and one over the ditch, to reach the Ox Trail. In twelve more minutes I was home. Mrs. Snow, wearing her I-told-you-so look, helped pull my rubber boots from my feet to find that there wasn't too much water in them, but my feet were very cold and my right hand began to ache as the warmth returned.

We did not have steamed clams that night, either. Nor did I ever find my clam fork, but I did rescue one rubber glove weeks later.

15

A MARSHFIELD GHOST

⚓

EVER SINCE I FIRST MOVED to Marshfield twenty years ago, I have heard about the pirates and the ghost seen at the famous Norwood house built by Daniel Phillips in 1750.* Situated in the triangular area across from the Coast Guard Radio Station on South River Street, it still stands majestically on the hill overlooking the South River and the ocean, and is now the attractive home of Mr. and Mrs. Kenneth Alman and their three daughters, Lucy 10, Jennifer 8, and Susan 6.

The Phillips family of Marshfield descended from the Phillips who landed at Plymouth in 1637. Thirteen years later Nathaniel Phillips acquired a large tract of land bordering on the marshes in Marshfield, an area that had been owned by Peregrine White.** The original house the Phillips family lived in was built down near the marshes. This later became part of the Governor Emery estate.

In 1750 descendant Daniel Phillips built what was consid-

---

* As is usually the case, there are many versions of the affair. I must admit that some descendants of Phillips have no knowledge of the ghost while others completely refute the tale. On October 22, 1905, the best account appeared in the Boston *Sunday Herald-Traveler*.

** The first English child to be born in New England.

ered a mansion in those days. Located high up on the hill, it overlooked the ocean.

Daniel Phillips was a Tory, like most of the other large property owners of Marshfield. He was one of those said to have been against the Marshfield Tea Party of 1773, and at the outbreak of the Revolutionary War he was seized by the colonists as a traitor and cast into jail at Plymouth. All his personal property was eventually confiscated. Later he was released on his promise to leave the country.

Nevertheless, he had invested considerable money in England, and was handsomely rewarded for what had been a highly speculative financial activity. Reaching England at the height of the Revolution, Phillips transferred his gains to Spanish doubloons, and sailed to Halifax, Nova Scotia.

His love for his homeland remained, however, and he found himself yearning for Marshfield. Around 1785 he wrote to old friends on the South Shore, who assured him that he was now more than welcome to return.

Choosing a schooner, he purchased it and hired a crew. Soon he transferred his gold aboard, covering the doubloons with a moderate load of lumber. Before long Phillips was back in his native land. A week later, after sliding over the North River bar at high tide, the schooner worked her way up to a point less than a mile from his home and where she grounded. The bags of gold were unloaded and carried over the marshes to the foot of the hill on which the house still is situated.

Night was coming on, and the group realized that there was not enough time to carry the heavy bags of treasure up to the house. They made camp temporarily and buried the gold in the back of a cavern nearby. Phillips and his three attendants kept guard alternately while the others slept, for prowling marauders were not uncommon.

The next day the gold was taken up to the house and

secreted in the cellar. That night Daniel Phillips and his men slept soundly and with a feeling of security.

Unluckily, a group of piratically inclined individuals * had sent a lookout ahead. This man detected the strange craft coming into the river. After Phillips left the cave with the doubloons, the pirates visited the area and picked up a few stray coins where the treasure had been buried. Then, waiting until eleven at night, they broke into the house and murdered Phillips and his crew. Whether or not the killers discovered all of the gold and carried off all or part of the treasure has never been revealed. There are those who claimed that both pirates and defenders had slain each other. In any case, there was such a feeling of horror in the quiet, orderly Marshfield community that the entire incident was hushed up at once.**

As the years went by children were warned against going near the bloodstained house, while women out riding alone whipped their horses to a fast clip and drove by the residence in a hurry.

All known evidence points to 11 P.M. as the time when the crime was committed. On many occasions after the event, those near the house at that hour swore that their horses would snort and then bolt down the road in wild flight. People pedaling by on bicycles at dusk claimed to see ghosts on the lawn, supposedly the spirits of the murdered men.

In this and many other ways the ghost tradition was built up. Every Phillips generation repeated the story with some members of the family declaring that they had often seen the ghost of their murdered ancestor, Daniel Phillips.

Then came the year 1905.

October was said to have been the month when the crime

---

* This same gang later buried two bushels of gold watches at First Cliff.

** A mysterious intruder is said to have visited near the house thus lending credence to the possibility that some gold still remains.

was committed, and in that year of 1905 Carleton Bennett of Boston moved into the Phillips house. He had as cook a boy from Dorchester, Ralph Lee. One night, Bennett returned from Boston relatively late. His account follows:

"At ten o'clock I had laid aside my book to go to bed. But the embers of the cedar logs in the old fireplace glowed entrancingly. I sat for a long time gazing into the dying fire. The odor of the cedar permeated the room like incense. It was so soothing that I could not make up my mind to go upstairs to bed.

"Instead, I went over to the couch in the corner of the parlor, and, half sitting, half reclining, I looked out over the distant ocean, which was roaring furiously after a northeast storm. The full moon was up, making a path of light over the water. I was fascinated by the beauty of the scene, and was thinking that all my surroundings were as idyllic as a dream.

"As I looked out upon the moonlit scene I heard an unearthly groan, and became aware of a presence. Turning my eyes toward the back parlor, where the moaning came from, I watched a white figure which glided from the darkness of the back parlor into the glow of the moonlight before the front window.

"I felt a numbing chill creep over me. Here was the ghost at last. Summoning all my senses, I proceeded to observe it accurately. The figure was tall and powerfully built. It had on long, coarse stockings reaching up over the knee and overlapping short knee breeches. The upper garment was a sort of coarse woven blouse, and on the head was a curious three-cornered, high, pointed hat—the everyday working costume, in fact, of a man of the period just following the Revolutionary War.

"A moment only the figure stood there, then turned, fully

facing me, and retraced its steps to the rear room, in the direction of the old stairway and the mysterious closet.

"In the instant only that I saw its face I photographed its details on my mind. It had small but regular features, somewhat like those of Mrs. Lindley who lived in the house in 1904. It also resembled Phillips Brooks, particularly the big, lustrous, burning eyes."

It was at this moment that Lee, the servant, began to shout at the top of his voice. Then he came running down the stairs from the upper rooms.

"I saw him! I saw him!" cried Lee. "He came down the stairs after me!"

After Bennett had quieted Lee, they talked about the ghost. Bennett was so disturbed he visited a doctor who blamed the whole affair on eating too much rich food.

Nevertheless, the ghost story continues through the years. On another occasion I visited the house while the Djerf family resided there. We toured the residence and went down to the Coast Guard property to visit the mysterious cavelike depression in the bank. One member of our group at that time suggested that some of the gold might still be in the back of the cave, but a metal-detector failed to reveal anything of startling significance.

Now, with the Alman family established at Norwood, the name used since 1905, there are new indications of the ghost's presence.

My visit to the Alman residence in September 1969 revealed that not only are there many secret and semisecret locations in the house today, but that in the short time the family has resided at 1299 South River Street there have been unusual manifestations.

When seven-year-old Jennifer realized that she was moving

A MARSHFIELD GHOST

into a house where much of a peculiar nature had taken place, she asked if "all these people" would ever come back, and she was answered in the negative.

However, the ghost evidently is using the telephone. When I visited Jennifer's mother and her grandmother, Mrs. Ruth Alman, a former Milton resident, I was told that the first time they used the telephone there were many strange voices heard in the background of the conversation.

I was escorted around the house and inspected the closets and panels. I discovered it was possible to look down into the cellar from two different vantage points. There is a boarded-up area in the living room closet which at one time led to the basement, while another section of the house reveals a sort of peephole through which one may glance into the cellar.

My particular interest, however, led us into the attic, where Mrs. Alman and I were able to remove a solid skylight. Then, by climbing on a fragile chair, I could get a view of the surrounding terrain, Marshfield Beach, and the Atlantic Ocean. Whether or not this skylight was used at the time of the murder will probably never be known.

Indeed, I am interested in the future activity at this fascinating house on South River Street.

After we toured the house, we attempted to discover the cave or tunnel in the hill nearby, but failed completely. Located on the Coast Guard property, it has probably been covered over since my earlier visit some years ago with Dana Djerf. Two coastguardsmen, Chief Warrant Officer Harold Warren and Chief Warrant Officer Robert Sanders endeavored to help us discover the cave, but not one of us succeeded.

16

THE BATTLE OF CHELSEA CREEK

⚓

It was a special Saturday long ago when I was shown the site of America's first naval engagement, although at the time I did not learn its full significance.

It was the occasion on which Grandma Rowe took me on one of her historical excursions to Boston, a destination requiring, in those days, a roundabout route on public transportation. As I remember it, we took the Narrow Gauge Railroad from the Winthrop Beach Station to the East Boston Ferry Station.

We soon arrived by trolley at our journey's first point of interest, Chelsea's Marginal Street where stood a row of once-elegant houses, each with pillars resembling those seen on the facades of ante-Civil War mansions on Southern plantations.

Stopping at one of the pillared buildings, Grandma Rowe told me to pay strict attention.

"Here it was, Edward, that the grandfather you never saw lived with me in the summer of 1865, just after our wedding. Your Grandfather Joshua was still in the Navy, and it was then I learned about America's first real naval engagement at Chelsea Creek.

"I want you to remember our visit here this morning, and

also where I take you this afternoon, for I won't be around always to remind you."

After we had walked along the waterfront we climbed back aboard the trolley car, and soon were in the tunnel under Boston Harbor. We continued underground to the subway station at the corner of Tremont and Boylston streets and went upstairs to the sidewalk, where Grandma took me into the Boston Common cemetery.

There in the graveyard she pointed out several stones, including that of Henry Purkitt, the youthful participant in the Boston Tea Party, part of whose tea I later acquired and still have.

Then we visited the stone of the first Chinese gentleman ever to die while sailing into Boston Harbor.* Then we went to the so-called sidewalk grave of the artist Gilbert Stuart, over whose remains more than a thousand people are said to walk daily, as the tomb goes under a Boston Common sidewalk. Stuart is best known for his Athenaeum painting of George Washington, famous all over America.

But the real reason Grandma Rowe took me into the cemetery was a large stone on which there was a statement certifying that there were bones there taken from the Boylston Street subway excavations.

I found out years later that the gravestone commemorated in particular the burial of the British who perished in the Battle of Chelsea Creek, even though the inscription was vague and did not mention how many were buried there. The bodies, believed to have been 107 in number, were taken to the Common immediately after they had been landed on Boston's Long Wharf a few hours after the battle, and in 1895 moved a short distance.

---

* Chow Manderien, who fell from the masthead of a vessel as she entered Boston Harbor. He was nineteen when he lost his life, September 11, 1798.

There are two main sources of information regarding this first real naval engagement in the history of our country.* The first is from Samuel Bixby's diary.

> Saturday, 27th. May [1775]—A number of men (about 600) marched to Chelsea, with two cannon, in order to burn some hay, and drive off a number of Cattle and sheep from Hog and Noddle's Island. There came an armed schooner against them from Boston, and ran aground between the islands and began a battle. Our men burnt the vessel, without the loss of a man, and she kept a continual fire all the time, till she was set on fire. She carried twelve cannon and four swivels.

> 27th. Saturday. About 200 men were detached to go to the Point (Dorchester), to guard it. About 9 or 10 o.c., in the evening, we heard the cannon roar, and the small arms crack for about an hour, in the direction of Marblehead, or Medford, as we thought. We have since learnt, that it was Col. Putnam, & his men at Noddle's Island, where he engaged the regulars, and took 300 sheep, & 200 lambs. One ship ran aground, & they burnt it. He also took some cattle.

I now quote the second source, General William Sumner's account:

> "Saturday, the 27th of May, 1775, a small party of the American Army at Cambridge received orders from Gen. Ward to drive the stock from Hog and Noddle's islands. Advantage was to be taken of the ebb tide, when the water would be fordable from Chelsea [Revere] to Hog Island, and from Hog Island to Noddle's Island, it there being about knee-high. This detachment, composed of Massachusetts and New Hampshiremen, numbering from two to three hundred, by some accounts, and six hundred by another, was led by

---

* Arguments could be started and continued until Doomsday, but Chelsea Creek without question is the first real naval engagement.

THE BATTLE OF CHELSEA CREEK

Col. John Stark of New Hampshire, afterwards of Bennington fame.

"Col. Stark, with his detachment, first crossed from Chelsea [Revere] to Hog Island, and took from it four hundred sheep, represented, erroneously, we think, as stolen by General Gage and deposited there for safe-keeping. They then passed over to Noddle's Island, to rescue the cattle there from their British keepers. The party had killed a few horses and 'divers horned cattle,' and taken away alive a few more, when a signal gun was fired from an armed schooner, lying at anchor near Winnisimmet ferry ways. The British admiral hoisted a red flag at mainmasthead, and sent the schooner, which mounted four six-pounders and twelve swivels, an armed sloop, and a large number of marines from different men-of-war, up Chelsea creek [river], to cut off our return to the main land. The barges conveying these marines were eleven in number, and all were mounted with swivels.

"A heavy fire was now opened from the sloop and schooner, under cover of which the marines advanced upon our men, who were busily engaged upon the Island, in the prosecution of their object. In the meantime, General Gage sent over from the city, four hundred regulars to reinforce the marines previously stationed on [Noddle's] Island. The provincials, under this heavy fire, retreating to a ditch in the marsh, kept themselves undiscovered, until they had opportunity to fire with effect upon the enemy; thus early adopting a practice, for which they were so celebrated during the war, of reserving their fire until sure of their aim, and which, in this instance, resulted in killing some and wounding others of the unsuspecting regulars. They then recrossed to Hog Island, where they were joined by the remainder of the party from Chelsea [Revere], the regulars, who remained upon Noddle's Island, firing upon them at the same time very briskly by platoons.

"Having cleared Hog Island of all the stock, and a sharp fire still continuing between them and the schooner, sloop, boats, and marines, the provincials drew up on Chelsea [Revere] Neck, and sent for a reinforcement. General Putnam with three hundred men and two four-pounders, came to their aid, and, being the highest in rank, he took command of our united forces, which now amounted to about a thousand men. The gallant and patriotic Warren, also, too ardent to remain at a distance, hastened to the spot as a volunteer, and by words and deeds encouraged the men. Putnam reached the ground about nine o'clock in the evening, and took in at a glance the true state of things. Perceiving Noddle's Island occupied by a large body of the enemy, and that a galling fire was kept up by the schooner, sloop, and boats, he with his customary coolness went down to the shore and hailed the schooner, which was within speaking distance, offering the men good quarter, if they would surrender. The schooner answered with two cannon shot, which was immediately replied to by two discharges from the cannon of the principals. A heavy fire ensued from both sides. The armed sloop, and a great number of boats sent from the ships, came to the aid of the schooner, and at the same time a large reinforcement of marines, with two twelve-pounders, was sent to Noddle's Island. For two hours the engagement was severe, until the firing from the schooner ceased. The fire from the shore was so hot that her men found they must perish on board their vessel, or make their escape from it. The love of life conquered, and they hastily took to their boats, leaving the schooner, and all she contained, as booty for the provincials. The barges attempted to tow her back to her station through the sharp fire of Putnam's men; but, unable to endure the severe fire, they were compelled to quit her. The Battle now becoming more general, continued through the whole night;

THE BATTLE OF CHELSEA CREEK

and during the action, a large barn, full of hay, and an old farm-house, on the Island, were burned.

"The schooner drove ashore on the Winnisimet ferry-ways, [then westerly of Chelsea Bridge] and a party, consisting of Isaac Baldwin and twelve others, of the provincials, after taking from her whatever was valuable, rolled bundles of hay under her stern, and set her on fire and burned her up. The reason for burning the schooner, of course, was the fact, that, the harbor being in the possession of the British, they would not be able to keep the vessel in their own hands.

"The provincials took from the schooner '4 double fortified four-pounders, 12 swivels, chief of her rigging and sails, many clothes, some money, &c., which the sailors and marines left behind.' The account honestly adds, 'they having quitted in great haste.' . . .

"The sloop still continued her fire, which was vigorously replied to from the shore, and a heavy cannonade was commenced upon the provincials with the twelve-pounders from a hill upon Noddle's Island, called West Head, near to, and directly opposite, the Winnisimet ferry-ways. But Putnam, inspired with the same dauntless courage with which he entered the den of the wolf,* heading his men, and wading up to his middle in mud and water, poured so hot a fire upon the sloop, that, very much crippled and with many of her men killed, she was obliged to be towed off by the boats. It is a striking illustration of the courage and impetuosity of Putnam, that he and his brave followers attacked and crippled this sloop with small arms; that, leaving their cannon, they waded within musket distance, and there fought the heavy armed vessel, heedless of the great disparity in weapons and of their dangerous position. . . .

"Soon after the disabling of the sloop, the firing ceased,

---

* Years before Israel Putnam had entered a wolf's den, killed the wolf, and had then been hauled out still clinging to the wolf.

excepting a few scattering shots between the marines on Noddle's Island, and the party at Chelsea. During the whole of the following forenoon, however, the *Somerset* man-of-war, of sixty-eight guns and 520 men, was continually firing upon the people on the Chelsea side, who had gathered together in great numbers to see what had occurred upon the Island. It is remarkable, that in this long and well-contested engagement, not a man belonging to the provincial army was killed, and but three or four were wounded, and one of these by the bursting of his own gun; while the loss of the enemy in killed and wounded was very severe. . . ."

The different reports of the battle give various estimates of the number of killed and wounded. The belittling account by General Gage is similar in character to his report of the battle of Lexington and Concord. The following extract from the *London Gazette* of the period is typical:

"Whitehall, July 18, 1775. Lieutenant-General Gage in his Letters to the Earl of Darmouth, dated June 12, 1775, gives an Account, That the Town of Boston continued to be surrounded by a large Body of Rebel Provincials, and that all Communication with the Country was cut off; that the Rebels had been burning Houses and driving Sheep off an Island that has easy Communication with main land, which drew on a Skirmish with some marines who drove the Rebels away; but that an armed Schooner got on shore at High Water, there was no possibility of saving her, for as the Tide fell, she was left quite dry, and burned by the Rebels. Two men were killed and a few wounded."

As an offset to this overwhelming underestimate of the British general, we quote a paragraph from historian Gordon. Says he: "The regulars were said to have suffered very much, not to have had less than 200 killed and wounded . . . The loss had a good effect on the provincials. The affair was a matter of no small triumph to them, and they felt upon the occasion more courageous than ever."

In the year 1895 Boston workmen at the edge of Boston Common were digging on Boylston Street near the corner of Tremont as part of a project to complete a subway through downtown Boston.

Suddenly one of the workers struck a fragment of bone with his pick and dislodged a human skull! All work immediately ended for the moment, but after the excitement had died down one man was delegated to set aside any human remains uncovered.

A pit was ordered dug in the nearby Boston Common cemetery, and as many bones as could be found of the British who died in the Chelsea Creek battle were placed in the pit. Later a substantial marker was erected over the bones.

On March 23, 1970 a group of Bostonians visited the cemetery and gathered around the stone marker. Two historians, Gregg Benjamin of the Bostonian Society, and bookman George Gloss, stood at the gravestone during a brief service in honor of the men killed 195 years before. The present uninspiring inscription follows:

> HERE WERE RE-INTERRED
> THE REMAINS OF PERSONS
> FOUND UNDER THE BOYLSTON STREET MALL
> DURING THE DIGGING OF THE SUBWAY
> 1895

PART TWO

Atlantic Tales

PART TWO

Atlantic Tales

1

THE *QUEEN MARY* SINKS A CRUISER

⚓

AT THE HEIGHT of the Second World War, I was aboard the *Queen Elizabeth* returning from the North African invasion. When about eight hundred miles from our goal, Halifax, we were told that the sister craft of the *Elizabeth,* the *Queen Mary,* had knifed through a cruiser sending hundreds of British sailors to their death.

We heard that the collision had taken place quite a few months before, and each of us began to wonder how this strange accident could have occurred.

Years later while vacationing in Bermuda, I discovered and interviewed a survivor of the collision. From that moment on, I pieced together for my own satisfaction what really happened on October 2, 1942, when the *Queen Mary,* nearing the British Isles at the Forelands, cut through and sank the H.M.S. *Curacao.*

It was a considerable period of time before I had the information to satisfy myself that I knew enough of the entire story. Nevertheless, anyone attempting to discover crisp, nautical language or accurate naval or maritime explanations should consult the British Admiralty records, and not this chapter. What I have put together is an account of the disaster told in a manner I believe will be fairly clear to the average landsman.

The 81,235-ton *Queen Mary* had been built for fast passenger service across the Atlantic. In World War II she and her sister, the *Queen Elizabeth,* carried thousands upon thousands of soldiers into many parts of the world, using their superior speed to evade enemy submarines. Thus each craft exchanged peacetime attractiveness for the grim realities of war, and when they sailed into Boston Harbor they appeared as inconspicuous gray craft. On one occasion at the height of the war they were both tied up at Boston's Commonwealth Pier, to the delight of all who saw them.

To both layman and shipbuilder, the construction of the *Queen Mary* must forever remain an accomplishment of magic and skill. In 1840 Samuel Cunard had built the first real ocean-going craft and named her *Britannia*. Two hundred and seven feet long, she had engines of 740 horsepower. Less than a century later, the *Queen Mary* was launched, 1,018 feet long, with a beam of 118 feet. Her depth from keel to masthead was 234 feet, and her funnels were so immense that three express locomotives could run abreast through any of them.

Launched on September 26, 1934, the *Queen Mary* was the first craft to be commissioned in the service of the combined Cunard and White Star lines.

Both the *Queen Elizabeth* and *Queen Mary* had built up their accommodations for wartime transportation until at least 10,500 men could be carried on each crossing. The soldiers had to sleep on alternate shifts, using the same beds or bunks for their slumbers. The usual time-consuming activities, such as attending movies, going to concerts, and carrying out air-raid drills kept the men fairly busy on the journey across the Atlantic. Then came a day in a fall crossing of 1942 when those aboard the *Mary* were informed by "scuttlebutt"

THE *QUEEN MARY* SINKS A CRUISER

that the British Isles were not too far away and they would soon dock in Great Britain.

The rendezvous with a cruiser and fleet of destroyers was imminent, and a craft noted for her antiaircraft ability soon hove in sight. She was the H.M.S. *Curacao,* whose master, Captain Wilfred Boutwood, D.S.O., had an excellent record of escort duty.

Good visibility allowed the *Curacao* to identify the three stacks of the *Mary* from a distance of no less than twenty miles, and before eleven o'clock that fateful morning Captain Boutwood had the *Curacao* in position five miles forward of the *Queen Mary,* with a group of destroyers in advance of him.

Boutwood believed that the most favorable position to answer an air attack was a mile astern of the *Mary,* but as the *Queen Mary* could outdistance him in speed, the length of time during which he could help in case of trouble was limited to whenever he could stay close astern of the *Mary.*

Shortly before noon Captain Boutwood communicated with the *Queen Mary,* asking for her course and speed. Writing of the incident years later in his book *An Agony of Collisions,* Peter Padfield * stated that when the *Mary* replied she made a mistake: her answer of 108 degrees should have been 106 degrees.

Naturally the *Queen Mary* was on an evasive or zigzag course to avoid submarine attack. The figure-eight plan, as it was called, was quite involved. It consisted of holding the 108-degree course to starboard for four minutes, then changing twenty-five degrees to port for eight minutes, after which she'd turn again to starboard on 131 for eight minutes. The final three courses were four minutes at 106, eight on 131,

---

* To whom we waved from our canoe when he was a crewman on the *Mayflower II* coming into Plymouth Harbor, just after the slight collision between the *Mayflower* and a government craft.

and then eight on 81, after which the combination known as figure eight was begun all over again.

It was the task of the *Curacao* to keep out of the way of the *Queen Mary*, usually steering at 108 degrees. According to records, Boutwood radioed to the *Mary* at half-past twelve that he was proceeding at twenty-five knots on a course of 108 degrees.

Unfortunately around one o'clock the *Curacao* began to fall away. Captain Boutwood set a new bearing of 105, but even that didn't bring him close enough. He now ordered the course at 100 degrees. Believing that he had compensated enough, he returned to 108, but soon realized that by so doing he had entered the danger zone of the *Queen Mary*'s evasive-action figure-eight courses.

About this time, the bridge officers on the *Mary* also were concerned because they believed the *Curacao* was getting too close for comfort. Senior Officer Robinson was on the bridge, and he approved a change of course. Nevertheless, he kept watching the cruiser, now on the port bow. Then came lunch-time. Robinson went below, his place was taken by Junior Officer Wright.

Some time later Wright shouted out "hard-a-starboard," causing Captain Illingsworth to come out on the bridge. He asked Wright what was going on and Wright explained that he thought the cruiser was much too close. Illingsworth studied the situation.

"You need not worry about her. These fellows know all about escorting," were the captain's comments. Wright now relaxed, his fears at rest. At four minutes past two the *Curacao* again began to close in on the *Mary*. The time came for Wright to order the next course change, which was to 131 degrees. Robinson soon returned from lunch, noticing at once that the *Curacao* apparently was on a converging course at a distance of less than a quarter of a mile. He didn't like what he saw, and called out "port-a-little."

On came the cruiser.

"Hard-a-port," he shouted. The cruiser still came at them.

It was now possible for the horrified officers to look down almost into the funnels of the cruiser as she cut the distance closer and even closer.

Then, to the amazement and shock of the *Mary*'s officers, the *Curacao* began heading across the *Queen*'s bow. But every man watching realized she was not going to make it. As the forward section of the *Curacao* slid across dead ahead of the liner's bow, the *Queen Mary* hit the cruiser 114 feet forward of her stern. After striking the *Curacao*, the *Queen Mary* rolled her over, cut through her, and sailed on, barely slowed by the impact. The two severed fragments of the cruiser began to sink slowly into the sea.

The horrified watchers noticed that the bow of the *Curacao* started to right itself to port, while across the *Mary*'s wake the stern of the cruiser at first was seen high in the air. Then, swiftly, she started to go down. Scores of sailors began jumping into the sea.

Captain Illingsworth rushed out on the bridge, fearing a bomb had hit, but learned the truth. Ordering speed reduced to ten knots, he sent a message to the destroyer escort *Bulldog* explaining that a collision had resulted when the *Curacao* had attempted to cross the *Mary*'s bow. With U-boats all around, wartime restrictions prohibited him from stopping to help save the lives of those overboard.

Three hundred and thirty-eight men perished. Because of the collision the *Mary* herself had some plates buckled on her port side, but with a collision mat lowered in place the speed was continued at thirteen knots.

Later, reaching port, the *Queen Mary* was repaired and continued to transport troops for the remainder of the war.

As in the case of other awesome marine disasters such as the *Titanic, Empress of Ireland,* and *Andrea Doria,* responsibility had to be decided, and in June 1945 the court met. On June 12, 1945, Justice Pilcher, Trinity House Masters Captain G. C. H. Noakes and Captain W. E. Crumplin began the case.

Costs had to be settled. If the *Queen Mary* was to blame, payments would be made on a civilian basis to families of those who were lost. If not, Admiralty pensions would be awarded.

Cunard lawyers claimed that standard practice involved escorts keeping out of the way of transports. Even if she, the *Queen Mary,* had been overtaking, the *Curacao* was the craft which should "give way." Admiralty representatives responded by saying that the *Mary* had not been following her declared zigzag course at the time.

In Captain Boutwood's testimony, he stated that as soon as he realized a dangerous situation was developing, he took control.

"From the moment of assuming command of the handling of the ship I did all I conceived was the best possible way to avoid a collision," he stated.

"Within perhaps a minute and a half or two minutes, I realized that there was no chance of saving any part of the ship. . . . After I gave up hope of saving the ship I instructed the officers who were with me to go down and take charge of what ratings * they could get hold of."

Captain Boutwood explained that he never ordered "abandon ship," but when he heard it given he realized that whoever gave the order was "justified in giving it. . . . I am

---

* Ratings were sailors without high rank.

absolutely certain that not long before the impact I had in mind the possibility of averting disaster by going hard a-port in order to swing myself clear, but it was not possible because the swing involved was quite out of the question in the time available."

Justice Pilcher decided that the *Curacao* had had no set course to follow and it was her duty to stay out of the way. He commented on the neglect of those on the cruiser to signal the *Mary* to find out what particular zigzag the liner was executing if they were in doubt.

The eminent jurist was critical of the *Curacao*'s lookout. Pilcher also found it difficult to believe that Officer Robinson on the *Mary* should be blamed for not taking more aggressive action at the helm. Indeed, he was favorably impressed with Robinson, who gave his evidence "well and clearly and no fault was found with his demeanor in the witness box. I formed the view that he was endeavouring to tell the truth and to give me the best picture he could."

In his ruling Justice Pilcher concluded that on that October 2 day, "after 1:40 P.M. the *Queen Mary* carried on with her zigzag and that Captain Boutwood's observation or his recollection are at fault." He completely exonerated the liner *Queen Mary* from all blame.

The British Admiralty appealed Pilcher's ruling, but almost two years went by before the appeal was acted upon. This time there were three judges, Lord Justice Scott, Lord Justice Bucknill, and Lord Justice Wrottlesley. After listening to all evidence, Justice Scott stated that there were special circumstances, and that the usual overtaking rule should be reversed, and that the craft being overtaken should keep clear.

This Justice Scott regarded as a complete vindication of the *Queen Mary*'s action, "the very fact that the *Curacao* put up the wildly erroneous contention of fact, that the *Queen Mary* abandoned her zigzag eight, is conclusive that the

Curacao's watch upon her movements was utterly inadequate. That very great fault in lookout was aggravated by her failure to signal to the *Queen Mary*."

Scott now stated that the disaster was caused by Boutwood's failure to understand that the *Queen* was then on an eight-minute leg to starboard which he knew was 131 degrees.

In spite of this Lord Justice Bucknill disagreed with Scott on many fundamental points, and stated that those on the *Mary* waited too long to make their decision.

In fact, Bucknill stated his surprise "that these two fine ships, officered by British sailors of high standing and experience, should collide with one another in the way they did." He also decided that much blame could be placed on Captain Illingsworth's order to Wright about not worrying as the *Curacao* would keep out of the *Mary*'s way. "If Captain Illingsworth had been on the bridge of his ship at the critical time, I feel confident that he would have ported and got onto a parallel course with the cruiser."

He then suggested that the blame should be divided with two-thirds on the *Curacao* and one-third on the *Queen Mary*.

Lord Justice Wrottesley agreed with Bucknill's judgment, and supported his division of the blame. Thus two-thirds of the Justices agreed that one-third of the blame was on the *Queen Mary*. Both parties appealed to the House of Lords, which upheld the verdict on February 8, 1949. As a result of this decision, contrary to what the average marine-minded person usually thinks, it is not necessarily the responsibility of a navy craft to keep out of a transport's way.

I wonder how many officers on the bridge of either craft that fatal day had read a book which I often peruse in the library of my Marshfield home.

On page 356 of the third edition Reginald G. Marsden's *Collisions at Sea*, he states the following:

"A vessel is not justified in delaying to take precautions

until the last moment; or in trusting to being able to 'shave' clear of the other. If by doing so, she frightens the other into taking a wrong step, and a collision occurs, she will be responsible for the entire loss."

Which, of course, is small consolation to the widows and relatives of the 338 officers and men who were lost on the *Curacao* that October day in 1942.

2

MARGARET RETURNS HOME

⚓

IN THE SPRING OF 1856, Captain James Peterson of Machiasport, Maine, who never looked forward to a long, lonely voyat sea without his wife, Margaret, told her he would like to take her to Cuba with him on the bark *Dublin* to get a cargo of sugar. At first she demurred, and her mother objected as well, claiming that yellow fever was raging in the Cuban area. Finally he won her over. To do this he promised faithfully that should she become ill, he would bring her back no matter what happened.

The *Dublin* sailed away, finally reaching Sagua LeGrand, Cuba. There the cargo was loaded, and there Margaret became ill with yellow fever. Margaret Peterson died on June 8, 1856, at the age of twenty-eight.

Captain Peterson now was faced with the task of keeping his word with Margaret and her mother. At the time he had been told of how John Paul Jones had been buried in a lead coffin and the lead coffin filled with rum.

Captain Peterson decided to use a cask of rum, rather than wait for the construction of a lead coffin. Then, with full religious ceremony, the chaplain of the *North Carolina,* at the moment in a nearby port, officiated at the strange service in which Margaret's mortal remains were immersed in the cask and sealed up. The cask was carefully chocked in the hold and the long, sorrowful trip back to the United States began.

In this way the remains of Margaret Peterson arrived in Boston Harbor. There at Central Wharf the cask was transferred to another craft, the brig *Stanley,* which a week later sailed into Machiasport with Captain Peterson and his wife's remains aboard.

Four days later, with proper ceremonies, the funeral was held at the Machiasport church and Margaret was buried a short distance away in the cemetery in back of the Machiasport church.

After several more voyages to the tropics, Captain Peterson married again, this time a girl named Mary, born in 1840. He died December 24, 1910, but his second wife lived until February 25, 1916. It is not known if there are any descendants living today.

Incidentally, there is quite a story about John Paul Jones and his lead casket, which gave Peterson the idea for the preservation of Margaret's remains.

When the United States realized the importance of having the remains of the illustrious naval fighter back in this country, General Horace Porter was given the task of locating the body. Five lead caskets were uncovered in the Paris cemetery where Jones had been buried, and all but one lead coffin had a marker on it.

The unmarked lead casket was taken out and opened up. Contrary to belief, it was discovered that Jones had been embalmed in alcohol and not rum. The remains were compared with the Houdon bust of Jones and accepted.

Sealed in a new triple casket of pine, lead, and oak, the remains of John Paul Jones were brought back to this country. Memorial services for him were held at Annapolis, Maryland, on April 24, 1906.

3

DERELICTS

⚓

THE MARINE AREA between Boston and Bermuda has had more than eight hundred derelicts or about one for each mile between the two locations. Stories of derelicts and their strange, unmanned adventures have always fascinated me. When we learn that at the height of the days of sail there were no less than forty-eight of these derelicts destroyed in one single year, we realize that indeed they presented quite a problem.

In the summer of 1870 a dangerous derelict was sighted off the coast of New England. The cruiser *Atlanta* fired a torpedo into her, but she did not sink. Two more torpedoes were fired with no effect. Reversing his engines, the captain of the *Atlanta* prepared to ram her. The *Atlanta* hit the abandoned craft square amidships and sent her straight to the bottom. Unfortunately, a large part of the *Atlanta*'s bow broke off and went down with the derelict. Had the sea been rough, the warship might also have gone to the bottom, but she steamed for Boston, where she was drydocked and repaired.

Of course, the most celebrated case of the abandonment of a craft was that of the *Mary Celeste* about which I have written in several books. In 1872 she was found in good condition off the shores of the Iberian Peninsula and was brought into Gibraltar by a prize crew.

What has often been called the most famous of all derelicts was a British naval vessel, the *Resolute,* abandoned in the ice around 1875 in Latitude 27° 40″ North. Her crew got away safely, and later the *Resolute* was sighted off Cape Mercy by a United States whaler and taken into Boston Harbor. The United States government completely refitted her and sent her across the ocean to England. Long afterwards, when the ship was broken up, the English had a beautiful desk made from her timbers, a desk now in the White House at Washington, D. C.

Another unusual incident connected with the abandonment of a ship took place shortly after the crew of the *John Blake* fled their craft off Cuba in the year 1885. While the men were rowing to land in the boats, they sighted a ship lying on a sandbar—actually another derelict. Getting her off the shoal, they sailed her all the distance to England, where they were awarded salvage for their services.

On January 28, 1899, the English bark *Siddartha* sailed from Jacksonville, Florida. Running into a bad gale, she was abandoned at sea in a waterlogged condition. The *Siddartha* became one of the most famous derelicts of all time, sighted on no less than fifty-seven occasions while adrift at sea. Three attempts were made to set fire to her and send her to the bottom, but she refused to sink. Finally a British warship was able to destroy her.

In October 1905 the Swedish bark *Orion,* laden with salt, was picked up at sea by the *Exeter City* after her crew had been taken off by the *Etruria.* Rerigged, remanned, the *Orion* sailed again. A year after this she was again abandoned in a storm and this time, spotted by an American warship, she was sent to the bottom with one torpedo.

On January 19, 1906, the coal collier *Dunmore* was abandoned at sea in mid-Atlantic. With disabled engines she was thought to be sinking.

During the next six weeks she was reported by no less than sixteen craft, and the *St. Louis* had to alter course to avoid running her down. Finally the British Admiralty searched for her, found her, and she was destroyed by gunfire.

In October 1907 the captain of the steamer *Phoebus,* on arriving in New York, reported that he had met a Dutch schooner evidently abandoned by her crew in mid-Atlantic.

A lamp still burned in the cabin and a lifeboat was in its place in the davits. She had nineteen tons of fish aboard. As the distance was too great to tow her into New York, she was sunk by gunfire by the *Phoebus.*

In the autumn of 1923 the *Governor Parr,* an American schooner, was abandoned three hundred miles south of Newfoundland. Rather than sink, however, the *Governor Parr* had other ideas, and started out on a cruise all her own. Some weeks later the crew of the *Saxonia* boarded her, finding her waterlogged. Several times in the next few weeks she was sighted, and around Christmas the cutter *Tampa* was sent out to find her.

She was discovered and taken in tow, but the *Tampa* ran out of coal before getting her close to port, and cut the hawser.

The following June she was sighted by the steamer *Olen,* which reported the *Parr's* bowsprit, anchor, and deckhouses still intact.

In July she was off the Canary Islands. A tug from Lisbon was sent out to destroy her, but weather changes sent the tug back to port.

On August 8 a liner from Africa discovered the *Parr,* and put aboard drums of paraffin to ignite her. On August 11 she was seen still burning by the *Umtali,* and four days later the *Iberia* reported that she was barely afloat.

The *Ada Cummings,* which floated around the North Atlantic for 549 days, was another derelict ship to attract considerable attention. From her abandonment off New Jersey, she drifted across the ocean almost over to Ireland. Then she came down to a point off Portugal, after which she floated out into the Sargasso Sea. When she finally came ashore on the coast of Colombia, South America, she was broken up.

The world's record for length of time as a derelict at sea is held by the *Fanny Wolston.* Abandoned in mid-Atlantic late in the nineteenth century, she was seen later off New York and then sighted in the Gulf of Mexico. Set afire on several occasions, she simply refused to sink. From the time of her abandonment until she was last sighted, no less than 1,408 days had elapsed.

Another unexplained derelict was found off the coast of Australia near Wyndham. Her sails were set and the hull was quite sound and seaworthy, but there were bloodstains on the deck. No one, dead or alive, was aboard and the mystery was never solved.

A large iron sailing craft, the *Arno,* was abandoned at sea, and the *Normannia* found her in midocean on her beam end. Her wheat cargo had shifted and she was about to capsize. Shortly after, the steamer *Merrimac* fell in with the derelict, and put a prize crew aboard. They trimmed ship and brought her into Liverpool, where they received a tidy sum in prize money.

Let us shift from derelicts to bottle messages, about which I've written on many occasions.

On February 23, 1937, the St. George Hotel lifeguard at St. Catharine's Bathing Beach, Richmond Boyd, found a message in a bottle.

This bottle was one of four hundred cast overboard on July 14, 1929, at a point twenty-three miles south of Long Island, and twenty-three miles southeast of Scotland Lightship off the United States coast. This was a campaign organized by the Brooklyn *Eagle* to cast some light on the question of why Long Island and other nearby beaches were so frequently littered with garbage floating in from the sea.

Less than one hundred of the four hundred bottles have been returned. The first one was found at Long Beach, eleven hours after it struck the water twenty-three miles away. The one found by Richmond Boyd had wandered over the ocean for seven and a half years. Some were reported from the Bahamas and from the Azores, at various intervals. It is estimated that because of the Gulf Stream three bottles which found their way to the Azores between March 1930 to June 1931 traveled at least six thousand miles, skirting the Irish coast, before heading south.

Each bottle contained a slip offering the finder one dollar reward if he would return it to the *Eagle* with the information about the time and place where it was found.

The bottle found by Richmond Boyd, it will be remembered, was covered with barnacles on the cork. The message in the bottle was wet, though there was no water in the bottle. Mr. Boyd suggested that the reward be sent to the Red Cross, but said he would like to know the time and place where the bottle was set adrift, and the above information was received from the *Eagle* in an article.

There was one interesting fact recorded in connection with the bottles. About this time there was a decided decrease in the amount of garbage floating back on the beaches. This was attributed to the fact that the garbage scows had formerly been dumping inside the legal limit, and with the *Eagle* campaign this ceased.

* * *

For the actual story of a visit to a derelict, let us quote the diary of Charles Dixon, the chief officer on the merchant ship *Erin's Isle,* then in Latitude 29° 30″ South, Longitude 23° 80″ West.

"Sunday, November 17, 1901:

"I was sitting on that part of the quarterdeck where I could have a view of all that was going on, and also ahead of the vessel, reading one of Max Pemberton's most interesting stories, when I happened to look up, and about nine miles ahead was what appeared to be a steamer bound to the eastward. . . .

"The apparently abandoned vessel was two points on the starboard bow, so that if we kept our course we should pass it at a distance of about a mile and a half or two miles. I then went down in the cabin to notify the captain (who was having his afternoon doze) of what was in sight, and that if he wished to find out all about her we should have to alter our course. He told me at once to alter the course so as to pass close to the dismasted vessel.

"The time began to pass faster when we began to argue and speculate as to the cause of the wreck's present condition; whether the masts had been cut away to save the vessel, or whether a sudden squall had dismasted her; or was she burnt out?

"At 4:15 P.M. we were then about a mile and a half from the wreck and it easily could be seen that she was an iron vessel. We read her name, the *Norfolk Island,* of Glasgow. As we pulled around to the lee side so that we could get a view of the deck, it nearly took my breath away to see such a sight; the other side had looked so promising. She had been completely burnt out, so as to be useless, and apparently had not a thing of value on her."

* * *

Dixon went aboard with three men and found that she had been loaded with coal which was still smouldering. A few vestiges of life aboard the ship remained, among them the works of the cabin clock with the hands stopped at three o'clock, and the ship's bell. For some strange reason the galley had suffered the least damage and the stove and cooking utensils were still intact.

The men climbed "pretty well" all over the vessel looking for salvage, crawling about on the eight-inch-wide deck beams with a drop of twenty feet to tangled iron, wire, and cinders below.

Standing by himself on the derelict, Chief Officer Dixon tried to imagine the sensations of one left alone on a vessel in that state. He was out of sight of his own ship, the day was gloomy, and the uncontrolled rudder made a mournful sound. He realized how helpless a human being would be in such a position, and he experienced such a feeling of despair and hopelessness as he never wished to experience again.

"One of the most curious things I noticed on board, close to the foremast where it was broken off at the side of the ship, was a piece of sail caught on the bulwarks, where even the iron was bent with heat. How the canvas was not consumed is more than I can solve, and I have given it serious thought. Someone might offer a suggestion. I wish they would for there is something uncanny in the thing which worries me. There was also a wooden pulley in the same place, also intact.

"It was now nearly half-past five, and although the sun was still above the horizon the sky was so heavily clouded that it was quite dark, and as there was nothing to be gained by remaining longer I called the men left in charge of the boat. They came alongside and we started for our own vessel, then about a mile and a half away, where we arrived about 6 P.M.

"About 7 P.M. we saw the last of the *Norfolk Island*. As she faded from our sight in the gathering mists of evening she presented a picture of such desolation that it left an impression to be long remembered as a fitting close to an incident that is likely to remain unique in the writer's seafaring career."

4

ANDREA DORIA AGAIN

⚓

ALTHOUGH IN TWO of my previous books I've written about the 1956 marine disaster which occurred when the *Stockholm* crashed into the *Andrea Doria,* I have never recorded the subsequent judicial investigation of the collision because in all fairness I had wished to include the *Andrea Doria* findings conducted by the Italian government's committee in Rome during the same period. More than a decade has passed since the Italians interviewed their last *Andrea Doria* crewman, but the results so far have never been made public. I hope that some day the findings will be announced to the world, but have decided to wait no longer to reveal the New York conferences and testimony.

Therefore, after covering the human interest angle of the crash in my 1957 *Legends of the New England Coast* and following it in 1967 with emphasis on scuba diving to the *Andrea Doria* in *Incredible Mysteries and Legends of the Sea,* in this volume I am going ahead without the Italian release and present the important details of the other findings. I have never covered this predominantly legal aspect of the story before.

Here is a brief outline of the disaster. The *Andrea Doria*

collided with the *Stockholm* on July 25, 1956. Of the 1,706 people on board the *Andrea Doria* all but 46 were saved from the collision that occurred more than forty miles to the south of Nantucket Island, Massachusetts. When the crash came the collision caught the passengers and crew unprepared. The Italian craft soon settled over on her starboard side, and ever so slowly began to sink.

The sea was kind to the stricken liner, for the potential for death was actually greater than the number of 1,503 who perished when the *Titanic* sank to her doom. When the *Andrea Doria* finally disappeared beneath the waves shortly after ten o'clock the next morning, the *Ile de France,* the *Stockholm,* the *Cape Ann,* the *Thomas,* the *Allen,* and the *Hopkins* had saved all but forty-six people. The *Andrea Doria* now lies in 222 feet of water in Latitude 40° 29" North and in Longitude 69° 51" West. The nearest part of her 697-foot hulk is 144 feet down from the surface of that South Nantucket sea area, and she is more than forty miles south of Sankaty Head Light on Nantucket.

In the rooms of the Boston, Massachusetts, Marine Society * I interviewed several of the other members who were veteran sea captains. They told me that after making a deep study of all the evidence of what actually caused the accident, they decided, strangely enough, that if the radar screen had not revealed the other's presence, there would have been no accident. Not altering course, the two craft would have passed each other harmlessly in spite of the foggy night. As it was, the Swedish officers aboard the *Stockholm* thought the passing would be port to port, while the Italians on the *Andrea Doria* believed it was to be starboard to starboard. These opposing beliefs added to the confusion.

Less than two months after the catastrophe, officers and officials representing both the *Andrea Doria* and the *Stock-*

---

* I am a member, holding certificate number 2738.

holm met in conference in New York City, so that all concerned could discover as much as possible about what really took place. Thus each group would find out what the others had planned to do and what they actually had done.

The first important representative of the *Stockholm* to speak was Third Officer Ernest Carstens-Johannsen. In his testimony Carstens revealed that his view of the radar an hour before midnight indicated that the *Andrea Doria* was twelve miles away from the *Stockholm*. Then, at a distance of ten miles Carstens began estimating positions on the plotting board and found that the approaching craft was two degrees to port. When six miles away he marked the approaching ship as four degrees to port. He then estimated that the *Andrea Doria* would pass at least one hundred yards to port at the point of nearest distance.

His first visual sighting through the partial fog was twenty degrees to port and 1.9 miles away. Therefore he ordered the helmsman to proceed to starboard. When the craft had turned two points, he called out "Steady as you go." This, in his opinion, would not allow the *Stockholm* to get within a mile of the *Andrea Doria* at any time. Almost immediately, to his horror, he saw the starboard lights of the *Andrea Doria* and the green sidelight, and realized a collision was probable.

Attorney Edward Underwood, of the opposition, queried Carstens.

"Is it true that you did not sound any whistle signals before the collision?"

Answering in the affirmative, Carstens stated that he had never heard of ships signaling each other in clear weather. Carstens did mention the fact that one of his helmsmen "rather often" was not too careful concerning a tendency to yaw * but stated that on the night of the disaster there had been no yawing.

* To swing off course either to port or to starboard.

Carstens was then queried concerning the so-called mysterious disappearance of the night order book which might have been of vital importance after the collision, but he had no logical explanation. He acknowledged that there might have been a patch of fog. On the other hand, he never admitted during the entire testimony that he even suspected fog, claiming there was bright moonlight to starboard.

He explained that when he finally changed course, his reason was to get more safety clearance and to exhibit his own red light to better advantage.

Having become excited by Carstens' narration, Underwood now challenged Carstens, asking him if the real reason was not that he suddenly realized he was on a collision course with the *Andrea Doria* practically dead ahead. Carstens' lawyer now leaped from his seat and objected to Underwood's tone. Nevertheless, Carstens finally replied in the negative, but admitted that during this period he had telephoned to the crow's nest and his telephone faced aft. Thus he would for a time have his back to the oncoming Italian luxury liner.

Carstens testified that if the Italian craft had sounded her whistle in this period, it would have aided him in attempting to prevent the collision, but he never heard it. Later there did come a blast, but by this time there were too many other conflicting noises.

The next important witness was Captain Piero Calamai of the *Andrea Doria,* who stated that he had been extremely active on the bridge the night of the disaster, continuously since three o'clock in the afternoon. He had spotted the *Stockholm* on radar from a distance of seventeen miles and she was off to starboard. In a moment the *Stockholm* apparently swung to starboard, heading right into the *Andrea Doria*. The Italian captain emphasized the point that he observed every rule of the road known to navigation. When five miles away, he directed a swing to port of four degrees for safety, at that time noticing a let-up of the fog. When two miles away the captain strode out onto the starboard wing, where he found the mate anxiously taking in the situation.

"Why don't we hear him? Why doesn't he whistle?" Third Officer Fiannini kept calling. A moment later both the third mate and Calamai saw a glow. Probably the *Andrea Doria* was then slightly more than a mile away with the *Stockholm* two points to starboard. Even at a mile away, a collision was almost inevitable.

Then, turning at least twelve degrees to port, the *Andrea Doria* proceeded in an attempt to escape the collision, but it came too late, and the larger craft was hit under the bridge. Beginning to list almost at once, a few moments later the *Doria* had reached a position leaning seventeen and a half degrees to starboard, even then making it impossible to launch the portside boats.

Calamai was later asked if he had special training in the use of radar, but he admitted none. He also stated that he knew very little about stability, nor did he have a working knowledge of the *Doria*'s center of gravity.

By now observers at the hearing realized that the aim of the Swedish group was to establish the idea that the *Andrea Doria* went to the bottom not primarily as a result of the collision, but because of electric failure which prevented closing the watertight doors. Instability of the ship itself was also considered.

Then the question was brought up as to whether or not the *Andrea Doria* engineer handled the situation correctly.

The Italian captain was on the stand for ten days. The vigorous questioning finally brought a protest by the Italian attorneys that the entire affair was becoming a "trial by ordeal" of Captain Piero Calamai, and he was allowed to leave the stand.

The next important witness was Captain Gunnar Nordenson of the *Stockholm*. For more than a third of a century, he explained, he had sailed on similar courses in that area without trouble. Nordenson stated that Third Officer Carstens had done nothing wrong at any time during the incident. The captain testified that a red wax-pencil plot had probably been taken by the third mate himself, but it had disappeared in the later confusion.

The unfortunate captain, becoming concerned at the height of the questioning, suddenly fainted under the tension in the courtroom. Carried to an open window, he was revived. The following six weeks he spent first in the hospital and then convalescing. Returning to court, he appeared to have aged considerably. Nevertheless, even under constant repetitious grilling, he never admitted that Carstens had made an error of judgment on the bridge regarding the fog. At first Nordenson stated that he cut speed in the fog, but when the log books were shown him, he had to admit that speed had never been reduced. He was then asked the question as to whether he would have reduced speed when close to a fogbank.

"I do not have to answer that question," he replied.

Peter Larson was the man at the wheel at the moment of collision and he backed Carstens' testimony about the helm orders immediately before the two craft came together.

Others who testified were the boy who had been up in the crow's nest and the apprentice who was lookout on the bridge's port wing. The latter was interrogated as to whether or not he had heard Carstens' comments after the crash.

He answered in the affirmative, quoting Carstens as saying: "I cannot understand why they could turn so."

The youthful lookout testified that when he noticed two white lights he called the bridge from his perch in the crow's nest. He had informed the bridge that the lower light was to the left of the higher. The Swedish motorship then went to starboard.

All officers and men questioned on the *Stockholm* stated that when the *Andrea Doria* was sighted visually without radar, she was off to port, her lower masthead light was to the left of the higher masthead light. Therefore the passing, as they thought, would be port to port. Across on the *Doria* the third officers saw the glow of lights of the *Stockholm* to starboard. Captain Calamai also saw them. The *Stockholm* began to turn, and when Calamai identified the masthead lights, the lower was to the left of the higher, and the red sidelight came in sight.

Actually, the two rival claims are impossible to associate with each other. The conflict in the statements of the officers from each craft are simply untenable, and one group must be wrong. It is generally agreed that at the moment of contact the *Stockholm*'s angle of approach was at least one hundred degrees. All testimony indicates that the angle of collision must have been substantial for the *Stockholm* to penetrate so deeply into the *Andrea Doria*.

Without question, the *Stockholm* could never hit the *Andrea Doria* and pivot her to starboard. Therefore we can assume from the evidence that the *Andrea Doria* turned to port and then the *Stockholm* noticed the *Andrea Doria* dead ahead, decided to pass port to port, after which the *Andrea Doria* saw the *Stockholm* to starboard and turned to port.

In general, the simplest way to explain the disaster is to consider two cars approaching each other on an east-west highway. They approach an intersection running north–south at about the point where they would pass each other. Both turn south at the intersection—and collide. Of course this is oversimplification, but the average person who drives should understand it.

Carstens turned correctly to pass port to port, but Calamai, in the fog, turned toward the *Stockholm*, thus negating Carstens' swing. Therefore the two giant craft began to swing toward each other, and collided.

Just why the *Andrea Doria* should almost immediately list to seventeen degrees is another matter. Built with the standards of the 1948 Convention in mind, she was supposed to float with good stability if only two compartments were flooded. The general belief of the experts is that only one compartment was damaged below. When I published my thoughts on the *Andrea Doria* more than thirteen years ago I brought up the point that either the Convention's standards were inadequate * or that the craft's builders did not adhere to the standards. Writing in 1970, however, I offer a third reason which could enter into the picture. Captain Frank H. Peterson of the Boston Marine Society told me that quite often, although of course it is against the law of the sea, fuel tanks, when they are supposed to be refilled with salt water for the sake of stability, are ignored and remain empty. This could have caused the extraordinary seventeen-degree list so soon after the collision when the liner did not respond after the crash and right herself.

A committee of the House of Representatives stated that the *Andrea Doria* could have met tests of the 1948 Convention *provided* she kept the tanks filled.

Incidentally, more than half the ships afloat would have difficulty staying afloat if they suffered a direct hit such as the *Stockholm* gave the *Andrea Doria*.

This should be the last word on the collision, unless the Italians eventually release their findings. Every member of the crew, officers and men alike, was called in and examined on the crash.

As the scores of competing airlines around the world estab-

---
* *Legends of the New England Coast*, p. 14.

lish schedules that make ocean transportation almost secondary in importance, now more than ever the shipping firms realize the importance of keeping their own schedules according to plan, regardless of fog and storm. The next few years will determine the future of passenger ships all over the world.

5

DOGS OF THE ATLANTIC

⚓

Milo

IN 1856 an enormous Newfoundland-Saint Bernard dog named Milo came to live at Egg Rock Lighthouse off Nahant, Massachusetts, with the family of the first keeper, George B. Taylor. Milo soon made himself at home with the seagulls, the ducks, and other wild life of Boston Bay. As the stone masons were finishing the lighthouse tower, they left a small hole in the little square addition which served as an entryway, and Milo thus had a private entrance to the edifice.

One day keeper Taylor took a shot at a great loon, wounding it, but not too seriously. The bird started to fly away and fell into the ocean. Eagerly Milo scrambled down on the rocky ledge which leads into the sea and jumped into the water. Seeing the dog approaching, however, the injured loon took off to fly in awkward fashion a quarter mile away before coming again. Milo continued his pursuit, and in a short time was less than a hundred yards from his goal. Just as the dog felt sure of his victim, away soared the loon again, necessitating another long swim. This unusual contest was watched from the lighthouse until the loon and dog vanished in the distance. Before long darkness closed in on the ocean. When Milo did not return that night, the family began to wonder if the dog had drowned in the sea. Late the next afternoon, however, Milo was seen swimming toward Egg Rock, not from the ocean but from Nahant. In the darkness he had evidently missed the Rock. After swimming ashore at Nahant, he had remained there to rest during the night, and then left for his home the next day.

It is believed that Milo rescued several children in and around the Rock, but all details are lacking. Because his fame spread far and wide, an artist drew a picture of Milo with a child, Fred Taylor, resting between the paws of the giant canine. The picture, known as "Saved," became famous all over America.* At the time of the picture's greatest popularity a sad accident befell the boy who posed with the dog. While passing through the swirling waters of Shirley Gut, Fred Taylor, then about eighteen, was drowned.

Be-Be's Adventure

One of my most unusual North River marsh adventures took place on November 10, 1966, when I went out to dig a half-bucket of clams at the Hanover flats. For those of you who are interested, the Hanover flats are owned by Scituate, and we of Marshfield pay ten dollars a year for the privilege of clam digging there.

The trip started out in the normal way with our beagle Be-Be firmly standing in the bow of our canoe, her two front paws up on the peak and her two hind feet delicately placed

---

* John Macauley of the Black-Watch Kennels in Pinehurst, Massachusetts, comments on Milo. "You call the dog Milo a Newfoundland-Saint Bernard. The dog is actually a Landseer of the Newfoundland line. Shortly after 1844 Sir Edwin Landseer suffered from a mental depression, which to some extent influenced his work. . . . His later animals took on almost human expressions and attitudes, which is shown particularly in 'Saved,' 1886. . . . Today the Landseer is completely accepted as a Newfoundland."

on the seat. I was the other occupant of the canoe, using my tandem paddle in the stern. When I paddle alone I reverse the canoe, sitting in the bow seat and facing the regular stern.

There was a high southwest wind which caught the canoe near our landing at the end of the Old Indian Trail in back of our house. Soon I made the necessary adjustments and was able to reach the mouth of Branch Creek where it flows into South River, formerly known as the North River.*

By three o'clock the tidal flats were rapidly being exposed as the extreme low tide would occur less than half an hour later. The North River and surrounding areas have on occasion no less than a fourteen-foot rise and fall of tide.

I pulled the canoe high on the beach in the clam-digging area, soon realizing that except for a few venerable, forlorn seagulls who had seen better days, Be-Be and I were alone on the flats.

Mrs. Snow and I have moderate demands as regards clams, and when I had dug my thirty-second clam that day, I decided to stop for a moment. Then I heard a strange noise directly behind me. Turning at once, I saw nothing but another dilapidated gull flying over my head at a height of about twenty feet. The gull seemed to indicate that she was interested in one of my broken clams. Her voice, a cross between the old Model T punch horn and a love-sick goose, made me realize that never in my life had I heard a similar cry.

Be-Be at once indicated an interest far beyond the call of duty. When the gull disappeared in the general direction of Fourth Cliff, Be-Be started after her. I stopped Be-Be just in time with an admonition stern enough for her to obey. Then I returned to my clam-digging activities.

I dug for quite a while, deeply engrossed in the actual dig-

---

* I realize the meanderings of the river can be very confusing to a new reader. For an explanation, see the chapter On the Marsh.

ging of the often elusive bivalve. Suddenly I had a feeling that all was not well.

I was correct. This time Be-Be had vanished. Once before when digging on the Hanover Flats with daughter Dorothy, I had caught Be-Be making a quick run across toward the Fourth Cliff. On that occasion it was only after three hours of hard searching that we found her near the path that runs up to the end of the obsolete Fourth Cliff radar tower.

On this occasion I had a strong presentiment that trouble was again in store for me. Dropping the clam fork, I began to follow the dog's tracks, and was soon running in the soft sand of that part of Hanover Flats. By the depth of her paw marks I knew she was running as fast as only a dog with an objective in mind can, and I was extremely worried about what her objective might be.

Four minutes later I reached the edge of the swift outgoing tide directly across from Fourth Cliff. There Be-Be's tracks ended at the water's edge, and there was only one thing I could do.

Wading into the outgoing tide I soon was over my head and swimming. The November salt water was not too cold, and in a moment I was clambering up the opposite bank.

Looking up and down, I tried to locate Be-Be's paw prints, but could not find them. Several times I ran across the sandspit, often the scene of the catching of stripers of giant proportions. Unfortunately, that same general location is where more than a score of people have drowned since the turn of the century. If she was caught by the rapid current, could Be-Be have been swept out to sea? I called and called. That was my first mistake. Hearing me, as I found out later from the Fourth Cliff residents, she realized she was in trouble because she had run away, and huddled under a bush out of sight.

Minutes later, thinking that perhaps Be-Be had gone

farther down the beach to make her way back across the channel to the Hanover Flats, I swam back and hurried to the canoe to search in vain. Then I paddled to Fourth Cliff again.

Seeing the residence of my good friend Willard Thomes in the distance, I ran stumbling up to tell him my problem. He agreed to drive me back to my house to get Mrs. Snow and our car. Twenty minutes later my wife and I started back by road to the scene of Be-Be's disappearance. Reaching the Fourth Cliff, we met William J. Conroy, the government caretaker, and discussed our problem.

Suddenly I heard what I thought was Be-Be's bark coming across from the Fourth Cliff bar. Then I saw scores of seagulls soaring up from their positions and being driven off the bar. This made me fairly sure that Be-Be was active in the area. Nevertheless, by the time we reached the location Be-Be was out of sight.

Then down by the water Mrs. Snow noticed an object she thought was Be-Be's bobbing head. To our amazement the object disappeared under water. A moment later it came out again, then vanished completely. Mrs. Snow was about to wade into the water and rescue what she feared was a drowning dog. Suddenly a head appeared forty feet away—that of a seal!

For the next five minutes, three different seals appeared, one after the other, only to vanish in the water. We found out later from Mr. Conroy's wife that each year the seals do their courting at the mouth of the North River.

Then Mrs. Snow, who was some distance from me, noticed caretaker Conroy hurrying down on the bar. He had sighted Be-Be under some bushes. Mrs. Snow rushed up and put her scarf around Be-Be as a leash.

The search was over. Be-Be was safe.

King

I have come across many stories of dogs and the sea, but there are few that offer such a combination of canine heroism and ability of perception as the story of the dog known as King.

The list of disasters along the rocky Newfoundland shores is a long one, but the tragedy which befell the British transport *Harpooner* was among the most dramatic. Aboard were 385 men, women, and children returning from Quebec to London as an aftermath to the War of 1812. Most of the soldiers were attached to the Fourth Veteran Battalion of the British army. There was also a canine passenger on board, King by name. Before leaving Quebec, the *Harpooner*'s master, Captain Joseph Bryant, had purchased this fine Newfoundland dog, and the captain and King were soon close friends.

On Saturday morning, November 9, 1816, the *Harpooner* was proceeding on her charted course past Newfoundland when a violent gale of snow and rain hit the area. Soon mighty seas were pushing the transport off her route toward the great cliffs of Saint Shotts. At eight o'clock that night the second mate's watch was called, and an hour later came the cry dreaded by all sailors: "Breakers ahead! Breakers ahead!"

A moment later the *Harpooner* hit heavily and then slid off one reef, only to crash against another. The vessel began to fill, and settled over on her larboard beam, half submerged but still supported by the rocky ledges which surrounded her.

In the midst of these disastrous events the dog King rushed up to his master and seized his coat sleeve, pulling him in the direction of the cabin. The dog was just in time, for Captain Bryant found the cabin ablaze from several lighted candles which had overturned in the crash. The captain, with the help of a dozen sailors, soon put out the flames. He now knew that King was not only a good friend but a reliable assistant.

A short time later a mighty wave picked up the *Harpooner*, lifted her completely off the ledges, and sent her wallowing in the heavy seas closer to shore. All was now hopeless confusion. Many men, women, and children rushed up on deck; scores of others drowned in their cabins.

Again the ship struck on a gigantic undersea ledge and lodged fast on the rocks there, but the masts were toppled by the blow. Several passengers tried to float ashore on them but were soon dashed to death at the foot of the cliffs.

By four o'clock the next morning, when the storm seemed to let up, Captain Bryant knew that he had to devise some way of getting his passengers ashore, for he realized the *Harpooner* could not stay afloat much longer. As the first step in his plan, he asked his mate, Mr. Hadley, to take four men in the jolly-boat and try to reach a giant offshore boulder.

Ten minutes later the men pushed off in the jolly-boat, the mate frantically trying to steer with the tiller as his crew rowed with all their strength. Several giant waves swept in and nearly capsized them, but finally they managed to reach the shelter of a huge rock a hundred yards away from the *Harpooner*. Just as they were about to land, the jolly-boat smashed to pieces under them. The five men scrambled to safety, however, and soon they had climbed up onto the highest point of the rocky area. There they discovered to their disappointment that the rock was still a good distance from the shore itself. Nevertheless, it was so high that they would be safe there indefinitely, and it was large enough to accommodate the entire company of survivors.

The mate now shouted across to Captain Bryant; "Let your log line float in so we can secure it." The captain signaled to show that he understood. Released, the log line began to drift in toward the rock. It came closer and closer, and then suddenly the current swept it away. Time and again the log line was rereeled and let over, but always the current proved too strong.

Parts of the ship were now breaking off and drifting toward shore, and Captain Bryant realized that at any moment the *Harpooner* might break up altogether and everyone would be lost. Then he had an idea born of desperation.

Calling his dog, King, the captain talked in an encouraging tone to the huge animal as he tied the log line to the dog's collar. Then he pointed to Mr. Hadley on the rock.

"Go get Mr. Hadley," shouted the captain, and a moment later King sprang from the rail into the sea.

Across on his perch at the rock, the first mate began whistling and calling to the dog.

"Come on, King; come on, King!" he shouted.

Fifty yards from the ship, however, King encountered a heaving mass of wreckage which swept him under the surface. When he emerged, it was seen not only that a small timber had caught in the log line, but that King was having difficulty breathing, and Captain Bryant ordered the dog pulled back to the ship. The order came just in time, for King was choking because of still another fragment of wood twisted between the line and his collar.

"I'll know better now," said the captain, and removed King's collar.

"Do you still want to try it?" he asked King. In answer, the dog barked eagerly, wagging his tail.

"All right, then, but this time we'll do a better job of it."

The captain looped the log line around King's haunches and secured it with a bowline. He patted the dog once or twice and then ordered him to jump. Springing into the swirling seas again, King made for the rock where the mate was waiting with his men. This time King swam much more easily, and the men played out the line with care as he neared his goal. Soon he was caught in a giant swell. Then, with a smashing thump, he hit high up on the rock within a few feet of the waiting men. Before they could reach him, however, the undertow snatched the dog back into the boiling foam at the base of the Saint Shotts cliffs.

When the next wave broke, the men were ready. The mate and the others had locked arms, forming a human chain. As King was again lifted high on the rock, he swept in past Mr. Hadley, who made a frantic try for him and missed. But as the undertow began to pull the dog out again, the log line came in near enough for the mate to grasp it. "Hold on," he shouted to everyone, and the men fought with all their might to prevent the undertow from carrying King back into the ocean.

For a split second it seemed that both men and dog would be dragged out into the sea, but the sailors clung desperately to the rocky crevices on the ledge, and the crisis passed. A moment later King was safe on the rock well above the water as the wave receded, and the men were able to pull him to safety. When the next swell thundered against the mighty boulder, King and the five men were beyond its dangerous reach.

The mate shouted to the captain that King had arrived safely with the log line. The master of the *Harpooner* now tied a heavier line to the end of the log line and signaled ashore for the sailors to pull away. Finally, the rope reached the rock. The sailors then retrieved from the sea enough timbers to build a makeshift tripod. When the tripod was secured to the rock, several of the *Harpooner*'s crew decided to attempt swinging hand over hand along the hundred yards of line between the ship and the rock.

The *Harpooner* had struck at nine o'clock Saturday night, November 9, and it was almost Sunday noon when the first sailor swung out and started for shore. He landed on the rock amid cheers from the other survivors. A short time later a block was rove on and a sling arranged. One by one the survivors were hauled up onto the huge boulder. Only one passenger who attempted the trip failed to gain the rock. This unfortunate man was struck by a gigantic sea as he swung out onto the line, lost his hold, and fell to his death in the ocean!

Each trip in the sling took ten minutes. By late Sunday afternoon there were still over 140 people left on the ship. But the storm seemed to be going down, and so a group of the more adventuresome decided to risk throwing themselves into the sea and swimming for shore. Several were successful, but most of them perished before reaching land.

Around four o'clock Sunday afternoon it was agreed that the women should try to ride the sling. The first woman to make the attempt was a soldier's wife who was expecting a child at any moment. Her husband was placed in the sling first in order to hold her in his arms, and then the trip shoreward began.*

All eyes were upon the couple as they moved slowly toward the rock. Then a wave swept over the pair. When it had passed, they could see that wreckage had caught in the block. The next wave freed the line, however, and the soldier and his wife neared the great rock where the men awaited them. Now the most difficult part of the task was at hand, hauling the double load of humanity up the face of the boulder.

Going down the line hand over hand the men reached the couple, now almost submerged by the surf. Finally they pulled the husband and wife to safety. Less than two hours later, sheltered from the wind and spray by the other survivors, the soldier's wife gave birth to a baby boy.

By now the situation on the *Harpooner* was desperate. The vessel could not last much longer. The sun had set and there

---

* Winslow Homer was inspired to picture the scene. See p. 49 in *Secrets of the North Atlantic Islands* for my copy of Homer's sketch.

were still over a hundred survivors waiting to be taken ashore. At seven o'clock Sunday night, the heavy rope, frayed by constant working and swinging across the sharp rocks, snapped in two. There was no way of replacing the line, and many gave themselves up to despair. The tide slowly rose again, and great waves swept completely over the wreck. The *Harpooner* now began to go to pieces.

The first break came at the stern around midnight. Then at four o'clock Monday morning, the *Harpooner* split in two right up to the forecastle. In the mad scramble for safety, dozens were swept overboard to their death, and soon the ship was almost bare of human life. Captain Bryant remained aboard his ship until almost the final moment, when a gigantic wave caught him and pulled him under. He was never seen again. Whether or not King watched the unsuccessful attempt of Captain Bryant to reach shore has not come down to us.

The very last person to leave the broken vessel was an old subaltern, Lieutenant Mylrea of the Fourth Veteran Battalion. Over seventy years of age, he remained on the vessel until everyone else had either been rescued or lost. Then he thought of his own life and leaped into the sea. Miraculously, he floated in to the rock and was pulled to safety. Of the last one hundred aboard the *Harpooner,* more than fifty were drowned.

The 177 survivors remained crowded on the rock until dawn. The men had been able to start a fire, and carried the soldier's wife and baby near its warmth.

At daybreak Monday morning, November 11, 1816, it was low tide and the storm had gone down enough for five men to wade ashore. A mile away they found the home of a fisherman. They were taken to Trepassey, and by Wednesday evening, November 13, all but five of the 177 survivors had reached that town to be billeted in the homes of the sympathetic people there. Near the wreck at Saint Shotts, in the fisherman's house, the soldier, his wife, and newborn baby were recovering from their terrible experience. All survivors reached Quebec the following spring.

In the tragedy of the *Harpooner* 208 persons lost their lives. King, the dog, saved the lives of more than 155 of the 177 survivors. Someone, sometime, should erect a monument on the great cliffs of Saint Shotts in memory of King, the heroic dog.

Rubens

Rubens, a large curly-haired Newfoundland dog, belonged to Colonel Robert Battersby. He came to the colonel in 1848 as a puppy. The next year the colonel and a friend, with a horse named Blucher and the dog Rubens, left New York for the newly discovered goldfields of California. They were among the first to go by way of Vera Cruz, Mexico, crossing overland to Acapulco, and then taking ship for San Francisco.

During the overland journey, sharp stones injured Rubens's feet, but his master made him shoes of horsehide which gave him comfort. Rubens was easily the master in any situation where local dogs were concerned. He would send them to their kennels by a swing of his paw or an ominous growl.

The travelers stopped in Mexico City for some time, but finally set out along the Guarvucca, one of the largest rivers of Mexico. They traveled for several days until they came to the forbidding pass where the river escapes through the Sierra Madre mountains to the sea.

It now became dark and gloomy, and here a seldom-used trail crossed and recrossed the river. At the first of the fording places the colonel unwound his lariat from the saddle bow and motioned to Rubens to cross the stream.

Taking one end of the lariat in his mouth, the dog swam

over. After landing on the opposite shore, Rubens wound the rope several times around the trunk of a tree on the opposite bank. He then held the loose end between his teeth as the horsemen crossed, steadied by the rope. Altogether, Rubens performed this feat 117 times while the party forced their way through the canyon.

At Acapulco they had to wait forty days for a craft bound to San Francisco. The vessel proved to be the British steamer *Unicorn*. Their relief at the arrival of the craft turned to dismay when the captain of the *Unicorn* flatly refused to allow the dog on board because of his belief that dogs brought bad luck.

Later in the afternoon as the captain stood in the Acapulco plaza, he felt a tap on his leg, and there was Rubens with a letter in his mouth. He read the message aloud:

Dear Captain:
I am Rubens, Col. Battersby's dog. I came all the way from New York across Mexico with my master. I have taken care of him for three years. I swam the torrent for him 117 times in one day. If you leave me behind, I don't know what will become of him, but am sure I shall never see him again. Please, Captain, take me too. —Rubens.

When he finished reading the letter, the captain agreed that Rubens could go aboard the *Unicorn*.

Landing in San Francisco the colonel set himself up in the gold-assaying business, and Rubens became a well-known figure along the waterfront.

Within a few years Rubens became famous up and down the coast for saving lives, with probably nine lives rescued as his total. He could swim out and bring in a rowboat which had drifted away and perform many other feats of daring. One day Colonel Battersby saw a friend's boat far out in San Francisco Bay, practically a mile from shore. Its owner told the colonel that the craft was too far away, and that the dog could never bring it in. Swimming out to the rowboat, Rubens grasped the painter in his teeth and towed the craft back to its berth.

Rubens was also considered expert in killing rattlesnakes in the California mountains.

In 1852 Rubens and his master returned to the east coast. The canine lived for the rest of his life on the colonel's country estate in New Jersey.

Rubens died suddenly in 1853 while attending a cricket match on the Hoboken Cricket Grounds. Colonel Battersby thought so much of Rubens that he contracted with a taxidermist to mount the dog. Rubens was placed in the entrance hall of the colonel's mansion where the canine remained until the outbreak of the Civil War.

Maine's Owl's Head Dog, Spot

One day, as I was sitting in the dining room of the Owl's Head Lighthouse keeper's home, his daughter Pauline Hamor told me the story of her springer spaniel Spot, who loved the giant signal bell near the lighthouse, and the boats of the bay. Spot's entire interest seemed to be centered on the lighthouse, the fog bell, and the shipping that passed the promontory. He always watched for boats to sail by the light. As soon as they would get near enough to the cliff to hear a signal, he would run over to the bell rope and give it a few quick tugs with his teeth, pulling with all his strength until the peal of the bell echoed out over Penobscot Bay. Then, as the craft answered with either whistles or bell, the happy dog would dash down to the water's edge and bark at the vessel. It was a joyous life.

One of the best loved of all craft that sailed by the light was the Matinicus mail boat, captained by Stuart Ames of

Rockland. Quite often Mrs. Ames would call up the light station to ask whether they had seen the mail boat coming from Matinicus, and in this way Mrs. Ames had a little advance notice about the time to put dinner on for her husband.

One wild stormy night, when the snow-laden wind was cutting in across Owl's Head, the lighthouse telephone rang. It was Mrs. Ames, terribly worried about her husband who had been scheduled to land his mail boat at Rockland several hours before. She asked if there had been any sign of the boat.

"My husband speaks so often of your dog and of his ability to ring the lighthouse fog bell. Do you think that Spot might be able to hear the mail boat's whistle?" asked the almost frantic wife.

Keeper Hamor replied that he would let the dog leave the house to see what might happen. But after a half hour outside in the gale, Spot returned and scratched at the door to be let in. He had a dejected air which told the others that he had not heard the mail boat. Shaking the snow from his shaggy coat, Spot warmed himself at the fireplace, and then went over to his favorite place in the corner. Just as he started to settle down to go to sleep, Spot raised up on his haunches, his ears alert and every muscle in his body tense with expectation. Everyone in the room knew that Spot had heard the mail boat whistle.

Springing up from his corner, Spot scampered across the hallway and barked to be let out. The others watched him scramble through the great drifts as he fought his way to the lighthouse bell. Unfortunately, he was unable to reach the signal rope, for the drifted snow was then several feet high. Prevented from ringing the bell, after several futile efforts to reach the rope Spot made his way along the edge of the cliff where the wind was sweeping the snow clear, and soon he reached the point nearest to the ocean. There Spot began to bark furiously.

Keeper Hamor, after struggling into his warm coat, went out into the storm and followed the dog. Soon he, too, could hear the whistle of the mail boat. He realized that if the dog's bark could be heard on the craft, Captain Ames in turn would know where he was and be able to get his bearings in spite of the storm. Sure enough, after a period of violent barking, there came an answer out of the blizzard—three distinct blasts of the mail boat's whistle—a signal indicating Ames had heard the barking dog. From that moment the Matinicus mail boat was assured of charting a safe course for Rockland, Maine.

Two hours later a grateful wife called up the Hamor residence and expressed her thanks to the spaniel Spot who had saved the mail boat from disaster. Spot was then sleeping soundly in his corner, possibly dreaming of his friend, the captain, and his beloved mail boat which had reached port from Matinicus.

The spaniel died many years ago and is now buried at Owl's Head near the fog bell he loved so well.

Bing

On December 10, 1919, the S.S. *Ethie,* a coastal steamer of 414 tons, smashed aground on Martin's Point off Curling, Newfoundland, and began to break up in the violent storm and heavy seas then hitting the coast. It was impossible to fire a line or launch a boat, and no member of the crew dared to swim ashore.

A Newfoundland dog, Bing by name, did make the swim ashore with a lifeline gripped in its teeth, and all ninety-two passengers and crew members were eventually pulled to safety.

Richard T. Dalton, who witnessed the rescue, vouches for the truth of the tale.

Salty

On August 7, 1969, an unusual presentation was made aboard the MV *Rocket II*, during her visit to Boston Light.

A plaque, including a picture of the dog Salty II, who had forty-three puppies during her relatively long career at Boston Light, was presented to Engineman Richard Fennelly of Boston Light by Representative T. Harold Gayron of Lynn, to be hung in the vestibule of America's oldest beacon.

Actually, in the last twenty years, there were two dogs named Salty at Boston Light. The first Salty enjoyed a long career of greeting visitors at the lighthouse on Little Brewster Island, but died in a strange accident some twelve years ago while the men were filling in the great cistern at the light.

It was the custom for the water boat to deliver several thousand gallons at the light twice a year. The water was piped into the great cistern near the lighthouse, and when this was done, the men took off the relatively small hatch cover to the cistern for the hose to drop into the great tank.

It has never been properly explained how Salty entered the cistern, but her lifeless body was discovered in the water several hours after she was missing.

The new dog, Salty II, arrived at the light as a black retriever puppy about a year after the death of Salty I. She proved to be a greater problem than Salty I as she developed the habit of following visiting groups I would bring across at low tide to Great Brewster Island half a mile away.

Eventually it became necessary during our visit to lock Salty II in the keeper's residence so that the keeper and his assistant would not have to spend the next few hours capturing Salty and coaxing her back to Boston Light before the tide came in.

Litter after litter of puppies were born on the island, and the adventures of the puppies were many. They persisted in following Salty's habit of crossing over to Great Brewster Island, and as several were not strong enough to swim against the current, they drowned attempting to return to Boston Light.

Finally came Salty II's last litter, in 1969, and it proved too much for the aging canine. She died the same day after delivering her last puppy.

To animal lovers Salty II can now be placed in the same category as other beloved pets of Boston Harbor. There was a dog at the Minot's Lightship which swam out to get the papers from the passing tugboats.

At Thompson Academy on Thompson's Island the boys thought so much of their famous greyhound that at her death about a century ago a tombstone with a bas-relief of the dog and a suitable inscription was placed at the cemetery end of the island.

The climbing cat of Deer Island Light, Boston Harbor, whose picture I included in my book on the lighthouses of New England, was a favorite of visitors as well as the keeper.

Other pets include the canary which was at Minot's Light when we visited there in 1935, and the pet seal at Billy McLeod's Grape Island about which he told us more than a third of a century ago.

General

The Newfoundland breed of dog, which figures so often in this chapter, is powerful, intelligent, and docile. They often measure six and a half feet from nose to extremity of bushy tail. In its own country it is said to bark only when greatly irritated, and then, with a manifestly painful effort, it produces a sound which is outstandingly harsh. It is said that a Newfoundland dog rarely goes mad or gets rabies. It is well known that these animals can swim very fast, dive with ease, and bring up objects from the bottom of the water. We are told that "other dogs can swim, but not so willingly or so well."

Some years before 1834, a Newfoundland dog was kept at an English ferryhouse at Worcester, Massachusetts, and during his relatively short span of life he was credited with saving at least four persons from drowning. This Newfoundland, whose name has not come down to us, would often lift up smaller dogs by the scruff of the neck and throw them into the water, when the dogs' masters had been ferried to the other side and they were afraid of swimming across. Then he would swim with them to the other side of the ferry crossing.

A native of Germany, while hiking through Holland with a huge Newfoundland dog, was walking one night along the side of a canal, when his foot slipped and he fell into the canal some distance below. The next thing he knew, he found himself in a cottage on the other side of the canal, "surrounded by peasants," who had been restoring his life by artificial respiration. The peasants told him that one of them had been returning home from work. Hearing a commotion in the water, he looked down into the canal, to see a large dog, swimming along with a bulky object, at times dragging, sometimes pushing whatever it was in the water. Finally the dog reached shore at a tiny creek across from the place where the peasant was standing.

Watching as the dog nuzzled and pulled the object onto higher ground above the water, the peasant discovered that it was a man. The dog, having shaken himself, now industriously licked the hands and face of his master, and the peasant began to call for help. Everyone crossed over the first lock and ran down to where the dog was attempting to bring the man back to life.

Descending to the beach, the people picked up the man and carried him into the nearest home, where he was eventually restored to consciousness. The two bruises on the man's body, one on the shoulder, the other on the neck, were both found to have teeth marks. It is believed that the Newfoundland had first attempted to pull the body at the shoulder, but finding the man's head was remaining under water, got a new hold with his jaws at the neck, so that the man would still be able to breathe.

When the peasant had noticed the pair in the water, the dog was keeping his master's head out of water by holding him at the neck. Writing a century and a half ago, the dog expert Brown stated that "it is therefore probable that this gentleman owed his life as much to the sagacity as to the fidelity of his dog."

Sphinx of Bermuda

On the many occasions when we have stayed at or visited the Hotel Inverurie in Bermuda, I have been attracted to the statue, slightly larger than life size, of the Great Dane named Sphinx. Standing impressive and conspicuous, the statue has been on the Inverurie grounds for many years.

The story of Sphinx has been told in several different ways. When the Inverurie was a private home, it was occupied by an army officer who lived fairly happily with his wife and three daughters. When a friend presented the officer with a Great Dane, he and the canine took to each other at once, to the subsequent unhappiness of the wife. When the comradeship grew even more apparent between the man and his dog, the wife, in desperation, decided to poison the dog.

One day Sphinx was found dead, and the officer realized what had taken place. He ordered a huge block of stone, and without ever speaking to his wife again, slowly began to carve the statue of Sphinx from the stone. Several years later he finished it and put it outside the residence where his wife would see it every day. Whether or not the wife died a normal death is still discussed at the Inverurie, for there are those who say that either the officer murdered his wife in a fit of insanity or he slowly poisoned her until she died. My historical expert in this particular case is Will Zuill, who simply states in his *Bermuda Journey* that the wife "eventually poisoned the animal." He does not even imply that the officer later killed his wife.

6

BARRATRY ON THE *FRANKLIN*

⚓

MORE THAN A THIRD of a century ago, when I first decided to write the story of the loss of the *Franklin* at Cape Cod, I was shocked to discover that Captain Charles Smith of the craft actually planned barratry, or the purposeful wrecking or destruction of a craft for profit.

In January 1970 Earle G. Rich of Cape Cod wrote to me that he had access to a rare letter concerning the disaster. It was written by Captain Elisha H. Baker to his sister in March, 1849. Mr. Rich has given me permission to include excerpts from the letter in this volume.

Captain Baker wrote:

"The ship *Franklin* of Boston came ashore on the Cape about four o'clock in the morning of March, 1st., from London, with thirty-two souls on board.

"The Captain and mate with some of the crew and one girl, eleven in number, attempted to land in the long boat and were upset and all drowned. That left twenty-one on the wreck. The ship then broke in two and the survivors took the bow, the sea at times breaking over them.

"There were three women among those on the wreck.

Two of them were married, one had her husband with her and a nursing babe. She had been brought up a lady and had wealthy friends, was an only daughter and granddaughter. Her husband held the child and supported her the best he could, and said she held on until the blood came through the ends of her fingers, but at last there came a heavy sea that took her away and the last he saw of her she was washed over his head. She was very composed while on the wreck and spoke encouragingly to the others, and to her husband. He and the child were among those that were saved. He lost all that he had, clothing and household goods. The girl that was lost in the [small] boat was his sister. He is still here hoping that the bodies will be washed ashore. He is now sick and says he wishes God had seen fit to have him and the child with the others.

"The other woman had two children, one of three years and one eighteen months. She had a brother to help care for the children. Her husband was in Boston. They all got ashore safely. Her husband heard of the wreck, and knew she was on board. He came immediately to the Cape, not knowing whether she was living or dead, until he got here and when he found his wife and children safe, such a meeting as they had is not often witnessed here or elsewhere.

"After the ship broke, the bow they were on moved toward the shore. As soon as it was possible for a boat to leave we pushed off to them and succeeded in getting the remaining twenty-one off. While some were trying to save the sufferers, others were saving the things that came from the ship. Such a sight you never saw. There were parts of the ship and cargo, sails and rigging all along the shore. She had quite a valuable cargo consisting of Linseed Oil, Wool, Oil of Lemon, Hartshorn, Nutmegs and many other kinds of merchandise. One-half of her cargo, if not two-thirds, never landed. What has been saved has been carted down to the shore by the orders of the Agent. Those who saved it contend for salvage.

"While I am writing I hear that the poor unfortunate man's wife has been found with her wedding ring on her finger. Today the captain has been found and one man was found Sunday. That is all up to the present. Such a scene as this has been enough to sicken anyone of going to sea. There has been a contribution taken in both Meeting Houses for the sufferers. There was $17.00 raised to get them clothing. They are gone today, some of them in the Packet to Boston. We can feed and clothe them, but we cannot heal the broken hearts. The ship came ashore about off where Mr. Kinnecum lives. We got them off about three o'clock P.M."

The report later goes on to say:

"The Congregational and Methodist Societies raised a contribution in each of their churches, on the Sabbath succeeding the day of the disaster and chose a committee to meet with the Committee of the Wellfleet Benevolent Society, to consult concerning the best means of disbursing their charities.

"The Committee for receiving and disbursing the funds raised, report as follows:

Cash received.

From the Contribution of the Methodist Society	34.65
From the Contribution of the Congregational Society	24.52
From the Methodist Sewing Society	10.00
From the Island Sewing Society	10.00
From the Social Aid Society of Congregational Church	15.00
From Contributions in Truro	41.50
From private contributions in Wellfleet	18.50
From A friend in Boston	1.50
	$155.67"

But the full story of the *Franklin* does not end here, for after Captain Smith's death a document was found in his valise which was pulled out of the surf by a beachcomber named Isaiah Hatch. When dried out the document seemed to indicate that the wreck was a case of barratry. As I explain above, barratry is the term applied to any master of a vessel who destroys his ship in order to collect insurance or gain financially in other ways.

The document in question, dated Boston, July 25, 1848, disclosed the following facts.

Capt. Smith:
Dear Sir: I thought I would write you this letter and give you the copy of the Insurance Policies on the Ship. $7,500 at Boston, $7,500 at the Merchant's, there is also $5,000 upon the freight to Coasters Office. All the Insurance cost was $725.00, the Insurance ends at London. I send you this account for your instructions. Mr. John W. Craft and myself have every confidence in your promises and hope to see you in Boston in the short time of thirty days. I have the best way to abandon her, let her leak, and watch your opportunity to leave her, and before you leave her, roll a barrel of the Turpentine into the cabin and fire her. We will leave all this to your best judgment.

J. W. Wilson

On the strength of this evidence, the owners of the *Franklin*, J. W. Wilson and J. W. Crafts, were indicted by a federal grand jury to stand trial for their complicity in the bizarre case. They were later acquitted of the charges in court for lack of evidence directly connected with the wreck of the *Franklin*. The finding of the court termed the disaster an "act of God" not one of barratry.

The Boston *Transcript* for Saturday, March 3, 1849 records the loss of the "ship *Franklin* and ten lives" on Thursday, the first, stating that she went ashore at 9:00 A.M. The *Franklin* was an old vessel built at Newburyport in 1831. "The vessel and crew were insured in this city."

The next day's paper, however, changed the story. The *Daily Evening Transcript,* Monday, March 5, 1849, stated concerning the loss of the *Franklin:* "This melancholy wreck was attended with more loss of life than was at first reported. We learn from Captain Stevens of the packet schooner *Modena* from Truro that 15 lives were lost. The ship had anchored back at the Cape on account of head winds, when it increased to a gale, and she finally went on shore at 4:30 A.M. on Thursday, and not long after, broke in two. Captain Smith, his first officer, some of the crew and passengers, ten in number, attempted to reach the shore in a boat, and while leaving the wreck, Captain Stevens called to a young woman to jump into the boat. She attempted to do so, but the boat lurching, she fell into the sea and perished. She had no child as was reported. The boat made for the shore, and had nearly reached it when it 'pitch-poled' in the heavy surf, and all were lost. The first officer was seen swimming for some time, and nearly reached the shore, when the undertow took him and he was seen no more. Three men were washed off from the deck, and drowned.

"The survivors crowded to the forward part of the ship, while the rear was breaking off by degrees, and remained with the sea breaking over them frequently, until nearly dark, when they were rescued by the Wellfleet people, with the exception of a woman who was washed from the bow by a heavy wave, which spared her husband and child.

"The people on shore had launched their whaleboat three times during the day, and each time it was immediately filled by the heavy surf and they did not reach the wreck until a very short time before the bowsprit pitched into the sand, and the remnant left was not sufficient to have protected the survivors any longer. Providentially, as the forward part of the ship was beaten to pieces by the sea, it careened continually toward the shore, which is said to be an uncommon circumstance; otherwise most of those upon it would have been lost.

"A woman whose husband resides in this city was saved, with her two children. It is said her brother was also saved.

"The *Franklin* had a valuable cargo, comprising a large quantity of wood and linseed oil, some nutmegs, books, dry goods, etc. A considerable portion has washed on shore, but in such a state as to be of little value, although people are busily engaged in rescuing as much as possible. An agent of the underwriters has gone to the wreck.

"The vessel is entirely to pieces, and the fragments of the cargo and freight are strewed along the shore and upon the face of the waters, for miles. But very little of the cargo will be saved.

"Since the above was in type a letter dated Provincetown, 4th inst., states that the captain, who left the ship in the longboat, took with him a bag of gold, a lot of jewelry, a gold watch, etc., all of which were lost. The people left on board slipped the chains and drifted ashore on a part of the wreck. The remains of the hull and materials were sold by the agent of the underwriters for $130. Twenty-five casks of linseed, twenty-six bales of wool, six casks nutmegs, one hundred pieces light duck and bagging, seventy or eighty kegs of white lead or paint, a few casks of porter, six casks emery, five or six casks goat skins, three casks hartshorn, and several casks contents unknown have been saved."

The actual number of persons aboard the *Franklin* was thirty-three. Eleven were drowned. The following fall Thoreau visited Cape Cod, walking along the beach where the wreck had taken place. One night he and a friend visited the home of Uncle Jack Newcomb, better known as the Wellfleet oysterman. Thoreau writes of Newcomb as the latter described the *Franklin* disaster:

"He told us the story of the wreck of the *Franklin*, which took place the previous spring; how a boy came to his house early in the morning to know whose boat that was on the shore, for there was a vessel in distress, and he, being an old man, first ate his breakfast, and then walked over to the top of the hill by the shore, and sat down there, having found a comfortable seat, to see the ship wrecked. She was on the bar, only a quarter of a mile from him, and still nearer to the men on the beach, who had got a boat ready. . . .
" 'I saw the captain get out his boat,' said he; 'he had one little one; and then they jumped into it one after another, down as straight as an arrow. I counted them. There were nine. One was a woman, and she jumped as straight as any of them. They they shoved off. The sea took them back, one wave went over them, and when they came up there were six still clinging to the boat; I counted them. The next wave turned the boat bottom upward, and emptied them all out. None of them ever came ashore alive!' "

The lady mentioned as jumping into the lifeboat was one Miss Skehan, one of several members of that family aboard the *Franklin*. The little child whom the captain held was an eleventh-month-old girl, a sister of Miss Skehan.

The *Franklin* began to break up when the lifeboat left the vessel. It was said that the lifeboat was hit by breakers from twelve to fifteen times as it floated toward the beach. Shortly afterwards the *Franklin* worked its way over the bar and started for the shore. This encouraged the watchers on the beach, who launched a small boat into the tremendous swell then running, and started for the survivors. They let over a line held by the crowd on shore, one of whom was a woman, who, it is said, did more than her share.

When the rescue boat arrived at the *Franklin* they found that one woman had been washed overboard, but all the rest were able to climb into the boat and reach the shore in safety. By this time the *Franklin*'s wreckage was strewn up and down the beach. An inhabitant of Cape Cod, writing of the incident two days later, noticed a small boy who had been rescued from the vessel.

"I took the little boy saved up in my lap yesterday afternoon, and as I looked upon him and the little babe, his sister, also rescued, I could not help exclaiming in admiration of that providence, without which no sparrow falleth to the ground."

Some rather confusing testimony came out during the trial, such as that given by Captain McLean, who was a passenger on the *Franklin* when she was wrecked. I quote from the news coverage:

"Captain McLean, a passenger, said he was on board when the *Franklin* was lost. The weather was fine. The vessel struck between six and seven P.M. He asked the Captain in a direct manner how the ship came in that position. Captain Smith evaded answering. As the water was making breaches over the vessel, he said, 'My God, I fear she'll drown us.' He then went into the cabin. In the stateroom the witness saw a young woman and sat down and talked with her. The Captain had a carpet bag in his hand and the Steward being about getting up his chest. The Captain said, 'if we save our lives we shall be lucky.' It was the first intimation that he despaired of the ship. The ship parted just forward of the main rigging and commenced going to pieces. The boat was lowered, and the Captain was the third man to get into the boat. When the witness looked again, the boat was some rods from the ship when she was swamped. He saw the Captain strike out to swim, but he shortly disappeared."

Being asked whether he thought Captain Smith purposely allowed his vessel to go ashore, Captain McLean replied: "By allowing the ship to drag seven fathoms with one anchor when there might have been two thrown out, was a gross error of judgment, to say the least. I think both anchors with plenty of cable would have saved the ship. I think she dragged her anchor twice the ship's length before a second anchor was let down. There was some coolness between Captain Smith and myself, in regard to a female passenger, but no quarrel."

The wreck of the ship *Franklin* was no doubt the most controversial incident of its kind to be recorded in Cape Cod history.

Newcomb's Hollow, the scene of the tragedy, is now a town parking lot on Cape Cod, visited by thousands of people each summer, little aware of the heartrending drama enacted at that spot one hundred and twenty years ago.

PART THREE

Bermuda Treasure

1

LUSHER THE UNFORTUNATE

⚓

ON ONE OCCASION when I visited William Zuill, author of *Bermuda Journey,* I asked him if he had ever heard of Captain John Lusher, about whom I had heard stories.

"Why, yes," Will Zuill answered. "You must go out and see John Lusher. Lusher was a diver, particularly interested in the ancient Spanish treasure galleons. He's pretty old now and I've lost touch with him. I think that he is living at the Packwood House in Somerset. By all means go over and visit him."

That, indeed, was a good clue, and we lost no time in driving over to Somerset. There we found that unfortunately John Lusher had been transferred to the poorhouse two years previously.

Finally we were knocking at the door of the poorhouse. "I would like to speak with Mr. Lusher, if it is possible," I announced to the woman who answered our summons.

"For the Lord's sake, man, what do you mean? Poor old Mr. Lusher's been dead eighteen months or so!" This rather took the wind out of my sails, and I fell back a few paces and muttered my apologies. I am afraid the woman who runs the poorhouse thought I was having fun with her by asking to speak to a dead man.

As we went back down the lane and passed the old Saint James graveyard, three men walked toward us. Acting on a hunch, I decided to question them.

"Good morning, gentlemen," I began. "I wonder if you could give me a little information." I then told them that my purpose was to find out what I could about the career of Mr. John Lusher who had died in the poorhouse sometime in the fall of 1946.

"Yessuh, man, we can tell about Mr. Lusher," began the youngest of the three men. "He was a good man, about eighty-five year old when he died, and we all liked him. Yes, we certainly did. Why, one day—"

"May I be privileged to say a few words?" interrupted the second member of the group. He spoke in a much lower tone. "Mr. Lusher did reside at the Packwood House earlier, but in his later years he lived up here. He was a wonderful man."

He went on to tell me what he knew about Lusher, and before our conversation was over I had several important leads which took me from Somerset to Saint George's Island and back again to Hamilton. A conversation with Mr. Leon Fox in Saint George's and a story by Carol Booker in the *Bermudian* for August 1946 finally completed my material on this colorful deep-sea diver, Mr. John Lusher of Philadelphia and Bermuda.

John Lusher was born at Bermuda in 1854. He was always a diver, although during certain periods of his life he was active in other work. In his youth he moved to Philadelphia, but in 1912 the cold winters finally sent him back to the birthplace he loved, Bermuda. On his return he began the building of a forty-foot boat which may still be seen at Saint George's. The boat was called the *Endeavor* and its name is appropriate—it took thirty-two years to build.

But his diving experiences interested me more than any other of his many achievements.

One of Lusher's diving exploits was an expedition out to an ancient galleon many miles from Bermuda. Arriving at the location, Lusher went down in his diver's equipment and found the wreck without too much effort. There he discovered that coral encrustations had grown to rocklike consistency over the treasure room, and he sailed to the nearest port to obtain blasting materials. On his return two weeks later he found that his earlier visit must have been observed—a native gunboat was standing guard over the sunken ship. Captain Lusher learned later that others probably brought the treasure to the surface, but nothing to that effect was ever announced officially.

Another expedition was at Cape Comet, over seven hundred miles from Bermuda in a southwesterly direction. Captain Lusher descended to the ocean floor to locate a wreck which had fallen apart from age. Prying off a fragment of the hull, he discovered loose gold, exactly as it had slid from the great chest many years before. Again a native gunboat appeared, and Captain Lusher was ordered to leave the vicinity almost at once. He did get some "souvenirs" of that particular dive, however. A short time later he learned that the nearby island, a few hundred yards from the treasure ship, had been purchased by two thrifty Scotsman who found the gold later.

A third expedition took place just a few miles off Bermuda itself. It was on this occasion that Captain Lusher was so seriously injured that he could never again dive in deep water. For years he had studied all the old charts and records he could find and had read carefully the accounts of several Spanish wrecks in Governor Nathaniel Butler's book *History of the Bermudaes*. Finally he decided to try to locate the old *San Antonio*, wrecked in 1621. He equipped himself with the most modern devices he could obtain and started out in his little sloop accompanied by two helpers.

It took Captain Lusher many weeks before he found the

hulk. Once it was located, he returned day after day to the ship. He found old cannon, fragments of silverware and pottery, and countless other articles, but no gold coins or pieces of eight. Finally one night he realized that his money was running low. He determined to make one great effort the next day.

The morning dawned, warm, clear, and windless, and before ten o'clock Captain Lusher had gone overboard and was standing inside the cabin of the old ship. Hammering away slowly but surely, for any movement underwater is by necessity a labored one, Lusher suddenly crashed through what appeared to be a bulkhead and another cabin was revealed.

"Can this be the stronghold of the ship?" Lusher wondered, and smashed away at the hole to enlarge it to the size of his body. Finally he was able to lower himself down into the opening, where he could feel the shapes of what seemed to be treasure chests. Smashing his giant sledge against one of the trunks, he crushed in the cover, and quickly knocked it aside. He was right. The entire top of the chest was filled with what appeared to be either doubloons or pieces of eight.

In his eagerness to inspect the coins he completely forgot the dangers which constantly threaten all deep-sea divers. He grabbed two of the coins and tried to scrape them against each other, but in doing so he had to release his hold on the lifeline temporarily. Just then his foot slipped in the sludge and seemed to enter a small cavity in the treasure room. A second later a great weight crushed his instep and he thought that one of the chests had fallen on his foot. Reaching down, he was horror-stricken to find that he was in the grasp of a giant sea clam * two feet across and weighing hundreds of pounds. He was trapped far underwater by this relentless creature which had never been known to release a victim.

---

* It is only fair to record that scientists do not believe there are any such creatures in the area.

Agonizing, excruciating pains were running through his leg as the giant clam slowly began to crush the bones of his foot. Then an idea came to him. He forced his heavy iron hammer into the remaining crevice of the clam's shell until the creature, with a tightening grip, caught the hammer and held it firmly. But the clam had already reduced Captain Lusher's foot to a hideous pulp. It is probable that he fainted at this point. He remembered awakening at what seemed to be a short time later with a numbing sensation running through the whole of his leg.

Realizing that he would have to act immediately or die within a few moments, Lusher braced himself with his other foot and gave a violent tug on the lifeline as a signal to be hauled up. Steadying himself for the coming ordeal, he watched the line tighten. Soon the line jerked at his body, and its tugging threatened to cut him in two. At last he was ready for the supreme effort. With great pain, he pushed away from the galleon's timbers with all the strength left in his good leg and slowly but surely squeezed what remained of his other foot through the small opening. At this moment Lusher fainted for the second time. Half an hour later he regained consciousness on the deck of his vessel.

"What do you want us to do?" his frightened helpers asked him.

"Weigh anchor, hoist the mainsail, and start for a doctor on Saint George's at once."

Lusher collapsed again and four hours later regained consciousness in a doctor's office. His leg had been treated and bandaged. The doctor told Lusher that he would never again have the full use of his crushed foot. Lusher explained how he had barely avoided death.

"You're a lucky man to be alive, then," the doctor told him. "You're the first person I've ever heard of who has escaped from the giant sea clam. How did you do it?"

Captain Lusher then told the astonished doctor of his strange experience in the cabin of the Spanish galleon. He did not reveal, however, that he had just come across the treasure.

"You can never dive again," the doctor warned, but in this he was mistaken.

Captain John Lusher, broken and crippled by his experience, did shallow-water diving until he was seventy years of age. But never again did he venture out to the scene of his dangerous escape from that terror of the ocean bottom, the giant sea clam.

Those who knew him best said that he spent the rest of his life looking for a man who had three qualifications: first, youth and ambition; second, sufficient courage to dive far below the surface of the sea; third, honesty. Of course, Captain Lusher knew that a man with these three qualifications could be trusted with his great secret—the sunken treasure of a Spanish galleon.

John Lusher's crippled figure was a well-known sight in the streets of Bermuda for many years. His white hair and bushy beard almost encompassed his ruddy face but did not detract from his alert blue eyes. Often toward the end of his years he stopped to rest on one of the tombs of the Saint James churchyard, where, surrounded by the boys and girls of the neighborhood whom he had grown to love, he would dream again as he told them tales of his adventures under the surface of the sea.

But he never found the man for whom he was searching. John Lusher, his mission unaccomplished, died at the little Somerset poorhouse overlooking Margaret Bay. Perhaps someday a youthful reader will follow in the footsteps of this ancient Bermudian patriarch and tempt the fate that led Captain John Lusher to the very gates of wealth and then allowed him to die in poverty.

2

SAN ANTONIO

⚓

AN EXTREMELY MODEST ESTIMATE would indicate that twelve million accessible dollars still remain within twenty miles of Hamilton, Bermuda, itself—and that is no crack-brained figure, but the cold deduction of one who has made a lifelong study of the situation.

Since the sixteenth century the mighty Spanish plate fleets had used the islands of Bermuda as an important sea mark on their journeys to Europe from South America. In some years they carried as much as $11 million. Hurricanes frequently sent one of the treasure galleons to the bottom, and the locations of many of the wrecks were known in general.

Moreover, even the earlier English settlers at Bermuda found many evidences of the wreckage of several Spanish galleons. By the law of averages, the hulls of some must be located not too far from the islands themselves.

Late in the summer of 1621 a Spanish galleon, the *San Antonio*, sailed from Cartagena, bound for Cadiz, Spain. Her cargo was a mixed one, consisting of hides, indigo, and a substantial amount of treasure. On the night of September 13 the *San Antonio*, far off her course, crashed into a coral reef barely nine miles to the west of Bermuda. Led by Captain

Fernandino de Vera, the seventy members of the ship's company finally reached Mangrove Bay, Bermuda, where they were discovered by the inhabitants. Suspecting an invasion, the Bermudians notified Governor Nathaniel Butler. When Butler investigated, he learned that the Spaniards were castaways and gave them food and shelter. He claimed later that he acquired from the Spanish captain a deed allowing him to salvage the *Antonio* for his own enrichment because of the generous treatment he had given the shipwrecked men.

Months later, when the surviving Spaniards from the *Antonio* finally reached London, they complained at once to their ambassador, Count Gondomar. The survivors told the Count that they not only had been treated shabbily in Bermuda, but actually had been robbed by the Bermudians of valuables saved from the disaster. Count Gondomar made the most of the situation by writing an official communication to the Bermuda colony listing the complaints one by one. The affair was finally brought to the attention of the Star Chamber, but no action was ever taken on the alleged ill-treatment of the shipwrecked Spaniards.

Governor Butler went to work salvaging the treasure from the *San Antonio*. He knew that it was there—the Spaniards had given him full details of the gold, silver, and merchandise aboard. Week after week his men tried to bring the treasure to the surface, but as far as we know it is still there today. The Governor never recovered more than a few cannon from the wreck.

In the book he wrote some time later, *History of the Bermudaes,* Governor Butler mentions several other Spanish ships wrecked in the vicinity of the islands. Whether the great Henry Morgan, despoiler of Panama, ever visited Bermuda to bury treasure is a debatable point. Many think so. Those who maintain this theory are equally certain that Morgan never returned to get that substantial treasure. Perhaps some enthusiast with a metal detector may yet find Morgan's millions on or off Bermuda's shore, but anyone expecting to take gold or silver off the island without paying Bermuda's treasure-trove tax is doomed to disappointment.

3

RUSSELL PEARMAN

⚓

ONE DAY during a driving rain I telephoned Russell Levi Pearman, of Victoria Street, Hamilton, and he volunteered to meet me in town where I was doing research at the time.

"I understand that you discovered a substantial amount of gold in a very peculiar fashion," I began.

His answer was direct and to the point. "Would you like to hear the whole story?"

I agreed at once, and he began to speak, his calm voice and his ready vocabulary lending added charm to the narration.

"I am a furniture or desk maker by trade, and on February 22, 1938, I was dismantling a desk which I had bought from my uncle, George Richardson, who lived for many years on Saint David's Island. I was planning to use parts of the desk to repair another which I believed to be of greater value. My uncle's desk was thirty-six inches wide, forty-two inches high, and about twenty inches deep. It was made of walnut and soft pine, but the termites had consumed most of the soft pine.

"As I removed a section of the desk, I noticed a thin piece of wood in the center pigeon hole. When I removed it, I found a cavity or pocket in back.

"Of course, this surprised me, and I reached in carefully to discover if anything might be there. My hand touched paper first, and then I made my discovery—a hoard of gold coins, each piece wrapped in paper, the paper marked with the weight of the coin and the value.

"After sorting the coins, I found that they were of fifty-seven different varieties, dating from the early 1700s to 1820. The 1820 piece was a Brazilian doubloon. Most of the other coins were either Portuguese or Spanish, with a few German and several Italian pieces. Many of the coins were counterstamped to denote the West Indian island where they had been in circulation. Without question, the careful way they were wrapped indicated that they were a collector's hoard."

It was indeed a wonderful story which this modest Hamilton man told me, and I asked him if he had ever learned who had secreted the hoard in the old desk.

"I have never found out whose treasure it was," was his reply. "Not only that, I have never found out in what country several of the coins were minted. Even the experts were unable to identify them. When I went to New York City and showed them to several numismatists, they put the coins on exhibition at the Chase National Bank."

"Well, what did the Bermuda government take from you for the treasure trove?" I asked Russell Pearman, and he smiled in return.

"That's the best part of it all. Since the money was in a desk, it was not legally treasure trove. Treasure has to be underground, and therefore I didn't have to pay the government anything. The treasure was worth slightly more than ten thousand dollars. When I reported it to the Bank of Bermuda, it created quite a sensation. Everyone on the island started pulling apart their old desks, but mine was the only one that held golden coins."

"Would you like to sell me one of the coins?" I asked hopefully. "You see, I, too, have found buried treasure, and I would like to add one of your coins to my collection."

"I am sorry," he answered, "but we only have a third of the 151 coins left. My wife says that we have enough money, so I am not going to sell any more of the gold." And Mr. Pearman stuck to his statement. We shook hands in farewell, and I had finished my interview with a very lucky young man of Bermuda.

4

A LADY OF BERMUDA

⚓

ONE OF THE HIGHLIGHTS of our trip to Bermuda was a delightful visit with a lady of sixty-four years who had in her younger days discovered a hidden treasure. My wife and I were strangers to her, but when I mentioned mutual friends, we needed no further introduction.

"Well, young man," the woman began, "just what is it you would like to know about me? I knew that you were coming."

"Did someone tell you?" I asked.

"No one has to tell me those things. I just know that they are going to happen and they always do. You want me to tell you how I found gold, isn't that it?" When I nodded in agreement, she smiled and continued:

"I'd better begin at the beginning. Back when I was eight or nine years old, in the 1890s, I was a husky young lassie. My father ran a small boarding house over on Trunk Island in Harrington Sound. At that time the Mussons owned the island. Perhaps they were pirates way back. Father was a retired sea captain and never had more than eight or nine guests. In those days, although I was very young, I could do the work of three women, and father knew it.

"I remember the first day that Mr. Doughty came to the boarding house. All I recall about him now is that he came from the States and that his costume was most unusual. The nearest approach to it I've seen is the famous one-piece siren suit Winston Churchill wore during World War II.

"Well, Mr. Doughty was always interested in getting sea shells. He seemed fascinated by them, so one night I said to him, 'If you want some flat plate shells, I'll take you over to Hall's Island early tomorrow morning.' Mr. Doughty quickly agreed, and at four the next morning we met at the beach. I slid the boat into the water, and Mr. Doughty sat down in the stern. He was pretty helpless, or he pretended to be, so I did the rowing.

"We landed at Hall's Island, about three-quarters of a mile across the Sound, and soon pulled the skiff up on the shore. Reaching the crevice which led down to the hidden cave where the flat plate shells were, I warned him against climbing down into the opening. He was a big man, Mr. Snow, weighing about as much as you do, over two hundred pounds.

"I went down alone and a moment later landed on the edge of the little beach, where I soon found several shells. When my eyes became accustomed to the dark, I noticed a large box or chest jammed into the rocky crevice far back in the cavern. It was an iron sea chest about three feet long, eighteen inches high, and two feet deep. I tried to open it, but the lid would not yield.

"I shouted back up to Mr. Doughty, 'Some fool person has dropped a trunk down here, and I can't move it or open it to save the Lord.' He peered down through the crevice and shouted, 'We can go back and get a chisel; but I knew I had to get breakfast and wash the breakfast dishes. We returned to Father's house, and planned to row back that afternoon.

"It was almost four o'clock before we reached the island again, and we had to work fast. With the chisel I finally sheared off the hinges on the back of the chest, but try as I might, the lock could not be forced. So I pried and pried, and eventually the back of the chest cover pushed up from the chest itself.

"The first thing which caught my eye was a peculiar dagger, not straight-edged, but curved in and out. It was very rusty, and the handle was actually longer than the blade. Beautiful stones were on the handle—blue, green, and red. I know now that they were rubies and emeralds.

" 'Someone must have cut someone's head off!' I shouted up through the crevice to Mr. Doughty, who was peering anxiously down at me. By this time the tide had come in a little, and I was standing in water three or four inches deep. I only had one dress and one pair of shoes in those days, and it was quite serious if I ruined my shoes.

"Underneath the dagger I found what appeared to be a Mason's apron, made from the skin of a goat. Then I noticed that all along the top of the chest, in shelves, were small boxes. I opened one and found it contained coins. I didn't know enough about money then to tell whether the coins were gold or silver, but I pulled off my apron, which I still wore, and piled up the pieces in the apron. Soon they made quite a number, and when I tried to lift them the apron wouldn't budge.

" 'Send down your fish line,' I called to Mr. Doughty, and ten minutes later he had hoisted the heavy money up out of the cavern at Hall's Island. After replacing the heavy iron cover to the chest, I climbed out as fast as I could. I'd be late getting supper, and father would make trouble. Father was all right unless we upset his schedule, and I knew pretty well how much he would stand. Mr. Doughty was to keep the money and the dagger in his room, and we were to tell Father after we got the rest of the treasure.

"We landed back at the boarding house just in time for

supper, and that night I went to bed early—I had done a lot in one day. The next day it rained pitchforks, and since I only had one set of clothes and had to keep it for best, I couldn't go out at all. Father rowed Mr. Doughty over to the mainland during the day and when he returned that evening without Mr. Doughty, I mustered up my courage to ask a question.

" 'Father, where's Mr. Doughty?'

" 'Oh, he's gone away for a few days. He didn't say whether or not he would come back, but I don't think he will.' And that is the way I lost my fortune. The next two days were rainy, but when I finally had a chance, I rowed over to Hall's Island and went down into the crevice. Nothing remained; everything had been taken.

"I never could understand how Mr. Doughty managed to get the rest of that treasure. He couldn't row a boat, he didn't know how to swim, and yet he went away and the treasure went with him. How did he do it? I have puzzled about that for over fifty years, and I haven't worked out a solution yet. What do you think happened, Mr. Snow?" She paused, sat back in her chair, and waited for my answer.

I gave the matter considerable thought, and then decided I had worked out a possible solution.

"Perhaps Doughty hired a boatman to take him over to the island and arranged for him to come back two hours later. He brought along two empty suitcases, and he stripped down to a bathing suit and thus was able to squeeze through the crevice. The fact that the money and the chest disappeared proves that he did get through. Next he filled the suitcases with the rest of the money, brought them down to the shore, and pulled out the iron chest. He tied each article and then went to the top of the crevice and pulled it out." As I talked, I warmed up to the theory myself.

"Then the boatman returned, and two suitcases and the

empty chest were put aboard. Halfway between Hall's Island and what is now the shore near the Harrington House, the iron chest was dropped down into the water, where it may still be today. Doughty left Bermuda by the next ship and lived happily ever afterward on his ill-gotten gain. —Well, how do you like that solution?"

"No, Mr. Snow, that couldn't have happened. There was no one he could hire to row him. I'll probably never know what happened to the bulk of the treasure I found, but I did save quite a little of the gold and silver. And I want to give a piece of silver to your wife and a piece of gold to you." And this kind, entertaining lady of Bermuda was true to her word.

"Now I don't mind if you tell the story," she said as we took leave, "but keep my name out of it. I want you to promise me that." I gave her my faithful promise that we would never reveal her name. I did make movies of her and also took several stills, but have never broken my word.

"What if someone wants to write you suggesting a solution to the mystery? What if Mr. Doughty is still alive? Would you like to hear about it?"

"Of course I would, but let them write to you, Mr. Snow. You just send the letter along to me here in Paget, and I'll answer if it rings true."

And that is what we agreed to do. That afternoon we went down to the Harrington House and looked across at Hall's Island. It was pouring rain, and those who saw us staring out into the Sound at the deserted hummock of an island probably wondered at our interest. We saw the dim outline of a crevice and wondered if it was the one that had held the treasure chest.

5

ROBERT REPOSE

⚓

BEFORE MY VISIT to Bermuda in 1948 my friend Dick Johnson had told me about the coins picked up on the Bermuda shore when he had been visiting there the previous year. Dick remembered a brief reference in the local paper at the time. Naturally I wanted to meet the person who had found the coins, and I tried all the usual channels of information. Although we had asked almost everyone we met and had been given several leads, for various reasons the leads proved unfruitful.

Then one day at Bermuda we were trying to locate a Mr. Perenchief, who had photographed Captain John Lusher, the diver. I was told I could find Mr. Perenchief at the Bermuda News Bureau. When I arrived at the Bureau, only the office boy was there to greet me. He told me that Mr. Perenchief was busy at the tennis matches and would not be available.

The next day I returned and was told Mr. Perenchief would be back shortly, so I chatted with the office boy again. His name, it seems, was Robert Repose. When I showed him the old piece of eight I always carry, he said that he, too, had a piece of eight that he had found on the bathing beach the year before.

"Why, you're the boy I've been looking for all week," I exclaimed. "I want you to tell me all about it!"

"Well, it wasn't much. Father and I went in swimming one day down at the beach and Father picked up an old disk or what he thought was a coin and was about to scale it out over the water, thus chucking it away. He had found it in the rocks and sand among what seemed to be the remains of a chest. Then I picked up another round metal piece and decided to scrape it to find out what the coin was. I found they were real silver pieces of eight. One was dated 1742 and the other 1745, with each coin being of good value."

"I'd like to take your picture with your coin," I told Robert. "Would you be able to go home and get it?"

Robert readily agreed, and half an hour later I photographed him holding up his precious treasure coin.

"Everything happens to me since I started working for the News Bureau," he exclaimed. "Will you really have my name in your book?"

"Of course," I agreed. As we drove away, the last I saw of Robert Repose was his excited face with a very wide grin on it. Without question Robert and his father, August Repose, had come across the remains of a treasure chest. Probably the rest of the silver is within a few yards of the place where they found those two pieces of eight on the Bermuda beach. Indeed, when Robert Repose and his father each found a piece of eight on the Bermuda shore it indicates without question that there probably is a worthwhile buried or sunken treasure not too far from where Repose and his father made their lucky find.

6

JOHN DAVENPORT

⚓

I MUST ADMIT that the principal reason why Bermuda had beckoned to me was my interest in buried and sunken treasure.

When I learned of Bermuda's greatest hoarder, John Davenport, I was anxious to study his career.

It is at Saint George's Island that much of the romance and mystery of Bermuda still linger. In the year 1815, when young John Davenport of England arrived at Bermuda, he founded a business at Saint George's selling dry goods and sundry items. Soon Davenport was negotiating with the British garrison for the contract to sell beef, and before ten years had elapsed, he was supplying the army with everything Bermuda could furnish. He then noticed that many a sea captain who entered Saint George's Harbor was financially embarrassed for lack of cargo. Davenport advanced him money with which to sail home, taking a mortgage on part of his ship as security.

It was not long before Davenport became the most influential man on the island. Secretly amassing a substantial fortune from his various enterprises, he trusted neither Bermuda nor English banks, and devised an unusual method of concealing his wealth. He obtained a trustworthy carpenter and had him build fifty arrowroot kegs. Several times a year Davenport took one of the kegs and placed it in his room. When he had filled it with gold and silver, he carried it down into his cellar to be stored. Then he replaced the full keg with an empty one in his room and repeated the process. Incidentally, Davenport kept the only key to the cellar in a secret hiding place.

As he grew older Davenport became more and more obsessed with the possibility of being robbed. Finally he decided to remain at home continuously to guard his treasures. During the last year of his life, he and his trusted servant Joseph spent most of their time in the cellar, boring into each keg to make sure its contents were still gold and silver.

Finally Davenport died and the servants revealed his secret to the old man's sons. Arrangements were then made with the government to examine and take over the treasure hoard in return for bills on the London exchange, and what a strange ritual this arrangement necessitated! Every morning Robert Davenport, the eldest son, ordered a new keg brought up from the cellar, taken into the dining room, and emptied on the great table. After the checking had been completed, another keg was brought up, and then another, until finally, fifty-eight days after the counting began, the last keg was taken from the cellar.

Saint George's was a small town, and money bought much more in the days before 1850. It was a marvel that no less than $400,000 in gold and silver was brought up from Davenport's cellar. It was one of the largest miser's hoards ever discovered anywhere.

7

TEDDY TUCKER

⚓

I FIRST HEARD of Bermuda's Edward Bolton (Teddy) Tucker in 1955, when Bob Nesmith of Rye, New York, told me that both Teddy and I had been placed on a board of treasure finders and seekers from many areas of the world.

The earliest that any of my friends knew Teddy was in 1932, when at the age of seven Teddy rowed across the inner Bermuda Harbor to visit Norman Black and his wife, summer inhabitants of Cliff Island, Maine. Even then Teddy was interested in the mysteries of the sea.

"The first time we met Teddy Tucker," Black notes, "he rowed across the harbor from his home to welcome us to our new place in Trelone, Paget, near Pomander Castle, Bermuda. A young lad of about seven years, he handled his boat beautifully. Teddy rowed over to our wharf and climbed out. He said 'I am Teddy Tucker' and I said 'I am happy to meet you.' He pointed out his home across the harbor.

"He wanted to know if we liked fish. I said yes, if it was broiled. He was quite taken back because he meant live fish. He left with the promise to return tomorrow, at which time he brought some beautiful fish, shells, and corals.

"The next day he came with a pail of water and sea weed floating on top. He said, 'I brought you some sea horses.' I was very interested because I had never seen one alive. He said, 'They won't be any trouble. Just change the water four times every night.'

"These animals hung on the seaweed straight up and down. They were very fascinating. They were like coats hanging on hooks. I told him I was afraid I might forget to change the water and asked him to keep them for me and bring them over often for me to see.

"He said, 'They are very interesting. The father has a pouch like a kangaroo. The mother puts her eggs in the pouch and the father takes care of them until they hatch and can take care of themselves. The mother goes out and has a good time.'

"Another day he took me to see the turtles. They were in a cement pool with a wooden grating for a cover. These turtles were brought up by vessels from the West Indies. Thursday night was always green turtle night at the yacht club. Lots of people took it home for supper. The turtles were lifted up by tripods and taken on a scow to the club.

"Then he took us to see an octopus. We went to the next wharf and got down on our knees and looked into the pool and sure enough in a corner was an octopus. 'Now,' he said, 'do you want to see him turn black?' He poked him with a stick. Instantly everything got cloudy and the water turned black.

"Teddy's interest in diving began by meeting Alec Lawrence whose father brought him as a boy from Canada to work on the cement docks at the harbor. Teddy took us over to see the outfit. The diving barge was round, fat, and chubby. She chugged along and her name was *Grandma*.

"Teddy took us over to see the old-fashioned diving outfit and a helper who manned the air pump. Alec would go down at 8 A.M. and not come up until 12, have lunch and go down at 1 P.M. and come up at 4 P.M. No coffee break at all.

"Teddy could sit on his porch overlooking the harbor and see all the shipping that comes to Bermuda, the English vessels, and the famous old Bermuda boats. Then he saw the *King* and *Monarch of Bermuda*, built especially for the shallow runs; the racing yachts from New York and trade vessels; the Lady boat that ran from the West Indies to Canada carrying bananas. Three of these fruit boats were destroyed by the German submarines. The fruit boats would come into the harbor once a week flying flags and a band would be playing. It was a wonderful sight for a young boy.

"Near his home was a branch or arm to the harbor. In time of hurricanes all the small boats rushed there for protection."

In 1948 Teddy Tucker and his brother-in-law Robert Canton "teamed up to go all-out" seeking pirate treasure in the rich area around the reefs of Bermuda.

Professional divers with years of underwater experience, Tucker and Canton had worked at such ordinary projects as bringing up copper metal and other materials from the bottom in moderate depths. The son of architect Edward Tucker, Teddy found the project strenuous, steady, but after a "regular diet," almost boring.

Tucker and Canton earned a fair income from their efforts, but dreamed of the days when a real Spanish galleon would be discovered somewhere on the bottom off Bermuda, a galleon such as Phips of Maine had found in 1687. But Teddy Tucker realized that he'd have to continue his regular salvage work while hopefully diving for galleons.

"It is far too expensive," he once remarked, "for it is easier than you think to spend a hundred pounds a week.

"There are at least two hundred craft still undiscovered on the many reefs and coral ledges, but so far it has been a wild goose chase."

Nevertheless, Teddy's luck changed in 1951, when he went to the bottom eight miles from the mainland. Diving in shorts and a mask he sighted a number of round objects partly buried in sand thirty feet down.

Excitedly, he went to the bottom and found that the objects were six ship's cannon, each weighing at least five hundred to nine hundred pounds. Eventually the venerable specimens of ancient armament became the property of the Bermuda Historical Monuments Trust, and are on exhibition at the Government Aquarium at the present time.

Teddy knows instantly what type of object a piece of coral may be growing around, be it oblong, square, or round. For example, he knows that coral will never grow on gold, but is well aware that wood, iron, steel, or even clay are often covered by coral growth.

And so it was one day in August 1955, when he went to the bottom, that his gifted fingers running through the sand fastened on a cube of genuine gold cut from a bar. When gold is brought to the surface its brilliant yellow glow simply overwhelms the happy finder.

With the cube as a delightful inspiration, Teddy went to work with renewed energy. Making several thirty-foot dives every day, the Tucker-Canton team succeeded in bringing up truly marvelous artifacts. Important finds included swords, breastplates, gold and silver coins, and many other priceless artifacts.

Then came the *amazing* discovery which electrified the entire diving world, a beautifully worked cross containing seven perfectly matched Colombian emeralds set in gold! From that moment on Teddy became the hero of scuba divers everywhere, for he had discovered a fabulous cross probably belonging either to a bishop or a cardinal of the Roman Catholic Church.

Dr. Mendel L. Peterson, curator of the Smithsonian Institution's Department of Naval History, was so interested that he journeyed to Bermuda to inspect the treasure. After examining the find, he is quoted as saying that Teddy Tucker's cross of gold and silver is the outstanding marine archaeological discovery made in the western hemisphere in this century. Then Peterson actually identified a silver coin as from the first Mexican mint of about four centuries ago!

After the excitement died down, Teddy Tucker discussed his good fortune. Tucker said that the galleon he found, because of the position in which he discovered her, probably went to the bottom in a northwesterly gale. He estimates that the craft was lost before 1600, probably in January or February, the months when northwesterly winds prevail.

Possibly the galleon discovered by Tucker and Canton struck the outer reefs, was transfixed there, and went to pieces, for practically nothing identifiable of the hull is left. Samples of the timbers were sent to Hans Prien in the United States for examination. Although the material has been under water more than a third of a millennium, it was identified as coming from the coast of Spain or France.

After all this time the numbering and lettering on the gold brought up is still clear and legible. The famous Spanish coinage expert Robert I. Nesmith says that the numbers X to XXIV on the coins are probably tally marks given to the gold shipments on a specific galleon. One gold bar has the Roman numeral XXI and the name "Pinto." The gold came from either Mexico, Colombia, Rio Pinto, Ecuador, Venezuela, or Peru.

Nesmith tells us that the route the Spaniards followed was carefully planned. Vessels known as avisos * did much of the message-carrying between Spain and the New World, and an empty galleon starting out from the Iberian peninsula to sail

---

* Relatively small, fast, lateen-rigged, courier-type craft. They were like the felucca developed by the Arabs for sailing close to the wind.

back with treasure had a definite schedule. When she was loaded in the New World for her return to Spain, a speedy aviso would start out ahead of her to warn the plate fleet of her coming.

Eventually the Spanish realized that the galleons sailing too close to what they came to call the dreaded "Isles of Devils" often ended up on the Bermuda coral reefs, and this had been the fate of the galleon whose bones Teddy Tucker found in 1955 underwater beneath the shifting sands.

The treasures which Teddy Tucker has brought up include much more than gold and silver, for he has located swivel guns, ancient hand grenades, brass dividers, timing glasses, brass cylinders with sliding covers, and bronze mortars. He and his partner, Robert Canton, also recovered from the sea pewter plates, porringers, red ware food containers, pottery cruets, and Indian artifacts.

The cannon from one wreck were typical of the late sixteenth century. Four cannon were identical, although cannon rarely matched each other in this period. Nevertheless, this group included such dissimilar weapons that it was suggested the wreck might be a pirate craft. The inscription on the bronze mortar reads "Petrus Van Den Gein Me Fecit 1561." Research indicates that Van Den Gein was a sixteenth-century caster of mortars, bells and cannons, then living in Belgium.

The emerald-studded cross, Tucker's pride and joy, is said to be "one of the most valuable pieces of sunken treasure ever found." It was recently valued for insurance at close to $200,000.

8

HARRY COX

⚓

ANOTHER WORLD-KNOWN DICOVERER of treasure, Bermuda's Harry Cox, has also been very successful in locating fabulous hoards on the ocean bottom. In his spare time he takes out his own sea-going craft, the *Shearwater*. Cox's most important discovery has been declared "a find of major importance."

Cruising the edge of the barrier reef in late July 1968, he was attracted by scattered ballast stones which he observed in about twenty-five feet of water. Other than the stones there was no indication of the existence of a ship. Harry Cox went down alone in his diving gear with the late afternoon sun giving slanting light. After searching and exploring for some time he began a final series of probes as the air in his tank was almost gone.

"You can imagine my astonishment," he told me later, "when several coins slipped out of an eddy of sand. Suddenly, a gold bracelet appeared! I was pleasantly surprised, to say the least."

Later two other Bermuda divers, William Gillies of Smith's and Miss Pat Maher of Warwick, went down with Mr. Cox and uncovered other items.

The entire find included gold bars bearing Spanish markings, hammered gold bars without markings, a fantastic assortment of "mint condition" gold Portuguese cruzados four centuries old, a long gold double-linked chain, a gold manicure set backed by two gold caryatids, an assortment of pieces of eight, a pearl cross with seven pearls mounted on gold wire, ornamental gold rings, Venetian glass trading beads, and a mariner's astrolabe.

The astrolabe is an ancient mathematical navigational device whose history is said to go back two thousand years. Silvio Bedini, Assistant Director of the Smithsonian Museum, tells us that very few astrolabes have ever been recovered from shipwrecks.* To date, twenty-one examples have been recorded, according to Bedini, and three more are believed to have been recovered from Spanish or Portuguese wrecks.

It can be said that Cox found the third oldest astrolabe ever discovered in this hemisphere.

* Possibly the most famous astrolabe is the one that belonged to Humphrey Cole in 1574. It is still preserved in England.

PART FOUR

Adventures at Bermuda

1

WRECK OF THE *BONAVENTURA*

⚓

How many unidentified galleons and treasure ships have crashed to their doom on the outer reefs of Bermuda will never be known, but on November 17, 1593, the French vessel *Bonaventura* was wrecked at what was later known as Somers Island.

After landing at Bermuda, the shipwrecked men built a small eighteen-ton craft from the native cedar wood on the island. Henry May of England was aboard the ship and later wrote of the incident, accusing the officers and men of the ship of drunken incompetence.

Excerpts from May's account follow:

"As for tackle we made a voyage aboard the wreck before she split and cut down her shrouds, and rigged our own bark from her. Instead of pitch we made lime, and mixed it with the oil of tortoises, and as soon as the carpenters had calked, I and another, with each of us a small sticke in our hand, did plaster the mortar into the seames. No sooner than we laid it on it was dry and as hard as a stone.

"In this month of April 1594, the weather being very hot,

we were afraid our water should fail us and therefore made great haste away."

We know, then, that Bermuda's first recorded shipwreck was that of a French vessel and that the first ship ever built there was constructed by men from that wreck.

The next wreck was that of the *Sea Venture* in the year 1609. The *Sea Venture* was the flagship of Admiral George Somers, who was leading a mighty fleet of nine vessels toward the struggling colony of Jamestown in the New World. Aboard was my ancestor, Stephen Hopkins, who later came across to Plymouth on the *Mayflower*.

Just as the reefs and shoals off Cape Cod prevented our *Mayflower* from reaching her destination on the Hudson River, so the reefs and shoals of Bermuda prevented the *Sea Venture* from reaching Virginia.

The entire fleet encountered a terrific hurricane about two hundred leagues from Bermuda. The *Sea Venture* became separated from the rest and developed a serious leak which could not be controlled. A passenger, William Strachey by name, described the incident:

"Wind and seas were so mad as fury could make them. For mine own part I have been in storme before, as well upon the coast of Barbary and Algiers in the Levant and in the Adriatic Gulf.

"Yet all that I had ever suffered gathered together might not hold comparison with this. . . . There was not a moment in which the sudden splitting, or instant overturning of the boat was not expected.

"Howbeit this was not all, it pleased God to bring a greater affliction yet upon us, for in the beginning of the storm we had received a mighty leak. And the ship, in every joint almost, having spued out her Okam, before we were aware, was grown five foote suddenly deep with water above her ballast, and we almost drowned within, while we sat looking when to perish from above."

2

A SHIPWRECK OF 1780

⚓

AMONG THE COUNTLESS SHIPWRECKS on the rocks and reefs of Bermuda, one of the more mystifying in the island's history is that of an unknown vessel.

The disaster took place during the great hurricane of October 10, 1780, a storm that had not been equaled in the memory of the oldest inhabitant. The mighty wind that hit Bermuda pushed over giant trees, knocked down portions of buildings, and scattered slate all over the islands.* At Castle Harbor the above-mentioned vessel came in by Gurnet Rock and anchored under the lee of Castle Island.

When the center of the hurricane reached Bermuda, it brought the usual ominous, deathlike calm, but a short time later the storm hit again from a different direction. Castle Island's cliffs now lay directly before the mystery vessel, and the anchor began to drag. High on the craft a topsail whipped loose, and two officers, Richard Oldgate and David Foggo, went aloft to secure it. In an overpowering gust, the topsail, with the two men in its clutches, ripped away from the ship and blew across to come to rest near the Fishing Steps at

---

* The hurricane was known as Captain Musson's Gale as it occurred on the eve the famed captain was buried.

Castle Island. Two soldiers from the fort ran to the aid of the sailors though everyone believed that there was little hope of saving them. But soon the white sail made its appearance in the dark water, and the men were rescued.

All that long night the two rescued sailors and the soldiers peered anxiously out into the storm. They could see nothing. The terrible force of the gale did not diminish, and surf swept the island every minute. When the first streak of day came, the ship had vanished. There was no trace of either the vessel or of wreckage from her, and she was never heard from in any other port.

Sailors Richard Oldgate and David Foggo stayed in Bermuda and as the years went by married local girls. Around 1782 Oldgate built Mount Wyndham near Bailey's Bay. David Foggo is believed to have built Aintree Crawl. Many of their descendants still live on the islands.

What is mystifying about this wreck is the fact that although there were two survivors, the name of the craft herself has not come down to us.

3

MADIANA

⚓

ON THE NIGHT of February 9, 1903, Captain Roderick Fraser, master of the *Madiana,* was approaching the general vicinity of Bermuda's North Rocks.

Over a year and a half before, the lighthouse at Gibbs' Hill had met with an accident in which its reflectors and revolving mechanism had been put out of order. Instead of repairing the damage, those in charge of the light ordered the keeper to get by as best he could with sheets of tin and galvanized iron and to make what repairs to the machinery were possible. As any mariner knows, this was worse than putting out the light, and the flickering rays seen from the tower completely confused ships at sea.

Just before the disaster, which occurred at 3:40 in the morning, officers on the bridge of the *Madiana* had noticed a strange, fitful light over the starboard bow. The light was so peculiar that mysterious forces were suggested by some. Since the light resembled nothing ever seen at Bermuda before, the captain was summoned at once. Just then the cry "Breakers ahead!" rang out from the bow lookout and hard-a-starboard the helm went.

Then the erratic light on the headland seemed to become

stationary, and the bewildered men on the *Madiana*'s bridge had to make a quick decision. If it were Saint David's Lighthouse, which had no flash but rather a steady glow, they must adopt one course. If it were the revolving light at Gibbs' Hill, a flashing beacon, another course altogether would have to be followed. Captain Fraser announced that he would come about and wait offshore until daylight.

Unfortunately, it was too late. The *Madiana* was then already inside one of the coral reefs, and the new course brought her right on to the ledges. Luckily, Captain Fraser did not make the mistake made by the captain of the *City of Columbus* off Gay Head, Massachusetts, nineteen years before. That unfortunate captain had ordered the engines reversed, and the *Columbus* backed off the Devil's Bridge to go down in deep water at once, drowning one hundred persons in twenty minutes.

Captain Fraser's first impulse was also to back the ship off the reef. But, communicating with the engine room, he found that there was probably a bad gash in the hull of the ship.

"Full speed ahead," he ordered, and the vessel drove high on the coral reef. When the passengers were assured that the *Madiana* was secure on the reef, there was no excitement or panic. All aboard were later taken ashore by the tug *Gladisfen*. Dawn revealed that the ship was stranded three miles west of the North Rocks and that it had been the false, faulty light from Gibbs' Hill which had led her there. All passengers were eventually landed without incident.

A court of inquiry was rapidly set up. It was proved that most of the local mariners knew of the weird peculiarities of the makeshift Gibbs' Hill Light. Captain Fraser, of course, had not been there since the light was damaged, and had no way of obtaining this information. Perhaps to protect fellow Bermudians from blame, the members of the court of inquiry decided that Captain Fraser should have known—possibly by communicating in some mysterious way with the outer world —of the condition of the light. The poor man was officially censored for his lack of information.

When the people in the United States learned the decision of the court, they were astounded. *The New York Times* correctly attributed the disaster to neglect ashore rather than incompetency or carelessness afloat. It was a substantial time later that the British Board of Trade exonerated Captain Fraser from all responsibility in the disaster.

4

THE MAIL STEAMER *CURLEW*

⚓

On Tuesday, March 18, 1856, after making "upwards of eighty voyages," Captain Hunter of the *Curlew* was approaching his goal at Bermuda.

Strangely bothered by a dream of disaster he had experienced two nights before, he had been upset to such a degree that he decided to take a small amount of laudanum to quiet his nerves. He then retired late Monday night.

To allow you, the reader, the chance to decide from what has come down to us from 114 years ago, if anything of supernatural nature can be attributed to the disaster, I offer you first the local paper's account, then a letter written by a survivor of the disaster, and finally a letter from the important people of Bermuda to the captain practically absolving him from all blame and stating that his ability as a navigator had been fully established, and that the wreck was indeed an accident. How then can we explain what happened?

Here is the newspaper article:

"We are called on this week to record the total loss of the Mail Steamer *Curlew,* Captain Hunter, which sad event occurred on the morning of Tuesday last on the reef North of these Islands and about one and a half miles East of the North rock. As soon as the circumstances of the *Curlew* being on the rocks became known, boats from the two Ships of War at Ireland Island, with their respective Captains, G. H. Seymour, C.B., and G. G. Wellesley, C.B., from the Naval Yard, from Somerset and St. Georges, instantly proceeded to her assistance, but long ere they reached her she had settled down on the reef, the forecastle being the only part of her visible above water.

"As she had broken in two amidships and the after part had gone down in deep water there was every reason to apprehend that none of the mail bags would be recovered. Fortunately, however, that portion of the vessel which had sunk soon came to pieces, and we understand that seven out of the nine mail bags put on board at Halifax have been picked up, several of them floating two miles or more from the wreck. From the very high winds which have prevailed during the last few days, and from the fact of some of her cabin furniture and of her cargo having drifted on shore on the south side of the Islands, we are of opinion that the *Curlew* is a perfect wreck. We give below the particulars of the loss of the *Curlew*, kindly supplied by one of the passengers, Mr. Howes.

"The *Curlew* was constructed of iron, comparatively new, having been built in Scotland in 1852. She was 182 feet long and 22 feet wide. She was first employed in the mail service between New York, Bermuda and St. Thomas, and last between Halifax, Bermuda and St. Thomas.

"Those who have travelled with Captain Hunter, will regret exceedingly to hear of his misfortune, for all, in common with ourselves, who have had an opportunity of observing his watchfulness and good seamanship at all times, but particularly during the period of danger, speak of him in the highest terms of praise. Many of the persons residing in Bermuda who have crossed the ocean with Capt. Hunter, contem-

plate presenting to him some token expressive of their esteem for him as a gentleman and a thorough seaman.
"The *Curlew* belonged to the Messrs. Cunard of Halifax, and, we presume, was insured."

The letter from survivor Howes follows:
"Hamilton, Bermuda, 21st March, 1856.
"Dear Sir,
"I will here give you the particulars of the deplorable loss of the Mail Steam Packet *Curlew,* under the command of Captain Hunter. We left Halifax at nine o'clock on Friday morning last, and had a fine run, with moderate wind and sea, until early on Sunday morning, when the wind and sea increased considerably and remained high until Monday morning, when they moderated, and I believe that Captain Hunter was on deck nearly the whole night.

"The weather continued fine all Monday, and at night we had every prospect of being in about six o'clock the next morning, as Capt. Hunter expected to make the light about one o'clock. On retiring for the night I only partially undressed, as I intended to get up when the light was made, and remain on deck until we got in. Capt. Hunter left the cabin about ten o'clock to go on deck, and we retired.

"Early the next morning I was awoke by Mrs. Howes who called me and said, 'the Steamer is on the rocks.' I woke up and heard the vessel grating on the rocks, and told her to 'keep quiet, it was all right, we should soon be on shore,' as from the splendid run we had had and the fineness of the night and the confidence I had in the Captain, I was under the impression that we had struck going in between the Forts.

"Mrs. Howes said, 'but I tell you she had struck on the north side reef, get up, we shall all be drowned.'

"Just then the Steamer crashed on the rocks. I got on deck as quickly as possible and heard the chief Mate say, 'the Engine room is full of water,' and saw the sea breaking on the deck amidships. I rushed into the cabin and told Mrs. Howes and Dr. Dickey to hurry on deck, as the vessel was sinking under us, and the cabin would soon fill. While I was speaking to them, I saw the Mate rush into the saloon to the Captain's room, and heard him shriek out, 'Captain Hunter, the vessel has struck on the rocks.'

"The Captain replied, 'eh? what?' The Mate again said, 'she is sinking, she is filling, the Engine room is full of water.' Hunter rushed out exclaiming, 'Good God, what sort of a look-out have you kept, what have you been doing, where is she?' and rushed on deck. I immediately followed with Mrs. Howes and Dr. Dickey. The cabin filled immediately.

"The Captain ordered the boats out directly, but two of them were smashed in the attempt. The third was washed from the davits while Mrs. Howes and Dr. Dickey were getting out of her. The fourth was more successful, and the Captain ordered her to lay by us until he called to her to come alongside. The sea was then making a clear breach over the stern, and we were obliged to get into the main rigging, which we succeeded in doing; we remained there about an hour, and then got into the boat and lay off.

"It appeared to me that the vessel broke in two about the Engine room, and the stern sunk almost immediately. After remaining some time and seeing no boats coming to us, the Captain called the boat along side and sent all the people in her, except two—he with the chief Mate, and second Engineer, remaining on board the vessel. The Captain told us to make the shore as quick as we could and send assistance to him: we landed at the Naval Tanks between ten and eleven o'clock in the morning.

"The vessel appeared to me to have a full cargo, and there were ten head of oxen. It was about half-past four o'clock when she struck.

"Captain is a very attentive, temperate and careful man, and I have that opinion of his ability as a Seaman that I would as soon go to sea again with him, as any one I have ever been with.

"The Mails were in nine white leather bags, and were put into two state-rooms, on the starboard side of the saloon. —I remain, dear Sir, Respectfully yours, J. R. Howes."

The blame for the unfortunate disaster of course, fell on the shoulders of Captain Hunter, who never could comprehend how the wrecking of his staunch craft *Curlew* could have taken place. The following Saturday he sailed for Halifax aboard the schooner *G. O. Bigelow,* whose master was Captain Whittier. On the afternoon before his departure a group of leading citizens presented him with the following testimonial:

"St. Georges, Bermuda, March 22, 1856.
"Capt. Hunter,
"Late, R.M.S.P. *Curlew.*
"Sir,—The unfortunate loss of the Royal Mail Steam Packet *Curlew* under your command, on the coast of these Islands, on the morning of the 18th inst., and the distress of mind, in consequence, it has caused you, have very naturally called forth the sympathy of the Inhabitants of this Town on your behalf; assured as we are that the disaster was purely the result of accident (to which we need scarcely say all are liable), your ability as a navigator having been fully established from the circumstance of your commanding at different periods one or other of the Mail Steamers on this station for upwards of Eighty Voyages.

"The untoward event which has elicited this letter we sincerely hope will be looked upon by those more immediately concerned, in the same light that it is regarded by us, and that you will not be in the remotest degree, prejudiced or injured by the sad occurrence. It will afford us sincere pleasure to hear of your being again Commander of one of the steamers plying to these Islands; your kindness in all respects has gained for you the good will of every one, and we are assured that, if time permitted, the number of signatures to this hastily written document would be very greatly augmented by the inhabitants of the Town of Hamilton as well as others residing remote from St. Georges.

"We are, Sir, with sincere good wishes for your future welfare,

"Your Obedient Servants [Signed by the mayor and principal inhabitants of the town of St. George]."

5

THE SEA DEVIL

⚓

THE SEA OFTEN YIELDS unexpected denizens of the deep which on occasion come to the surface to frighten humanity. While fishing from my canoe back in 1945 I brought up an extremely ugly creature of brownish color, three feet long and two feet wide, which later proved to weigh ninety-one pounds. On coming ashore, I was quickly surrounded by scores of bathers, one of whom decided to help me take a picture of the monster.

Just as the shutter clicked, the creature made a vicious snap at me, and the resulting picture was published in newspapers and magazines all over the world. Uglier than the worst-appearing sculpin ever to be seen, this creature was indeed a horrible representative of the ocean. Two six-fingered hands projected out of the side of its body from the center of the stomach, while its grotesque, cavernous jaws were lined with scores of sharp, snaggly teeth. Its ponderous flippers seemed partly sheathed in medieval armor, while two long tentacles with strange, pointed feelers at the ends extended from the top of its head. Looking down into its throat, I saw what resembled two baby hands at the entrance to its stomach. Later I found that the creature was a *Lophius piscatorius*.

During my recent visit to Bermuda I came across another fish story which put my account into the background. The tale is of a sea devil that Pilot Fred Virtue of St. George's Island encountered on May 5, 1919.

Imagine an enormous skate fish, with fins or wings spanning nearly twenty feet across and having tremendous jaws full of teeth capable of grinding any obstacle in the manner of a stone crusher.

Let us turn to the pages of the *Hamilton Gazette* for May 13, 1919, and read what was recorded that day:

"Picture this giant Eagle-Ray (Milyobatis Aquila) popularly and appropriately nicknamed 'Sea-Devil,' coming at your boat with a malevolent intent, in the night time, 'flaring' the water just below the surface for many rods by the sinister force of its onward drive.

"And fancy the emotions of the pilot's crew as this uncanny visitor approaches—its great bulk outlined by a strange electric and phosphorescent glare in the dark waters! If you recollect the fact that one of these monsters was captured near Messina, weighing 1,250 lbs. (as recorded by the scientist Risse), then you will realize perhaps that our St. George's men experienced a real thrill of emotion when the local Sea-Devil pursued them right to the side of the 'Charybdis.' And you can also sympathize with their feelings of relief as they clambered up to the vessel's deck. But here is the true account as furnished by our enterprising East End correspondent.

"On Monday night last 5th inst., the 'Charybdis' was sighted from the pilot station at St. David's Island. Immediately afterwards, Pilot Fred G. Virtue left the shore in the gig 'Gazelle,' with the following crew: Jeremiah Lamb, Murray Fox, Thomas Fox, George Burcher, Ted Griffiths and Benny Lamb.

"The wind was light, the sea comparatively smooth, but a

little surly; the air quiet and just damp enough to be chilly. At about one o'clock on Tuesday morning the 'Gazelle' was some four miles off shore, St. David's Light bearing West. The crew were resting on their oars; the 'Charybdis' then lying dead, about one mile off shore of the gig.

"Pilot Virtue, who was sitting in the stern of the 'Gazelle' observed a flare of great size coming at right angles to the gig from the South. Neither the pilot nor the other men who saw the flare advancing under the surface of the water had the slightest idea as to what it was; but 'torpedo' suggested itself.

"The flare came on quickly, went under the after part of the 'Gazelle,' stopped the moment it felt the weight of the boat and lifted the after part of her clear out of the water as it came to the surface. As the boat careened the men thought they were on top of a whale. The after men unhung their oars and began to pound the big fish to make it move, the four forward men pulling as hard as they could to force the 'Gazelle' over the obstruction which they ultimately did. The flare in the water was not altogether a phosphorescent one, but long and white.

"As soon as the crew got the boat afloat and all oars hung, they struck a long, silent but very quick stroke for the 'Charybdis' and never eased until they were along side her.

"The sea devil followed them all the way and the flare caused by it was seen by the officer of the watch on the steamer. After the pilot boarded the vessel the monster disappeared.

"Pilot Virtue is quite sure that it was a sea devil. Had this particular one gone under the middle of the gig she surely would have overturned and the results would probably have been very serious.

"As the men pulled the gig off the fish it flapped its great broad wing-like fins and a great quantity of water went into the boat. When the gig's stern was on the fish the pilot had to hold on by both sides of the gunwale to keep from falling into the gig's bottom.

"Pilot Virtue said that none of the crew lost presence of mind during the dangerous period; scarcely a word was spoken until safely alongside the 'Charybdis'; 'but,' says Pilot Virtue, 'if I ever have another similar experience it will be the last for I shall never go night piloting in a gig again!' "

"The fish was fully ten feet each way which would give it 100 square feet of surface on its top side."

6

BERMUDA'S 1915 WRECK

⚓

ONE OF BERMUDA'S most thrilling shipwrecks in the entire first half of the twentieth century occurred at the height of the September 1915 storm, when the steamer *Pollokshields* was caught on the coral reef off the South Shore Hotel.

On Monday night, September 7, coastal inhabitants noticed that the seas were running tremendously high all along the shore, for a terrific gale was sweeping Bermuda. Then, early on Tuesday morning a shrill steamer whistle aroused the people of Paget. Soon, those gathered in the South Shore Hotel saw a steamer through the spray and mist between the Bermuda shore and the first line of breakers. There was the *Pollokshields,* hopelessly fast among the reefs. By her position, it could be seen that she had been heading north-northeast when she struck.

The watchers at the hotel studied the jagged line of reefs holding the wrecked ship in their grip. Gigantic breakers smashed the steamer again and again. Those ashore kept their eyes on the frightened group of men gathered together on the deck of the steamer. The survivors clung to the superstructure as the great combers attacked them. Meantime, those on shore made their plans. Men arrived, bringing with them what lifesaving apparatus they had at hand. Bermuda volunteers and many others organized on the beach, but they were helpless in the teeth of the wind and the sea.

Meanwhile several Bermuda residents familiar with storms and the coast wondered if a lifeboat might be found that could ride out the violent gale then raging. A boat built for battling with great seas, a whaleboat for example, might be practical. Mr. Antonio Marshall had a whaleboat, and he was willing enough to risk her, but she was a long distance from shore. The group then thought of Mr. Spurling who owned a dray.

A group was quickly organized to move the whaleboat to the South Shore to rescue the men clinging for their lives to the broken ship.

Then followed the overwhelming task of pulling and tugging the heavy whaleboat to Mr. Spurling's, after which the Spurling dray carried the great boat and fought with the wild wind that tried to capsize it. They urged the horses to their utmost on that midnight journey.*

When morning broke the men on shore looked out over a gray, boiling sea. Great crowds were out on the beach, watching the doomed ship transfixed on the coral reef. As far as could be seen, all her crew were still on the deck.

Now, with the whaleboat ready, the men stood by for the moment of launching. Then came a lull of calmness, and the boat was run into the sea. The surf was still tremendous and the waves hit with seldom-witnessed fury. As they left the shore, the whaleboat's volunteer crew faced the combined force of wind-driven spume and driving rain. They were skilled, chosen men. All were Bermudians with the exception of Mr. Antonio Marshall, skipper and whaleboat owner, who had been a whaleman. The others were Edward Dil-

---

* A woman later furnished the volunteers with hot coffee which proved "as good as six men."

worth, Charles DeShield, Gordon Bascombe, David Williams, T. Basden, and Reginald Minors.

The whaleboat rode out the first three waves, only to hit a towering breaker which capsized the oarsmen into a tangled mass of men, lines, and life preservers. Captain Marshall's second attempt was successful, and twenty minutes later the crew brought in six survivors from the *Pollokshields*.

Out on the steamer, several adventuresome sailors, equipped with life belt and life buoys, swam ashore, where they were helped up to the South Shore Hotel. Warm blankets and hot toddies awaited them.

The next three trips brought ashore ten, ten, and seven men, making with the others thirty-three in all ashore successfully. Sadly enough, it is said that had Captain Edwards not attempted to launch the lifeboat when the ship first struck, he might have been among the saved. The final rescue was that of three tiny kittens brought ashore in a bag.

Among those in the naval contingent who did outstanding work during the rescue was the Reverend Peyton-Burbery, R.N., while the wonderful skill shown by former whaling captain Antonio Marshall in his own boat will never be forgotten by those who were present.

It was a happy group of English, Greeks, Irish, Americans, and Belgians—all members of the *Pollokshields* crew—who ate a substantial dinner at the South Shore Hotel, after which they bedded down for the night, their worries temporarily over. In the morning a fine breakfast was given them. Within a fortnight the last crew member had left the island.

As an aftermath to the shipwreck, a marine court was appointed by His Excellency the Governor of Bermuda. It announced its findings on September 17, 1915. Convened under the provisions of the Wreck Inquiry Act of 1880, it was established for the purpose of inquiring into the circumstances under which the British S.S. *Pollokshields,* while on a voyage from Cardiff, Wales, bound to Bermuda, was wrecked on the southern reefs of these Islands on September 7, 1915, and became a total loss.*

Pertinent details from the report follow:

The S.S. *Pollokshields* encountered a heavy easterly storm which continued until the ship was wrecked at about 8 A.M. on the morning of the seventh on the barrier reefs opposite the eastern end of Elbow Bay. The ship was light and consequently had little hold in the water. Owing to the thick weather no observations were taken by the officers of the ship from noon of Thursday the second until the time of the wreck.

Assuming the recorded position of the ship on Thursday the second, when the last observations were taken, was correct, and that, according to the evidence, the ship's position at midnight on the same day, after twelve hours of dead reckoning, was eighty miles east of Bermuda, the court could not comprehend, if the course was altered as late as 1:30 P.M. on Monday the sixth, how the ship could have reached the position she was in at eight o'clock on Tuesday the seventh. In order to do this the ship would have had to steam as great a distance in eighteen and a half hours as she took eighty-five and a half hours to steam on her southerly course.

In the absence of the master of the ship, who was washed overboard and drowned shortly after the stranding of the ship, and in the absence of the ship's logs, engineer's logs, and the charts on which the ship was working, all of which were lost according to the evidence, and owing to the fact that the first and second officers were unable to give the court definite information as to the courses steered and distances made good, the court experienced great difficulty in deter-

---

* Another organization to do with wrecks was the Shipwrecked Mariners' Society instituted in 1839. The president was Sir James Graham, according to agent Montague Pasco whose address in 1856 was Boaz Island, Bermuda.

mining how far the master was responsible for the loss of the ship.

The court was of the opinion that soundings should have been taken when under the circumstances it was obvious that the master was not sure of the ship's position and that there is a possibility that had an anchor been let go on sighting land the wreck of the ship might have been avoided.

The court considered the immediate cause of the wreck of the ship was the thick weather prevailing on the morning of the seventh which prevented the land from being seen at a sufficient distance to permit the ship's course to be altered to avoid the reefs.

The court was composed of the Hon. A. F. Smith, President, Commander E. Hamilton-Bate, R.N., and Captain T. M. Dill, B.M.A.

The last time I flew over the *Pollokshields* there was very little left to photograph of her. Nevertheless, I returned from Bermuda with a color motion picture which clearly shows a fragment of the craft that caused so much excitement fifty-five years ago.

7

THE *LA PLATA*, WHICH NEVER REACHED BERMUDA

⚓

JUST HOW MUCH ANGUISH and suffering can a shipwreck survivor endure before he succumbs to what he believes is the inevitable and dies?

Most of us have heard of the story of Eddie Rickenbacker and his group floating in rubber lifeboats out on the Pacific after their plane's mishap in 1942. I have been asked if there is any record of a survivor from a shipwreck enduring similar agony and coming through the ordeal to live and write about it.

I offer the following observation from a participant in a disaster that overwhelmed a craft almost a century ago. *La Plata* left England on November 26, 1874, on a long journey which had Bermuda as her first destination.

No wreck of the last century aroused more intense contemporary interest than this cable ship bound from the Thames to South America. It had been the captain's plan to cross the Atlantic, leaving Bermuda far in her wake long before Christmas. Fate intervened, however, before many days had elapsed after the *La Plata*'s departure from Gravesend.

The following survivor's report "is as marvelous as any

that has ever been read of adventures at sea," according to the *Annual Register*. The story by Quartermaster John Hooper tells of the disaster in which sixty-eight people perished.

John Hooper already had considerable experience with the sea, having been shipwrecked on the *Flying Scud* off California, as well as having been injured while rounding Cape Horn on the *Morning Cloud*. However, he had no premonition of any difficulty when he signed on for the voyage on the *La Plata*. Let us step back into the past for the story as he wrote it ninety-seven years ago.

"The *La Plata* was an iron screw-steamer of 1,218 tons, barque-rigged, and with her machinery well aft. She was especially equipped for cable-laying, and when I joined her on November 22, 1874, which was a Sunday morning, she was ready for sailing from the Telegraph Works at New Charlton, Woolwich, where she was lying.

"The steamer had on board 183 nautical miles—that is, about 200 land miles—of deep-sea cable, and had also a great quantity of iron telegraph-poles and telegraph-wire. This was all dead-weight material, and with her 219 tons of coal the *La Plata* had a total weight on board of 1,200 tons. As this was mostly stowed in the after part of the vessel, with her bunkers filled with coal, you can understand that she was heavily laden by the stern. I want you to bear that in mind, and also the fact that we were to cross the Bay of Biscay in the winter-time.

"Many people in these days dread crossing the Bay at any time, even in the big splendid liners with their great freeboard. I wonder what they would have said to starting out in that little steamer, with so much dead weight on board that she was like a log in the water when we started.

"On November 26 we left the Thames for Rio Grand do

Sul. The steamer had a total crew of ninety-five men, which was a very large number, because it included the telegraph staff, engineers, and hands who were necessary for laying the cable in the deep sea.

"It was fine weather when we went down Channel, and it was a glorious morning when we dropped our pilot off the Isle of Wight and stood out to cross the Bay and get out into the Atlantic.

"I took a lingering look at the white cliffs of Old England, as did all my comrades who were on deck. I was to see them again, after such suffering as few men have ever lived to describe; but as for them, they had indeed said good-bye.

"I was one of the quartermasters of the steamer, so that when I was on duty my post was at the wheel. to steer the ship during my watch. Until Saturday, the 28th, things went well with us, then I knew that we should encounter the full force of a heavy gale. I knew also, that in such a ship, deeply laden as our own was, a heavy gale would be a dangerous one, yet I had no misgivings, even when I saw the great dark clouds gathering in the sky and noticed the huge swirl which was rolling up from the southwest.

"There are times when even the boldest sailors feel inclined to turn and seek shelter, and I dare say that more than one bold seaman on board would have been thankful to hear that the *La Plata* was making for some safe spot at which she could anchor until the gale had spent its force. But orders are orders at sea, and our own were to get the steamship out to sea.

"The promise of the stormy sky was speedily fulfilled. First the wind came on us like an ordinary gale, then it grew in strength and increased until, by midnight, it was blowing with the force of a hurricane.

"The steamer drummed and thrashed into the seas, which had risen to an enormous height and were sweeping her from stem to stern. It is nothing in these days of Atlantic leviathans for a magnificent monster to drive through any ordinary gale, and she can always be held up to any wind that blows and forced to face any sea that runs. But they have such enormously powerful engines—they have their two, three, or four screws, and they have no top-hamper; but the little *La Plata* had only a single screw, and low-powered engines, and she had to depend on the help of her sails.

"When we began driving into the storm we had as much sail set as we could carry, but the sails were blown out of the bolt-ropes, and as the ship was so heavily down by the stern, it was impossible to keep her head to the wind. Her bow was high out of the water, and wind and sea drove against it with such force that the vessel was almost blown round and became unmanageable.

"By midnight it was seen that we were in a position of serious danger, if not very great peril, and there was not a man on board who did not know that if she survived the storm at all it would only be through incessant watchfulness on the part of everybody on deck and in the engine-room.

"The very life of us depended on the engines being kept working and protecting the engine-room from the enormous masses of water which smashed on board. Time after time the Atlantic waves swept on board, with a deafening and terrifying noise, and a force that promised to smash the ship and overwhelm her.

"The almost incredible ill-luck which had followed me ever since I went to sea remained with me now. The privations I had been forced to endure had told on even my wonderful constitution, and when we began that hard fight with the gale, I was below in my berth, the doctor having ordered me to go there, because I had a bad sore throat, and was suffering from a very severe cold. I was unfitted to go on deck and cope with such bitter weather as was being experienced. Yet nothing could have been harder for me to endure than the misery of lying helpless in my bunk, hurled and thrown about by the dreadful labouring of the vessel, and knowing that any one of the seas which struck us might mean our destruction.

"It is bad enough at such a time of peril to be at one's post on the deck or on the bridge, but it is infinitely worse to be cooped up in the foul air below and battened down. If you are on deck there is at least a chance of salvation, but there is no hope whatever when you are imprisoned as I was in the *La Plata*.

"Time after time I heard the ominous thud which told of some big sea coming on board in the darkness of that terrible night; then, at two o'clock in the morning, there came a crash which told me that some serious mischief had been done on deck.

"I asked for tidings as to what had happened, and learnt that one of the boats had been torn from its fastenings and carried overboard. That was bad enough, but in such a gale you expect something to be swept away. Boats and stanchions and fittings can be replaced, and their loss does not greatly matter, but I heard also that a man had been carried away and had perished.

"No more depressing thing can happen at sea than a death on board ship, especially such a death as this, because it is the end that may come to any man at any moment. So terrible was the gale by this time that it was almost seeking death to go on deck; yet, in spite of my illness, which had exhausted me and left me almost as weak as a child, I could not bear to remain below any longer. Duty called me, and I felt bound to obey.

"How I clambered out of my berth and got on deck I do not clearly remember, but, bit by bit, I fought my way along the deck, struggling through the deep water with which it was now constantly filled, and dodging, as best I could in the darkness, the seas of the Atlantic.

"At last I struggled up to the bridge and took my post at the wheel, and from that moment until the ship went down I did not leave my place.

"I wish I could find words that would convey to you anything like a strong impression of the dreadful scene on which I looked from the bridge of the struggling steamship; but all I can tell you is that the sky above and all around was perfectly black, and yet there seemed to be enough ghostly, mysterious light to show what an awful, deadly sea was running.

"No light, however, was needed to tell us of our danger. We knew that too well from the terrific motion of the ship as she fell away into the trough, or was hurled high by one of the hills of water which swept upon her. It was impossible to do anything more than try to keep her up to it, and yet this could not be accomplished, for the reason I have given.

"Steam and steer as we would, the *La Plata* was driven back and hurled about, entirely at the mercy of the wind and sea. She was like some poor, frail human being striving to battle with the wind that has the power to lift him off his feet and throw him away like straw.

"For two hours in that night of turmoil—a shriek of wind and a roar of sea in which no human voice could be heard at a distance of more than a few inches—I held to my post and did what I could, more by instinct than by judgment, to help to save the ship. I craved for daylight, although I knew that the dawn would reveal a sea which would appall the stoutest sailor; but it would at least give us the chance of seeing an approaching wave, and doing our best to meet it.

"Mercilessly and incessantly the waves crashed on board and swept the deck, carrying away every movable thing, and many things that had been, as we imagined, firmly secured.

One boat had already gone; at four o'clock a sea bore down upon us which ripped the lifeboat out of its skids, wrenched bolt-ropes and every fastening from the deck, and swept the entire mass, a heap of shattered wreckage over the side.

"Again, hour after hour, until the dawn broke in the east, the sea continued its work of maiming and destroying. Still things went fairly well. The ship was making a gallant fight and was bearing her punishment nobly. Almost like a living thing she was settling to the contest with wind and water, and it almost looked as if the work of man would triumph over the forces of Nature.

"Then—about an hour after the cheerless dawn had shown on the horizon—there came to us a report which drove all hope from every heart. We were told that a plate in the engine-room had started, and that the sea was rushing in and threatening to extinguish the engine-room fires, to take away from us the very force on which our safety depended.

"Hope abandoned me as soon as I heard the tidings, for I knew that so far as the *La Plata* was concerned, she had received her sentence of death.

"From the time I first went on to the bridge until it was reported that the engine-room fires were drowned and that the ship was no longer under control, I had stuck to my post at the wheel, trying as hard as I could to keep her to it. I did not abandon my spokes until the mate came and told me that there was no hope, and that every man must fight for his own life.

"A few of the men seemed to be filled with despair, but, for the most part, the crew bore themselves like good Englishmen, and made ready to get the boats free from their lashings and skids, and to clamber into them—the idea being that when the steamship foundered the boats would float and could be rowed away. It was impossible in the sea that was running to attempt to lower them, because they would either have been swamped or smashed to pieces against the steamboat's iron sides.

"Captain Dudden, the commander of the *La Plata*, was on the bridge when I finally left it, but all my orders were given to me by the second mate. By the time I got on deck the steamship had been got round, and she was lumbering on before the wind and sea, continually pooped by the terrific following waves.

"The water came on board in such enormous masses that the after part of the ship was completely buried, while her fore part was high out of the water. First of all, I made my way to a raft which was on the bridge. The doctor and some of the telegraph men were clustering about the raft, evidently intending to cling to it when it was afloat in the water. It seemed to me that there would be no chance of my own salvation on the raft, so after helping to launch it to windward, I climbed down the bridge and struggled aft towards a lifeboat which the boatswain, whose name was Lamont, and some of the crew had got ready. This was the starboard quarterboat.

"How I got into the boat I do not know, but at last I found myself packed in her, waiting for some stroke of luck to come and get us into the sea, so that we should have a fighting chance.

"No sooner had I taken my place in the lifeboat than a tremendous sea swept on board, crashed on to the top of us, burst the lifeboat in two, and by sheer force of water, drove me and the rest of us deep down into the sea.

"Now, indeed, I thought that the end had really come. I seemed to go down and down and down into the green depths, until I was almost suffocated in the attempt to hold my breath, and until there seemed to be no chance whatever of rising again to the surface.

"I struggled with all the energy within me to get to the top, and at last I found that water getting lighter and lighter, and then I shot up again into the air and took a deep, long breath.

"I was still perfectly conscious, and saw that the *La Plata* was just on the point of sinking, and that wreckage was falling all around me.

"A number of men were struggling in the water near me, and one of them shouted, 'Look out, quartermaster, for her rigging!'

"I saw that I had been sucked over the sinking ship and that the mizzen rigging was crashing upon me. I tried to swim away, but before I could make more than a stroke or two, the mass was upon me, and I was netted just as a lion might be by hunters in the forest.

"The tangle of rope was over me, and for the second time I was carried down into the depths of the Bay of Biscay. The rigging had caught me over the back, and I sank face downwards. I think this time I went deeper than before, for I could no longer hold my breath, and began to swallow salt water.

"The end now seemed sure indeed, yet I made another despairing effort at salvation. I struck out and down—I did anything I could instinctively to clear myself of the toils—and again I had the joy of seeing that my limbs were free and that I was rising rapidly.

"I knew that in two or three seconds I should be clear of the water, yet as I rose to the surface my head struck a topgallant-yard and was cut open by one of the bolts. Stunned and bleeding though I was, I had strength and resourcefulness left to cling to the spar.

"It was while I was being sucked down by the sinking ship that I heard and felt a terrible explosion.

"The *La Plata* had sunk, and the noise was caused, not, I imagine, by the bursting of her boilers, but owing to the compression of the air.

"I was too much occupied with the thoughts of my own peril to pay any great attention to the foundering of the steamship. I looked about me and saw the boatswain not far away.

"The two of us struggled to a broken American air-raft which came floating past us. This raft consisted of a couple of air-tight india-rubber tubes, which were covered and connected with canvas. We knelt in it with our arms over the tubes, immersed in the water, and for the present, at any rate, safe.

"I had had time to look around me, and had seen the carpenter, who was clinging to a hencoop, swept off and drowned. In the distance, on the crest of a wave, I saw our only remaining boat, the port quarter-boat, running before the wind and sea. She carried fifteen men, who, after many hours of exposure in the Bay, were picked up by a passing ship and afterwards put on board a homeward bound steamer and landed in England.

"It was these survivors who first told the tidings of the disaster and reported that the *La Plata* had gone down with every soul except themselves. Not a word about the boatswain and myself, who were clinging to our frail support and were being hurled about by the angry seas of the Biscay in wintertime, up to our waists in water, with the seas breaking over us any minute, without food or drink, and with very little clothes on to keep off the piercing cold.

"There had been no time to make the air-raft thoroughly ready for the water, and the result was that although the air-tubes were sound they were not thoroughly inflated. This was, perhaps, fortunate for us, because we were able to get a better grip than we should have done if the canvas had been thoroughly rigid, and at the same time there was quite buoyancy enough to keep us both afloat.

"The boatswain and myself sat on the tube which was most fully inflated, pressing our knees against the other tube, and resting our feet on the canvas connecting the two.

"The raft had capsized and the framework had been shattered by the seas, the result being that we had nothing to cling to and were in the water up to the waist, with the breaking seas continually sweeping over our heads.

"After the ship had foundered and we were on the raft, I saw a man with a cork lifebelt on. He cried pitifully for help, time after time, but we could do nothing for him, and he drifted away and perished, like the rest of those who had been cast into the waters. Some of them were mercifully spared prolonged suffering, because they were taken down into the vortex, but I fear that many died a lingering death.

"Do you clearly understand the terrible position in which we found ourselves? We were not, remember, in an open boat, nor were we even on an ordinary raft. We were simply clinging to the more or less deflated air tubes, deep in the water, in the bitter air of a late November day.

"Only one thing kept us from perishing of exposure, and that was the fact that the water in which we were floating was part of that warm current, the Gulf Stream, which flows across the Atlantic and warms certain portions of the English Channel and the Bay of Biscay.

"The water itself was not cold, but the air was bitter. I remember that once I raised one of my legs into the air, to give it a rest, but the cold was so bitter that I was glad to put the limb back into the liquid warmth.

"The time came when the two of us, who had been talking more or less hopefully, got very silent, and when the hope which had risen within us because of our temporary salvation, gave way to dull despair.

"The afternoon wore on and the dark night came, followed by what seemed to be a hopeless dawn. Still we clung, sodden, starving, and parched with thirst, to our flabby raft, and all through that day we looked with bloodshot eyes to every point of the compass, hoping and praying for the help which seemed likely never to come. Lamont bore himself wonderfully well, and we did our best to cheer and comfort one another.

"Once or twice we saw ships—for we were in the track of the traffic to and from the Near and Far East—across the Bay. More than once it seemed as if our salvation was assured, because ships came so near and we clamoured loudly for help. At one time it seemed certain that we should be rescued, but the ship which could have saved us went away, although I am sure that we must have been within hailing distance.

"It was an American three-masted schooner, which seemed to be bearing down directly for us. That was on the Tuesday morning, when the gale had died away and there was fine clear weather. She got up to within half-a-mile of us, and then a dead calm came, and we had the unspeakable agony of watching her for at least two hours, and then, when the breeze returned, bearing away from us and leaving us to our sufferings and our doom.

"A consuming thirst was afflicting us, and yet there was not a drop of water to drink. In my despair I set to work to chew the edge of a medal which I was wearing when the ship went down and which had been presented to me by the Shipwrecked Fishermen and Mariner's Society. This relieved my thirst to some extent, and helped the day on.

"The weather varied, and a driving, bitter sleet succeeded the fine spell we had enjoyed. The wind and snow drove pitilessly down upon us, and added to the sufferings, which were now becoming unendurable.

"Both of us went almost delirious, and I, at any rate, began to have vivid pictures of sun-bathed fields and green trees, with plenty of clear, pure water to drink and more than enough food to eat. These illusions were shattered from time to time when my senses returned and showed me the cruel reality of the Bay in which we were drifting in the winter.

"For four full days and nights the boatswain and myself were in the water; then, on the Wednesday at noon, nearly a hundred hours after we had been castaway, we saw a Dutch schooner, and knew that she had seen us. She was the *Wilhelm Berklesorn*, bound to the Mediterranean.

"It was soon clear enough that, having spied us, they were not going to abandon us, but the breeze had freshened again, and the sea was so rough that there was no chance of running the little ship down towards us and rescuing us.

"After beating about for a long time the schooner bore down, and Lamont and myself did the only thing it was possible to do to secure ourselves. He had a lifebuoy round his waist, and as the schooner sailed past us, as near as she could get, he slipped away from the raft and managed to seize a rope they threw him and made it fast round his waist. He was too utterly worn out to try and secure it, but the Dutchmen had got him, and they did not mean to let him go until they had dragged him through the water and hauled him, terribly swollen and emaciated, on board.

"Then the schooner returned for her second shot, this time at myself. I was perfectly helpless, yet I managed to catch hold of a rope they threw, and which, by a stroke of luck, had fallen around me.

"I tried to grasp the rope with my hands, but no strength remained in them. I managed, however, to put the rope round my neck and to trip it with my teeth to prevent myself from being strangled.

"The way of the vessel through the water brought me alongside, and reaching over, the Dutchmen caught me by the collar of my shirt and pulled me on board. I collapsed on the deck, but had just breath enough left to utter a few words of thankfulness to God for His mercy in so marvellously preserving me.

"The schooner bore away for Gibraltar, and from that port, after being treated in a hospital, we sailed for Southampton by the P. and O. mailboat *Cathay*.

"It was reported at the time that Lamont died soon after being landed; but I heard afterwards that he did not pass away just then.

"As for myself, for a long time I was unable to get about at all, except on crutches; and ever since the disaster I have suffered greatly from the effects of my long stay in the sea."

8

SHIP OF SKELETONS

⚓

"A BOWSPRIT OF A BRIG, as supposed, drifted ashore here about three weeks ago, cut with an ax near the stem of the vessel, on which is cut on one side with a chisel or knife, the words *'Amity,* of Norfolk.' It is fresh and must have been lost lately."

"The schooner *Henry Lee,* of Brandywine, Delaware, was brought into Ely's Harbour, on Saturday last, by Captain R. M. Staples, having been found abandoned at sea."

During the scores of hours I have spent delving into the pages of thousands of issues of the Bermuda papers, items like the two above are but typical examples of the perils of the Atlantic in the area called the Bermuda Triangle.

Possibly the weirdest marine disaster in Bermuda history was that of a schooner about which I shall now write.

During the last week of the year 1833, on December 27, a native of Bermuda was fishing out of Ely's Harbor. The air was dead calm. Far in the distance he noticed a craft drifting lazily along in the current. Interested because of possible salvage, he sculled out to the object which proved to be a derelict, with her bow partly under water. On coming alongside, the Bermudian was terribly frightened to find that the vessel was manned by a strange crew of silent sailors sprawled in grotesque positions on the deck. When he clambered over the side of the drifting wreck, he discovered that every man aboard was a skeleton!

The wind was coming up, and the Bermudian hastily returned to his craft, unfurled the "leg-of-mutton" sail and headed for Ely's Harbor. Excited by his unbelievable find, he was hardly able to contain himself. Reaching shore, the fisherman told his news to other mariners, and a short time later a dozen fishing boats were on their way to the derelict on the deck of which was a ghastly crew. Eventually the men of Bermuda brought the derelict into Ely's Harbor, beaching her in shallow water.

In the year 1948, during the first journey Mrs. Snow and I ever made to Bermuda, I visited Packwood House in Somerset to obtain information concerning the famous Bermuda diver, Captain John Lusher, who had found a treasure galleon under the sea. Unfortunately, Mr. Lusher had died a year and a half before we arrived in Bermuda, most of his treasure still on the bottom of the ocean.

One of my informants, a man who had more than the usual interest in shipwrecks and ghosts, took me aside. "If you really want the most awful story of Bermuda, at least that I have ever heard, I have a tale founded on fact that should interest you.

"A hundred years and more ago my ancestor was there when the old *Liza Ann* washed into Ely's Harbor. Some still talk about it, but if you go down to the library at Hamilton, you'll find the tale in the papers of well over a century ago. A medal which had something to do with Ben Franklin was found on one of the skeletons."

I journeyed at once to the Bermuda Archives on Queen Street, and after long hours of impatient research I began to discover those facts which were important in putting together the details I hoped would solve the mystery.

When on January 3, 1970, I returned to Boston from our fourth trip to Bermuda, it was my belief that I had obtained in the archives of Bermuda enough information about the skeleton ship to begin working in the Boston and New England area, investigating the various depositories of newspapers, city records, and school files. My work in Boston is now finished.

In the year 1829 William Brown was one of six boys in the Washington Place Boylston School * of Boston, Massachusetts, to receive the Benjamin Franklin medal of achievement.

Franklin left a hundred pounds to the directors of "the free schools in my native town of Boston." The interest was to be annually "laid out in silver medals and given as honorary rewards." The Franklin medals were first awarded in January 1793 and continuously after that. Always given only to boys, since 1867 the medals have been limited to the Boston Latin School and several other high schools of the area.** In 1922 the number of medals was about thirty a year, and the total since 1793 has been more than four thousand.

*The other five boys were Joseph Bates, Edward F. Robinson, David G. Ranney, Jacob T. Woodbury, and Patrick L. Fahy.
** In January, 1793, the Committee decided that only boys would receive the medal, although Franklin made no such stipulation. Possibly Franklin intended them for boys only, as girls, when the will was written in 1788, were not admitted to public schools. It was also decided that a boy could not try for the medal in two schools at once. A boy then attended a writing school in the morning and a reading or grammer school in the afternoon. Changes were made in awards through the years. In 1867 a joint committee was set up between the Latin and English High Schools to control the Franklin fund activities. In 1914 the High School of Commerce was added to those eligible. In 1935 the Board of Superintendents of the Boston schools took over the awarding of the Franklin medals.

SHIP OF SKELETONS

On December 11, 1832, the schooner *Eliza Ann* sailed from Boston for Guyana on the island of Puerto Rico. Aboard was William Brown, one of the 1829 winners of the Boston Franklin medal. When he sailed on the *Eliza Ann*, owned by his father James Brown, a prominent Boston merchant, he wore his silver medal around his neck on a chain. William's brother James was also on board, while the master of the schooner, Captain Brown, was a nephew of the owner. A former Boston Customs inspector, Joshua Seaver, was a passenger on the schooner traveling for his health, and was accompanied by his brother.

Apparently the *Eliza Ann* vanished after leaving Boston. Nothing was heard from her for more than a year.

Then, as I have already indicated, in 1833 on December 27, a schooner was sighted off Ely's Harbor and brought ashore there. All Bermuda quickly heard of the "ship of skeletons" and the authorities decided to step in and take over. The officers in charge of the investigation ordered the human remains to be taken ashore. The bodies were examined one by one for clues. On one of the skeletons the name *J. Seaver* was discovered sewn into the clothing, while another yielded the name *N. Seaver*. Down below in the hold, a cargo of shook headings, beef, pork, mackerel, butter, cider, cherry brandy, and other assorted food was found. The beef, pork, and mackerel were branded "Boston," with the dates September, October, and November, 1832.

From the decayed state of almost everything perishable, it was evident to the investigators that the derelict had been adrift for many months.

It was conjectured that the craft, which proved to be a schooner, had capsized in a hurricane while most of the sailors were below deck. After her masts had gone, she partly righted herself.* Probably the men had died of thirst as the days, weeks, and months had gone by.

After careful examination of one of the skeletons, the investigators found a silver medal attached to a chain around one victim's neck. A scholar of the local school studied the medal carefully to see if it might give a clue of importance. Two days later he revealed the medal had been awarded to one William Brown, and the entire inscription was extremely informative.

> ADJUDGED BY THE SCHOOL COMMITTEE
> AS A REWARD OF MERIT TO
> WM. BROWN
> THE GIFT OF FRANKLIN

Underneath the inscription was a device of crossed pens over an open book.

The information revealed by the medal proved so interesting that it was shown to a visiting Boston sea captain, Marrell by name, whose brig also had been wrecked and taken into Bermuda. However, Captain Marrell stated that he had no idea who William Brown was.

"There are plenty of Browns in Boston," he admitted, "and also the name Seaver is not an uncommon one, but the only Franklin I've ever heard of is Benjamin Franklin, and he left Boston as a youth to reside in Philadelphia more than a century ago."

On January 4, 1834, the Bermuda paper published all pertinent facts concerning the derelict. Sometime later, when the newspaper reached Georgia, the Savannah journal reprinted the news item. The Savannah paper eventually reached Boston.

* A craft at sea can indeed participate in many uncanny, almost weird feats. See *Strange Tales from Nova Scotia to Cape Hatteras*, pp. 17–23, for my account of the *Cod Seeker*.

SHIP OF SKELETONS

On Saturday morning, February 8, 1834, all Boston was shocked and disturbed when its residents read the local *Statesmen*. Printed near the shipping news was the story from Savannah. I quote excerpts below:

"A Bermuda paper of the 4th Jan. received at Savannah reports that an American built schooner of about 66 feet keel was found among the reefs at the W. End on the 27th Dec.

"The above vessel is probably the 'Eliza Ann,' Capt. Brown, which sailed from Boston on the 11th Dec. 1832, for Porto Rico, and has not been heard of since. She was owned by Mr. James Brown of this city, and her loss is peculiarly afflicting to him as two of his sons were on board, and Capt. Brown was his nephew. Mr. Joshua Seaver, late an Inspector of our Customs, was a passenger for the benefit of his health."

A few years after the *Eliza Ann* appearance of 1833 an artist in Bermuda decided to record on canvas the view of the wrecked but still floating derelict with the skeletons sprawled on deck. His painting, which he placed at the top of the grand stairway in his Somerset home, was a masterpiece of terror and mystery, impressing all who were given the privilege of viewing it.

Sometime after the completion of the skeleton painting, a struggling young artist who was attempting to establish a name for himself heard about the Somerset work of art. He visited the older artist who finally consented to allow the youth to make a sketch from the painting. There were two points, however, that the younger artist should keep in mind, according to the older man.

First, the youth was often to be in charge of the house, as the older artist was then painting scenes some distance away on a Bermuda beach which appealed to him. Secondly, the sketching should always be finished before midnight, whether or not the older artist returned by that time. Otherwise it was within the realm of possibility that unusual events might occur.

Spending several days on the effort, the young man was working late one evening when he suddenly heard a clock striking midnight, the deadline concerning which his host had warned him. Taking out his own watch, he found that it had stopped at eleven-fifteen, for he had forgotten to wind it.

Hastily gathering together the material from his sketch pad, the young artist fled from the almost finished drawing on the easel and rushed down the stairs. About to open the door, he encountered several forms which to his upset mind appeared as skeletons. Not stopping to investigate, he hurried home.

The next time he visited the artist's residence he told the older man of his encounter. The owner admitted that on occasion he, too, had seen the apparitions after midnight.

"It is an unusual situation," said the older man. "The ghosts of skeletons!"

A few weeks went by, and the painter told his friends about the young sketch artist who had sighted the supernatural beings.

Then, suddenly, both artists vanished. When the weeks passed and then the years went by, the unlived in but fully furnished house showed definite signs of its vacancy and more and more deterioration. Soon it was known as the Haunted House of Somerset.

I had hoped that research into the career of artist Winslow Homer might offer a hint that he was the artist involved, as he did visit Bermuda and paint while there, but not only is there no painting including skeletons and a ship by Homer, but Winslow Homer was not in Bermuda at the time.

Sir Charles Wyville Thomson, whom I mentioned in my book *Fury of the Seas* six years ago, was visiting Bermuda during his H.M.S. *Challenger* voyage around the world between 1872 and 1876.

In some way he heard about Somerset and Ely's Harbor. Possibly he had been informed concerning the *Eliza Ann* and the skeletons, but let us ask him to tell what happened ninety-seven years ago.

"Sunday, April 20, 1873 After luncheon At Capt. Aplins walked with the Captain through Somerset Island & to a queer old place, a 'haunted house' beyond the Ferry. All the things lying about & the house furnished as it had been left about 20 years ago. Even the slips cut from the *Illustrated London News* of somewhere about the year [18]48 to make a screen. We could not get at the story. The negroes would not tell it."

Luckily, one of the three Bermudians interviewed by me in 1948 knew the story, and was not afraid, as others had been in 1873, to tell the details I have included in this chapter.

How should we explain the appearance of the skeletons who were seen by both the oil painter and the sketch artist? I am interested in knowing if anyone at Somerset has seen the skeletons at or near the property where the artist lived more than a century ago.

All sources are silent except one. I have been told that the artist's residence, after its long period of vacancy, was completely remodeled. The present owner is not interested in even discussing the former history of the edifice visited by scientist Thomson of the *Challenger* in April, 1873.

If I couldn't get the present history of the building, I was even more eager to attempt acquiring either the painting or the sketch of the "Ship of Skeletons." After a considerable amount of research in an effort to discover the oil painting of the older artist or the copy in pen and pencil of the younger, I met with utter failure.

Then, actually years later, when it had long been established that I very much wanted to obtain either the oil painting or the sketch, I was approached by a man who introduced himself as having information on the skeleton story. He stated that unless I assured him I would never reveal either his name or connect his name in any way with the painting or sketch, he would terminate our conversation and walk away in silence.

After recovering from my surprise, I assured him that I would do as he directed. He then told me that he could get a copy of the sketch on the condition that I was interested financially to a certain extent. Realizing that I was on the verge of success, I tried to suppress my excitement, but did a poor job of it. Nevertheless, my visitor left after giving me a promise that within twenty-four hours the sketch then in his possession would be mine.

I am now the owner of the sketch, and of course have included a copy of it in this book. But naturally I have my doubts about it. Was this sketch made in the twentieth century, possibly after some artist who knew what it was I wanted drew the picture accordingly, or was it the original nineteenth-century sketch, copied from the oil painting which now has probably vanished forever?

Regardless of its origin, I like to think that it is the youthful artist's effort, now more than a century old, and that he did a good copying job when he worked after the hour of twelve on that weird night now so long ago.

INDEX

Abbot, Captain William, 55, 57
Acadians, 6
Acapulco, 160, 161
Active (patrol boat), 69
Ada Cummings, 135
Adams, Charles Francis, 17
Adams, Charles Francis (son), 14
Adams, Melvin Ohio, 47, 48
Adams, Samuel, 8
Addie E. Snow, 55
Adriatic Gulf, 214
Africa, 134
Agony of Collisions, An, 123
Ainsleigh, Capt. Charles, 35-37
Ainsleigh, Jack, 36, 37
Aintree Crawl, 217
Akbar, 92
Algier, 214
Allen, 141
Allison, Keeper, 79
Alman family, 108
Alman, Jennifer, 104, 108, 109
Alman, Kenneth, 104
Alman, Mrs. Kenneth, 104, 109
Alman, Lucy, 104
Alman, Mrs. Ruth, 109
Alman, Susan, 104
Ambrose Martin boat yard, 57
American, 247
American Legion, 73

Americans, 233
Ames, Mr., 60
Ames, Capt. Stuart, 162-164
Ames, Mrs. Stuart, 163, 164
Amity (brig), 250
Anderson, Russell, 71, 72
Andrea Doria, 126, 140-148
Angier, Oakes, 6
Annapolis, Md., 131
Annual Register, 237
Aplins, Capt., 257
Arabs, 206
Arlington (collier), 36
Arno (iron sailing craft), 135
Assawompsett, 16, 17
Athenaeum, 111
Atlanta (cruiser), 132
Atlantic Hill, 91
Atwood House, 75, 76
Augusta boat, 65
Australia, 136
Austrian, 35
Azores, 136

Bagnall, George, 60
Bagnall, William, 60
Bahamas, 136
Bailey's Bay, 217
Baker, Capt. Elisha H., 170
Baldwin, Isaac, 115

259

INDEX

Balfour, Capt., 10
Bangor boat, 65
Barbary, 214
Barker, Otis, 57
Barnstable County, 85
Barry, John S., 11
Bascombe, Gordon, 233
Basden, T., 233
Bates, Joseph, 252
Battle of Chelsea Creek, 110-117
Battle of Lexington and Concord, 9, 10, 116
Battersby, Col. Robert, 160-162
Bay of Biscay, 237-246
Bay Colony, 24
Be-Be, 150-153
Beaver, 97
Bedini, Silvio, 209
Belgians, 233
Belgium, 207
Belknap, Jeremiah, 86
Bendall, Edward, 64
Benjamin, Gregg, 117
Bennett, Carleton, 107, 108
Bennington, 113
Berklesorn, (schooner), 248
Bermuda, 121, 132, 168, 169, 181-258
Bermuda Archives, 252
Bermuda Historical Monuments Trust, 205
Bermuda Journey, 169, 181
Bermuda News Bureau, 198
Bermuda Triangle, 250
Bermudian, 182
Bettinger, Fritz J., 70
Bettinger, Paul, 70
Beverly, Mass., 52
Bicknell, Dorothy Snow, 152
Bicknell, Laura Ann, Dedication page
Bigelow (schooner), 225
Billings, Hammett, 10
Billingsgate, 75
Billingsgate Island, 79-86
Billingsgate Light, 79-86
Billingsgate Point, 80
Biltmore Club, 31
Bing (dog), 164
Bixby, Samuel, 112
Black, Norman, 202-204

Black, Mrs. Norman, 202-204
Black-Watch Kennels, 150
Blackstone, Mr., 17
Blake, 133
Blucher (horse), 160
Blue Hills Observatory, 50, 51
Boaz Island, Bermuda, 234
Bolovitch, John, 35
Bonaventura, 213-215
Bonham (patrol boat), 69
Booker, Carol, 182
Boston Athenaeum, 111
Boston Bay, 31
Boston Common, 111, 117
Boston Common Cemetery, 111, 117
Boston Customs Inspector, 253, 255
Boston Edison Company, 51
Boston English High School, 252
Boston Harbor, 45, 61, 64-66, 90, 111, 122, 131, 133, 165, 166
Boston Herald Traveler, 15, 70, 104
Boston Latin School, 252
Boston Light, 28, 44-47, 90, 165
Boston Lightship, 55
Boston Marine Society, 141, 147
Boston, Mass., 3, 7-12, 17, 19-22, 24, 28, 38, 42, 45, 47, 49, 51, 57-59, 64, 69-71, 90, 92, 100, 107, 110-112, 116, 117, 122, 132, 141, 170, 172, 173, 252-255
Boston Massacre, 7
Boston-to-New York boat, 67-73
Boston State House, 12
Boston *Sunday Herald Traveler*, 104
Boston Tea Party, 8, 96, 97, 111
Boston *Transcript*, 173
Boston Weather Bureau, 51, 52, 61
Botovitch, John, 35
Bottle Imp, 34
Bottle messages, 135, 136
Boutwood, Capt. Wilfred, 123, 124, 126, 128
Bowley, Supt. George W., 37
Boyd, Richmond, 135, 136
Boylston School, 252
Boylston Street (Boston), 111, 117
Boylston Street Mall, 117
Bradford Manuscript, 11

INDEX 261

Bradford, William, 5, 11, 12, 17, 20, 86
Braintree, Mass., 64
Branch Creek, 103, 151
Brandywine, Del., 250
Brant Rock Lifesaving Station, 58
Brant Rock, Mass., 58, 71
Brewster Islands, 33
Bridge on the River Kwai, 34
Briney, Edward, 44, 48
Briney, Mrs. Edward, 44
Britannia, 122
British, 4, 11, 70, 110-116, 121, 128, 133, 134, 154, 161, 200, 233
British Admiralty, 127
British Board of Trade, 220
British Isles, 121, 123
Broad Street (Plymouth), 9
Brooklyn *Eagle,* 136
Brooklyn, N. Y., 11
Brooks, Frank, 72
Brooks, Phillips, 108
Brown, Capt., 253, 255
Brown, James, 253, 255
Brown, M. Henry, Jr., 31
Brown, William, 252-254
Brunswick, Me., 20
Bryant, Capt. Joseph, 154-159
Bucknill, Lord Justice, 127, 128
Bulldog (destroyer escort), 125
Burcher, George, 228
Butler, Gov. Nathaniel, 183, 188

C. G., 176
Cadiz, Spain, 187
Calamai, Capt. Piero, 143, 144, 147
Calf Island, 45, 46
California, 12, 160-162, 237
Cambridge, Mass., 92, 112
Canada, 203
Canary Islands, 134
Canoe Beach, 28
Canton, Robert, 204-207
Cape Ann, 141
Cape Ann, Mass., 22, 25, 52
Cape Breton Island, 60
Cape Cod Canal, 67
Cape Cod, Mass., 4, 5, 22, 24, 35, 36, 39, 55, 59, 74-87, 90, 170-178, 214

Cape Cod National Seashore, 86
Cape Comet, 183
Cape Horn, 237
Cape Mercy, 133
Capt. Musson's Gale, 216
Captain's Hill, 12
Cardiff, Wales, 234
Carol (Hurricane), 100
Carstens-Johannsen, Ernest, 142, 143, 145, 147
Cartagena, 187
Casco Bay, Me., 23
Cashman, Senator J. H., 73
Cashman, William H., 68, 69, 71, 73
Castle Harbor, Bermuda, 216
Castle Island (Bermuda), 216, 217
Cathay (mailboat), 249
Catholic, 16
Cedar Island, 29
Celeste, 132
Central Wharf, 131
Challenger (H.M.S.), 257
Chappel, Thomas, 88
Charlestown Navy Yard, 51
Charter St. (Boston), 57
Charybdis, 228-230
Chatham Lights, 75-78
Chatham, Mass., 41, 75-78
Chatham Naval Air Base, 38
Chatham Village, 77
Chelsea Bridge, 115
Chelsea Creek, 110-115
Chelsea, Mass., 29, 54, 110-117
Chelsea Neck, 114
Chinese, 111
Church of England, 16
Churchill, Winston, 194
Chase National Bank, 191
Ciarmataro, Joseph, 45, 46
Ciarmataro, Salvatore, 45-47
Ciarmataro, Victor, 48
Ciarmataro, Vittorio, 45-48
City of Columbus, 219
Civil War, 76, 77, 80, 110, 162
Clark's Island, 3-5
Cliff Island, 202
Coast Guard, 32, 37-41, 71, 73-75, 101, 108, 109
Coast Guard Station, 70

INDEX

Coast Guard Radio Station, 104, 108
Cod Seeker, 254
Coffin, Robert, 5
Cohasset, Mass., 54, 92
Cole, Chester, 100
Cole's Hill, 7
Collisions at Sea, 128
Collins, Capt. Michael, 79
Columbia (pilot boat), 54-58
Columbia, S. A., 135, 206
Columbian emeralds, 205
Columbus, 219
Commerce (tug), 70
Commonwealth Pier (Boston), 122
Concord, Battle of, 116
Congregational Church, 172
Congregational Society, 172
Connolly, Diver William, 88
Conroy, William J., 153
Constitution, 51
Cooper, Capt. Thomas, 57
Cortés, 16
Cox, Harry, 208, 209
Cox, Lawrence, 32, 33
Craft, John W., 173
Crest, The, 32
Crumplin, Capt. W. E., 126
Cuba, 130, 133
Cummings (derelict), 135
Cunard Line, 122, 126
Cunard, Messrs., 223
Cunard, Samuel, 122
Cunard Wharf, 64
Cunningham's Grotto, 99
Curacao (H.M.S.), 121, 123-129
Curlew (mail steamer), 221-226
Curling, Newfoundland, 164
Curran, Surfman, John, 56
Cushman, Elkanah, 6
Cushman, Mary, 12

Daddy's Rock, 95
Daily Evening Transcript, 174
Daily Ledger, 61, 62
Dalmatian pirates, 16
Dalton, Richard T., 164
Dapprich, Diver Douglas, 88
Dartmouth, Earl of, 116
Davenport, John, 200, 201

Davenport, Robert, 201
David Copperfield, 57
Declaration of Independence, 13
de Crisse (pirate ship), 88, 89
Dedham, Mass., 51
de Gorges, Sir Frank, 16
Deer Island, 28, 29
Deer Island Light, 166
Delaware, 250
Derelicts, 132-139
DeShields, Charles, 233
Des Moines, Ia., 44
de Vera, Capt. Fernandino, 187, 188
Devil's Bridge, 219
Dickens, Charles, 57
Dickerson, John, 7
Dickey, Dr., 224
Dill, George T., 85
Dill, Keeper Herman, 80-82
Dill, Mrs. Hosea, 85
Dill, T. M., B.M.A., 235
Dillworth, Edward, 232, 233
District of Columbia, 133
Diving, 64, 66
Dixon, Charles, 137, 138
Djerf, Dana, 109
Djerf Family, 108
Dogs, 149-169
Dolly's Rock, 103
Dorchester, Mass., 107, 112
Dorchester Point, 112
Doria, 140-148
Dorothy's Cove, 27
Doty, Edward, 5
Doughty, Mr., 194-197
Douglas, Edward, 69
Drake, Samuel Adams, 22
Dublin, 130
Ducharme, Joseph, 69
Dudden, Capt., 243
Dudley, Deputy Governor, 17
Duffield, Rev. Mr., 30
Dunmore (coal Collier), 134
Dutch, 20, 247
Duxbury Beach, 70
Duxbury, Mass., 6, 8, 20, 70, 100

Eagle, 136
East Boston, Mass., 35, 58, 64

INDEX

Eastham, Mass., 75, 81, 83-85
Eastman, Ralph M., 57
Ecuador, 206
Eddy, Harry F., 72
Eddyville, 44
Edwards, Capt., 233
Egg Rock, 149, 150
Egg Rock Lighthouse, 149
Elbow Bay, 234
Eldridge, Walter Walsh (Good Walter), 38
Eliza Ann, 253-255, 257
Elizabeth, 121, 122
Elizabeth and Ann, 28, 30
Ellingson, Andrew, 57
Ely's Harbor, 250, 251, 253, 257
Emery, Governor, 104
Empress of Ireland, 126
Endeavor, 182
England, 7, 8, 11, 14, 15, 17-20, 105, 133, 135, 154, 200, 213, 236
English, 4, 187, 200, 204, 233
English Channel, 246
English ferry house, 167
Erin's Isle (merchant Ship), 137
Essex County, 22
Essex, Mass., 52
Ethie, S.S. (coastal steamer), 164
Etruria, 133
Etrusco, 70
Exeter City, 133

Fahy, Patrick L., 252
Fairfield, Capt. William H., 54, 55
Fanny Wolston (derelict), 135
Faunce, Elder Thomas, 6
Fawcett, Capt. John, 57
Fawcett, Joseph, 57
Fawcett, Warren, 90
Fennelly, Richard, 165
Fiannini, Third Officer, 144
First Cliff, 106
First Parish Church of Hingham, 92
Fishing Steps (Bermuda), 216
Flaherty, Leo, 22
Florida, 133
Flower Hill, 103
Flying Santa, 74
Flying Scud (wreck), 237

Foggo, David, 216, 217
Forbes, Charles, 60
Forefather's Day, 8, 9
Forelands, 121
Fort Heath, 29
Fort Scammell, 6
Fort Standish, 19
403 (barge), 35
Fourth Cliff (Scituate), 93, 151
Fourth of July Celebration, 64
Fourth Veteran Battalion, 154, 159
France, 18, 206
Francis, 90
Franklin, Benjamin, 251, 252, 254
Franklin medal, 251-254
Fox, Leon, 182
Fox, Murray, 228
Fox, Thomas, 228
Franklin (ship), 170-178
Fraser, Capt. Roderick, 218-220
French, 213, 214
Fulham Palace, 11
Furnival's Inn, 15
Fury of the Seas, 256

G. O. Bigelow (schooner), 225
Gaffney, George, 31
Gage, Gen., 9, 10. 113, 116
Gallop's Island, 46
Gardiner, Lady, 18, 19
Gardiner, Sir Christopher, 14-21
Gay Head, Mass., 219
Gayron, T. Harold, 165
Gazelle (gig), 228, 229
General Court, 22
Georgia, 254
Gerard, Francis, 31
German, 45, 47, 204
Germany, 33, 35-39, 167
"Ghanges Khan," 86
Ghosts, 104-109, 256
Gibbs' Hill, 220
Gibbs' Hill Lighthouse, 218-220
Gibralter, 133, 249
Gilbert, Point, 86
Gillies, William, 208
Gladisfen (tug), 220
Glasgow, Scotland, 137
Globe, 70

INDEX

Gloss, George, 117
Gloucester, Eng., 15
Gloucester, Mass., 25, 35, 39, 52, 60, 82
Gondomar, Count, 188
Good Walter, 38
Gordon, Historian, 116
Gorges, Sir Ferdinando, 15, 17-19
Gorsock, S. K., 91
Government Aquarium, 205
Governor Parr, 134
Grace Irving, 65
Graham, Sir James, 234
Grandma (diving barge), 203
Grape Island, 166
Graves Light, 61
Gravesend, 236
Great Brewster Island, 45, 46, 165, 166
Great Dane dog, 168, 169
Great Sea Rescues, 95
Greeks, 233
Griffiths, Ted, 228
Griswold, Frank, 69, 73
Grove, Mary, 15, 19, 20
Grover's Cliff, 30
Guarvucca River, 160
Gulf of Mexico, 73, 135
Gulf Stream, 136, 246
Gurnet Lighthouse, 10
Gurnet Rock (Bermuda), 216
Gurnet's Nose, 10
Guyana, 253

Hadley, Mate, 155-159
Hagar, Joseph, 97
Halifax, N. S., 105, 121, 223, 225
Hall's Island, 194, 195, 197
Hamilton-Bate, Commander E., R.N., 235
Hamilton, Bermuda, 182, 187, 190, 191, 226, 251
Hamilton Gazette, 228
Hamilton Sound, 193
Hammond, Capt. Charles, 79
Hamor, Keeper, 162, 164
Hamor, Pauline, 162
Hampton, 23
Handmaid (ship), 15

Hanks, Nancy, 19
Hanover Flats, 96, 150, 153
Hanover, Mass., 96
Harding, Herman, 75
Harding, Virginia A., 75, 79
Harding's Ledge, 88, 90, 91
Hardy, Grace, 75, 76
Hardy, Capt. Josiah, 75-79
Hardy's Wharf, 77
Harper, Earl, 72
Harpooner (transport), 154-160
Harrington House, 197
Harrison, Thomas, 88
Hart, Keeper J. Lelan, 45, 46
Hartford, Conn., 51
Harvard College, 4, 6
Hatch, Isaiah, 173
Haunted House of Somerset, 256, 257
Hayakawa, Sessue, 33, 34
Hedge, Capt., 90
Heitt, Capt., 85
Hemans, Felicia Dorothea, 4
Hen Island, 95, 96, 98, 102
Henry Lee (schooner), 250
Herald Traveler, 15, 104
Herbert, John R., 15
High Pine Ledge, 70
Highland Light, 39, 59, 80
Hill, Dr. Edgar, 71
Hindu, 54
Hingham, Mass., 92
Hingham packet, 90
History of the Bermudaes, 183, 188
Hoboken Cricket Grounds, 162
Hog Island, 112-114
Holland, 167
Holmes, William, 88, 89
Holy Cross Cemetery, 71
Homer, Winslow, 158, 256
Hooper, John, 237
Hope Leslie (novel), 15
Hopkins, 141
Hopkins, J. L., 84
Hopkins, Stephen, 3, 5, 214
Horgan, State Trooper, 72
Hotel Inverurie (Bermuda), 168
Houdon (artist), 131
House of Lords, 128

INDEX 265

Howard and Montgomery (boat yard), 54
Howes, J. R., 222-225
Howes, Mrs. J. R., 223, 224
Howland Tavern, 7
Hudson River, 214
Hull, Mass., 45-48, 91
Humarock Bridge, 99
Hunter, Capt., 221-226
Hutchinson, Sir Thomas, 16

Iberia, 135
Iberian Peninsula, 133
Idlewild Hotel, 69, 71
Illingsworth, Capt., 124, 125, 128
Illustrated London News, 257
Incredible Mysteries and Legends of the Sea, 140
Indians, 5, 7, 16, 17, 19, 20, 27
Ingalls, Keeper J. W., 85
Iowa, 44
Ipswich, Mass., 52
Ira Kilhren (schooner), 81
Ireland, 135
Ireland Island (Bermuda), 222
Irish, 136, 233
Irving, 65
Island Sewing Society, 172
Isle de France, 141
Isle of Wight, 238
Isles of Devils, 207
Italian, 45, 46, 48, 140-148
Italian Government, 140

J. D. King (collier), 36
Jacksonville, Fla., 133
Jamestown Colony, 214
Janiszewski, Diver Michael, 88
Japanese prison camp, 34
Jeffreys, Mr., 17
Jeffries Point, 58
Jesuits, 16
John Blake, 133
John's Peril, 27
Johnson, Dick, 198
Johnson, Thomas, 33
Johnson, Mrs., 33
Jones, John Paul, 130, 131
Jones River, 6, 100

——, Joseph, 200
Joseph, Mate, 88
Joseph's Beach, 27
Julian Calendar, 7

Kadosh (bark), 88-92
Katko, Marvin, 44
Keeley, J. J., 69
Kelly, Allen, 31
Kennedy, Sister Jean, Introduction
King (collier), 36
King (dog), 154-160
King George, 8
King (liner), 204
King Philip (schooner), 55
Kindston, Mass., 6, 100
Kinnecum, Mr., 172
Kirby, John W., 92
Knight of Malta, 16
Knight of the Sepulchre, 16, 21

Lady in Black, 15
Lakeville, Mass., 16
Lamb, Benny, 228
Lamb, Jeremiah, 228
Lamont, ——, 247, 248
"Landing of the Pilgrim Fathers," 4
Landseer (dog), 150
Landseer, Sir Edwin, 150
Landsward (barge), 35, 36
Lapans, Mr., 62
La Plata (cable ship), 236-249
Larsen, Peter, 144
Lawley yard, 15
Lawrence, Alec, 203
Lee (Boston to New York steamer), 67-73
Lee, Ralph, 107, 108
Legends of the New England Coast, 140, 147
Lehigh (tug), 41
Lehigh Valley Railroad, 39
Lemoine, Thomas, 28
Leuitel, Deputy Sheriff, 85
Levant, 214
Lexington, Battle of, 116
Liberty Pole (Plymouth), 9
Lincoln, Abraham, 19
Lindley, Mrs., 108

INDEX

Lisbon, Portugal, 134
Little Brewster Island, 165
Little Emily, 57
Little, Torrey, 58
Liverpool, 135
Liza Ann (schooner), 251
Lloyd, Diver, 65
London, Eng., 11, 17, 18, 154, 170, 173, 188
London Exchange, 20
London Gazette, 116
Long Beach, 136
Long Island, 136
Long Wharf (Boston), 111
Longfellow, Henry Wadsworth, 14, 15, 21
Lophius piscatorius, 227
Lothrop, Isaac, 6, 8, 9
Lothrop, Thomas, 6
Loveland, Keeper Joseph, 76
Lowell, James Russell, 49
Lunt, Mr., 77
Lusher, Capt. John, 181-185, 251
Lynch, John F., Introduction
Lynn, Mass., 28, 31, 165
Lyon (ship), 19

Macauley, John, 150
Machiasport, Me., 130, 131
MacLellan, Lester R., 70
Macy, Yeoman Thomas, 22-26
Madaket, 24
Madianna, 218-220
Magee, Mr., 72
Magee, Capt. James, 95
Maher, Miss Pat, 208
Maine, 6, 20, 23, 39, 57, 130, 162, 202, 204
Maloon, Clarence D., 31
Malta, 16
Manderien, Chow, 111
Mangrove Bay, Bermuda, 188
Manhattan, 98
Manila, 90
Manomet Coast Guard Station, 68, 71-73
Manomet, Mass., 70, 71
Manomet Point, 67
Manomet Point Road, 69

Marblehead, Mass., 112
Marconi Wireless Station, 75
Margaret Bay, 186
Marginal Street (Chelsea), 110
Maritana (Square rigger), 28
Marrell, Capt., 254
Marrington, Robert, 83
"Marry Mount" (romance), 16
Marsden, Reginald D. (author), 128
Marsh Monster, 94
Marshall, Capt. Antonio, 232, 233
Marshfield Beach, 109
Marshfield Committee of Correspondence, 10
Marshfield, Mass., 6, 10, 64, 93-109, 128, 150
Marshfield Tea Party, 105
Martha's Vineyard, Mass., 6
Martin, E. C., 57
Martin's Point, 164
Mary Ann Rocks, 67, 68, 73
Mary Celeste, 132
Mary (liner), 121-129
Maryland, 131
Massachusetts, 3, 4-22, 44-112, 128, 141, 148-153, 219
Massachusetts State House, 22
Massachusetts State Police, 73
Matthews, J. A., 90-92
Matinicus Island, 162-164
Matinicus mailboat, 162-164
Maverick, Mr., 17
May, Henry, 213
Mayflower, 3-6, 12, 214
Mayflower II, 123
Mayhew, Thomas, 6
Mayo, Mr., 83
McClearn, Lester, 31
McLean, Capt., 177, 178
McLeod, Billy, 166
McQueeney, James, 31
McQueeney, Thomas, 31
Medford, Mass., 112
Mediterranean, 248
Merrimac (steamer), 135
Merry Mount, 15
Mertis H. Perry (fishing schooner), 58-60
Messina, 228

INDEX

Methodist Society, 172
Mexican, 206
Mexico, 160, 161, 206
Middle Brewster Island, 44-48
Middleboro, Mass., 16, 20
Milo (dog), 149, 150
Milton, Mass., 50, 109
Minors, Reginald, 233
Minot's Light, 54, 61-63, 166
Minot's Lightship, 166
Modena (packet Schooner), 174
Mohaska County, 44
Monarch of Bermuda (liner), 204
Morgan, Henry, 188, 189
Morison, Samuel Eliot, 12
Morning Cloud, 237
Morton, — (writer), 86
Morton, Thomas, 15, 17, 18
Motley, John Lothrop, 16
Mount Wollaston, 17
Moxie (motorboat), 31-34
Murder, 44-48
Murphy, John, 31
Myrtle (lighthouse tender), 78
Mount Wyndham, 217
Musson family, 193
Mylrea, Lt., 159

Nahant Coast Guard, 32
Nahant, Mass., 27-30, 149, 150
Nantasket Beach, 90
Nantasket, Mass., 90, 91
Nantucket Island, 141
Nantucket, Mass., 6, 22, 24, 25, 141
Narraganset Indians, 27
Narrow Gauge Railroad, 48, 110
Natick Mall, 50
Natick, Mass., 50
Nauset, Mass., 79
Nauset Beach Life Saving Station, 83
Nauset Harbor, 37
Nauset Lights, 75
Navy, 110
Needham, Mass., 51
Nelson, Frank, 57
Neponset River, 14-21
Nesmith, Robert I., 202, 206
New Charlton, Woolwich, 237

New England Sea Tragedies, 70
New Hampshire, 112, 113
New Jersey, 39, 135, 162
New York, 11, 20, 35, 39, 42, 70, 72, 135, 140, 142, 160, 161, 191, 202, 204, 222
New York Times, The, 220
Newcomb, Uncle Jack, 175
Newcomb's Hollow, 178
Newfoundland, 134, 154, 164
Newfoundland dog, 154, 160, 164, 166-168
Newfoundland-Saint Bernard dog, 149
Ney, Keeper Samuel, 76
Nickerson, Keeper Simeon, 76
Nickerson, Mrs. Simeon, 76
Niger, H.M.S., 10
1948 Convention for Safety at Sea, 147
Noakes, Capt. G. C. H., 126
Noddle's Island, 112-116
Nordenson, Capt. Gunnar, 145
Norfolk, 250
Norfolk Island, 137, 138
Normannia, 135
North Africa, 95, 121
North Atlantic, 135
North Bennett St. (Boston), 57
North Carolina, 66
North Carolina (ship), 130
North End (Boston), 45
North River, 93-105, 150-153
North Rocks (Bermuda), 218, 220
North Scituate Lifesaving Station, 56
North Sydney, N. S., 60
Northern Avenue Bridge, 64
Norwegian, 57
Norwood (house), 104, 108
Nostra Senora de Crisse, 88, 89
Nova Scotia, 6, 60, 105, 121, 222, 223

Oakes, Uriah, 6
Ocean Avenue (Winthrop), 32
Ode on Freedom, 7
Of Plymouth Plantation, 11, 12
Ohio (steamer), 55
Old Colony Club, 6, 8, 9
Old Colony Memorial, 70
Old Indian Trail, 151

INDEX

Old Ironsides, 51
Old Peggotty, 57
Old South Church, 11
Oldgate, Richard, 216, 217
Olen (steamer), 134
Olsen, Capt. Ellis, 57
O'Neil, Eugene, 75
Orient, 90
Orion (bark), 133
Orleans Coast Guard Station, 37-41
Orleans, Mass., 35, 36, 38, 40, 82
Otis, Amos, 86
Otis, James, 8
Owl's Head Light, 162-164
Ox Trail, 103

Pacific, 236
Packwood House, 181, 251
Pacqua (steamer), 70
Padfield, Peter, 123
Pagent, Fred, 28
Paget, 197, 202, 231
Palmer, Diver, 66
Panama, 188
Paris, 18, 131
Parr, 134
Pasco, Montague, 234
Pashby, Matthew, 31
Pavonia, 70
Payne, Keeper Thomas K., 82-85
Payne, Mrs. Thomas K., 84
Pea Island, 28
Peaked Hill Bars, 75
Pearman, Russell Levi, 190-192
Pemberton, Max, 137
Pembroke, Mass., 96
Penobscot Bay, 162
Pentagoet, 55
Percy, Lord, 9
Perenchief, Mr., 198
Perkins ship, 92
Perkins, William, 90, 92
Perry (fishing schooner), 58-60
Perth Amboy (tug), 35-43
Peru, 206
Peruvian, 90
Peterson, Edward E., 57
Peterson, Capt. Frank H., 147
Peterson, Capt. James, 130, 131

Peterson, Margaret, 130, 131
Peterson, Mary, 131
Peterson, Dr. Mendel L., 205, 206
Peterson, Peter, 57
Peter-Burbery, Rev., 233
Phantom Clam-Digger, 94
Philadelphia, Pa., 55, 182
Philippines, 91
Phillips, Daniel, 104-106
Phillips Family, 104-106
Phillips, George L., 64
Phillips House, 104-109
Phillips, Nathaniel, 104
Phips, Sir William, 204
Phoebus (steamer), 134
Pierce, Capt. Robert F., 37, 38
Pike, Capt. Joshua, 60
Pilcher, Justice, 126, 127
Pilgrim Hall, 10, 11
Pilgrim Rock, 3-5
Pilgrims, 3-7, 10-13, 19, 20
Pinehurst, Mass., 150
Pizarro, 16
Plymouth American Legion, 73
Plymouth County, 48
Plymouth Fire Department, 73
Plymouth Harbor, Mass., 3, 5, 10, 95, 123
Plymouth, Mass., 3-10, 19, 73, 89, 104, 105, 214
Plymouth Police Department, 73
Plymouth Rock, 3-7, 9-13
Plymouth Superior Court, 45, 47
Plymouth Town Square, 9
Point Shirley, 33
Point Shirley Beach, 29
Pollokshields (steamer), 231, 235
Pomander Castle, 202
Pope Gregory Calendar, 7
Portland boat, 65
Portland (steamer), 54, 55
Portland, Me., 6, 39
Portland Storm, 54-63
Portugal, 135
Portuguese wreck, 209
Prien, Hans, 206
Prince Library, 11
Prince, —— (writer), 86
Proctor, Alden A., 69

INDEX 269

Provincetown Harbor, 59
Provincetown, Mass., 4, 12, 37, 38, 41, 80, 81, 84, 175
Puerto Rico, 253, 255
Pulpit Rock, 27
Purchase, Mary Groves, 20
Purchase, Thomas, 20
Puritans, 16, 19
Purkitt, Henry, 111
Putnam, Col. Israel, 112, 114, 115

Quakers, 22, 23
Quebec, 154, 160
Queen Elizabeth (transport liner), 121
Queen Mary (transport liner), 121-129
Queen Street (Bermuda), 252
Queen's Guard, 10
Quincy, Mass., 61

Race Point Light, 59
Ranney, David G., 252
Reamy, Milton H., 61-63
Reamy, Octavius H., 61
Red Cross, 136
Red Wing, 69
Reddy the Fox, 96, 98
Reed, Capt. John, 88
Reekast, Augustus, 46-48
Repose, August, 198
Repose, Robert, 198, 199
Resolute (British naval vessel), 133
Reubens (dog), 160-162
Revere, Mass., 112-114
Revolutionary War, 105, 107
Reynolds, Police Chief Frank M., 46, 47
Rhyme of Sir Christopher, 21
Ribbs, Edward J., 51
Rich, Earle G., 170
Rich, Shebnah, 86
Richards, Cliff, 91
Richardson, George, 190
Rickenbacker, Eddie, 236
Rio Grand de Sul, 237, 238
Rio Pinto, 206
Robbins, Dr. Maurice, 16
Robert E. Lee (steamer), 67-73
Robertson, Hudson, 31, 32

Robertson, Hudson, Jr., 31
Robinson, Senior Officer, 124, 127
Robinson, Edward F., 252
Robinson, Capt. Harland W., 67, 68
Robinson, William, 24
Rocket II (motor vessel), 165
Rockland, Me., 163, 164
Rockport, Mass., 52
Roman Catholic Church, 205
Roos, Hjalmar J., 45, 47, 48
Rosewain, Edward, 88, 89
Roslindale, Mass., 57
Roundhead Colony, 16
Route 133, 52
Rover (dog), 83
Rowe, Grandma, 110, 111
Rowe, Joshua N., 110
Rye, N. Y., 202

Sagamore, 68
Sagua LeGrand, Cuba, 130
St. Catherine's Bathing Beach, 135
Saint David's Island, 190, 228
Saint David's Lighthouse, 219, 229
St. George Hotel, 135
Saint George's Harbor, 200
Saint George's Island (Bermuda), 182, 185, 200-222, 225, 226, 228
Saint James Graveyard, 182, 186
Saint Shotts, 154, 157, 160
Saints and Strangers, 12
St. Thomas, 222
Salisbury, Mass., 22
Salmon, Robert, 27, 29
Salty I (dog), 165
Salty II (dog), 165, 166
Sampson, Earl, 69
San Antonio (Spanish galleon), 183, 187
San Francisco, 160, 161
Sand Hills, 56
Sanders, Chief Warrent Officer Robert, 109
Sankaty Head Light, 141
Sappho's Rock, 27
Saquish, Mass., 19
Sargasso Sea, 135
Savage, Capt., 84
Savage, Capt. (off Nahant), 28

INDEX

Savannah, Ga., 254, 255
Savannah journal, 254
"Saved" (painting), 150
Saxonia, 134
Scala, Tony, 31
Scammell, Alexander, 6
Scituate Harbor, 89
Scituate Lighthouse, 89
Scituate, Mass., 55, 57, 58, 70, 88, 93, 150
Scituate Pier, 90
Scotland, 137, 222
Scotland Lightship, 136
Scott, Lord Justice, 127, 128
Sea Devil, 227-230
Sea Venture, 214
Sears store, 50
Seaver, N., 253
Seaver, Joseph, 253, 255
Seaver, Joshua, 255
Secrets of the North Atlantic Islands, 158
Sedgewick, Catherine Maria, 15
740 (barge), 35
766 (barge), 35
Seymour, Capt. G. H., C.B., 222
Shag Rocks (Nahant), 28
Shawmut, 17
Shearwater, 208
"Ship of Skeletons" (sketch), 257
Shipwrecked Fishermen and Mariners Society, 247
Shipwrecked Mariners' Society, 234
Shirley Gut, 29, 150
Shoals of Chatham, 41
Shore Drive (Winthrop), 31, 32
Short Beach, 33
Siddhartha (bark), 133
Sierra Madre, 160
Sinbad the Sailor, 86
Skehan, Miss, 176
Smith, Ammi, 65
Smith, Capt. Charles, 76
Smith, Capt. Charles (*Franklin*), 170, 172, 173, 174, 177, 178
Smith, Hon. H. A., 235
Smith's Parish, 208
Smithsonian Institution, 205, 206
Smithsonian Museum, 209

Snow, 55
Snow, Alice Rowe, 33
Snow, Anna-Myrle, 27, 67, 93, 94, 101, 103, 151-153, 251
Snow family, 31, 100
Snow, Nicholas, 32, 33
Snow residence, 51
Social Aid Society, 172
Society of Mayflower Descendants, 11
Somers, Admiral George, 214
Somer's Island, 213
Somerset (Bermuda), 181, 222, 251, 255-257
Somerset (man-of-war), 116
South America, 135, 187, 236
South Boston, 48
South River, 97, 104, 151
South River Flats, 97
South River Street (Marshfield), 104, 108, 109
South Shore (Bermuda), 232
South Shore Hotel, 231, 233
South Wellfleet, Mass., 75
Southhampton, 249
Spain, 133, 187, 188, 206, 207
Spaniards, 206
Spanish, 15, 181, 187
Spanish galleon, 186, 204
Sparrow, Mr., 82
Spectacle Island, 55
Sphinx (dog), 168
Spooner, Deacon Ephriam, 6
Spot (dog), 162-164
Spurling, Mr., 232
Squantum, Mass., 16
Standish, Myles, 5
Stanley (brig), 131
Staples, Capt. R. M., 250
Star Chamber of Bermuda, 188
Starbuck, Richard, 24
Stark, Edward P., 69, 73
Stark, Col. John, 113
State Point, 69
State Street (Boston), 7
Stevens, Capt., 174
Stevenson, Marmaduke, 24
Stevenson, Robert Louis, 34
Stimson, Keeper Samuel, 76
Stockholm, 140-147

INDEX

Stone's Wharf, 31, 32
Storms of 1969, 49-53
Strachey, William, 214
Strange Tales from Nova Scotia to Cape Hatteras, 27, 254
Strawberry Hill, 90
Stuart, Gilbert, 111
Sullivan, Daniel, 72
Summer Street (Marshfield), 95
Sumner, General William, 112
Swallow Cave, 27
Swedish, 133, 140-147

T Wharf, 64
Tampa (cutter), 134
Tapley, Capt. James H., 36, 38-43
Taunton River, 20
Taylor, Fred, 150
Taylor, George B., 149
Taylor, Dr. J. Danforth, 35
Telephone Works, 237
Tewksbury, Capt. William, 28
Thames River, 236, 237
Thanksgiving Day, 4, 5
Third Cliff, Scituate, 88, 93
Thomas, 141
Thomas, John, 6
Thomes, Willard, 153
Thompson Academy, 166
Thompson's Island, 166
Thomson, Sir Charles Wyville, 256, 257
Thoreau, Henry David, 74, 175
Thornton, John Wingate, 11
Three Episodes of Massachusetts History, 17
Three Sisters of Nauset, 74
Titanic (disaster), 126, 141
Tobin, Surfman Richard, 55, 56
Tories, 8, 9, 105
Tower, Frederick, 78
Trelone, Paget, 202
Tremont Street (Boston), 111, 117
Trepassey, 159
Trinity House, 126
Trouant's Island, 93
True Tales of Curious Legends, 64, 90
Trunk Island, 193

Truro, Mass., 80, 172, 174
Tucker, Edward Bolton ("Teddy"), 202-207
Tucker, Edward, 204
Turkish pirates, 16
Turner, Rev. Charles, 8
Twelfth Bomber Command, 95
Twelfth Massachusetts Regiment, 65

U-Boat, 35-38, 73, 125
Umtali, 135
Underwood, Edward, 142, 143
Unicorn (steamer), 161
Union Church (Brant Tock), 58

Van Den Gein, 207
Van Dyke, 14
Varuna (pilot boat), 54, 55
Veader, Joseph, 60
Venezuela, 206
Vera Cruz, 160
Victoria Street (Hamilton), 190
Vineyard Haven, 41, 42
Virginia, 214
Virtue, Pilot Fred, 228-230

Wales, 234
Walford, Mr., 17
Walker, J. F., 82, 83
Wallstonecraft, Mary, 8
War of 1812, 154
Ward, General, 112
Warren family, 6
Warren, Chief Warrant Officer Harold, 109
Warren, James, 6, 8, 9
Warren, Joseph, 114
Warren, Mercy, 8
Warrington, Thomas, 88, 89
Washington, D. C., 133
Washington, George, 81, 111
Washington Place, 252
Watson, John, 6
Welch, Matthew, 31
Wellesley, Capt. G., C.B., 222
Wellfleet Bay, 81
Wellfleet Benevolent Society, 172
Wellfleet, Mass., 81, 83, 84, 172, 174
Wellfleet Oysterman, 175

INDEX

Wesport, 85
Wessagusset, 17
West Head (Noddle's Island), 115
West Indies, 203
Wharton, Edward, 23, 24
White, Cornelius, 6
White House, The, 133
White, Peregrine, 6, 104
White Star Line, 122
Whitehall, 116
Whittier, Capt., 225
Whittier, John Greenleaf, 24
Wilberforce, Lord Bishop Samuel, 11
Wilcox, District Commander, U.S.C.G., 73
Wilhelm Berklesorn (schooner), 248
Williams, David, 233
Willison, George F., 12
Winnisimmet ferry, 113, 115
Winslow, Edward, 6, 9
Winslow estate, 10
Winslow, Maj. Gen. John, 6
Winslow, Pelham, 6, 9
Wilson, J. W., 173
Winthrop Bar, 33
Winthrop Beach, 100
Winthrop Beach Station, 110

Winthrop Highlands, Mass., 29
Winthrop, Gov. John, 15, 18, 19
Winthrop, Mass., 27, 29, 31, 32, 69, 100
Winthrop Yacht Club, 32
Wolston, 135
Women's Liberation, 8
Wood End, 68
Wood End Light, 80
Wood, Irving, 69
Woodbury, Jacob T., 252
Woodsum, George T., 64
Woolwich, 237
Worcester, Mass., 167
World War I, 35
World War II, 121, 194
Wreck Inquiry Act of 1880, 233
Wright, Junior Officer, 124, 128
Wrottlesley, Lord Justice, 127, 128
Wyndham, Australia, 135

Yarmouth, 92
Yokohama, 90
Yorktown (battle), 6
Young, Capt. Arthur, 72

Zuill, Will, 169, 181

RENEWALS 458-4574

DATE DUE